*Postmodern Politics
for a Planet in Crisis*

POSTMODERN POLITICS FOR A PLANET IN CRISIS

Policy, Process, and Presidential Vision

DAVID RAY GRIFFIN
AND RICHARD FALK,
Editors

STATE UNIVERSITY OF NEW YORK PRESS

We are grateful to New Society Publishers for permission to reprint portions of "Our Life as Gaia," by Joanna Macy, which appeared in the book *Thinking Like a Mountain: Toward a Council of All Beings*, by John Seed, Joanna Macy, Pat Fleming, and Arne Naess (Philadelphia: New Society Publishers, 1988); and to *New Perspectives Quarterly* for permission to reprint material from the essay "Post-Modernism: The Stenography of Surfaces," by Todd Gitlin, *New Perspectives Quarterly* 6 (Spring 1989): 56–59, © New Perspectives Quarterly, Los Angeles, CA.

Published by
State University of New York Press, Albany

For information, address State University of New York
Press, State University Plaza, Albany, N.Y., 12246

Production by E. Moore
Marketing by Fran Keneston

Postmodern politics for a planet in crisis : policy, process, and
presidential vision / David Ray Griffin and Richard Falk, editors.
    p.   cm. — (SUNY series in constructive postmodern thought)
    Includes index.
    ISBN 0-7914-1485-X (CH : acid-free). — ISBN 0-7914-1486-8 (PB :
acid-free)
    1. United States—Politics and government—1989-   2. Presidents—
United States. 3. Environmental policy—United States.
    4. Postmodernism. I. Griffin, David Ray, 1939-   . II. Falk,
Richard A. III. Series.
JK271.P63   1993
353.03'23—dc20   92–22104
                                                CIP

10 9 8 7 6 5 4 3 2 1

Dedicated to
Maryanne Mott and
Herman Warsh

CONTENTS

PREFACE

This book arose out of our shared conviction that our world has little hope for survival, at least without misery beyond imagination, unless a radically new mode of politics emerges in America, a mode that we have come to call *postmodern*. We also share the conviction that the office of the presidency is crucial: There is little hope for the widespread reorientation that is needed unless this office becomes the radiating center of postmodernist transformation rather than modernist reaction.

Out of these shared convictions came the idea for a book such as this, which would seek, through a variety of voices, to sketch out various dimensions of what a transformation from modern to postmodern politics in America would involve, and some ideas as to how to bring this about. In selecting the contributors, we looked for people who basically share our postmodern sensibilities, who would write with wisdom about some aspect of the overall picture, and whose opinions would carry weight with our intended audience. We sought a rough balance of the three dimensions that need to be given equal attention: ecological sustainability, social equity within the nation, and peace and equity in the relations among nations.

The essays in this book were written after the 1988 presidential campaign and before the 1992 campaign. This fact, however, does not matter much. The kind of postmodern transformation of politics we envisage transcends any probable differences, as important as they may otherwise be, between the two elections. They also transcend, for the most part, the distinctions between Democrat and Republican. Most of the negative examples of presidential leadership do, it is true, refer to Republicans; but that is due mainly to the fact that we have had Republican presidents for the past twelve years (and sixteen of the past twenty). There is little doubt, to be sure, that we and the other contributors to this book will support the Democratic ticket this year. This does not mean, however, that we see a Clinton-Gore administration as the likely beginning of a postmodern presidency. It is true that Albert Gore has a far more informed and enlightened position on the environment than any previous candidate. It is also virtually certain that a Clinton-Gore administration would be far more progressive in terms of social justice within America than the Republican administrations have been. On the other hand, however, both Clinton and Gore supported the Gulf War and have in their campaign rhetoric staked out positions more militarist than Bush. They have, furthermore, fully endorsed the idea of continual economic growth—which, in our view, is inconsistent with ecological sustainability. Of course, it is possible that some of their campaign rhetoric is just that—rhetoric. Even if not, they are bright and compassionate men, and it is possible that, once in office, they would have the kind of conversion that John Cobb in his essay portrays a president as having. For now, however, we can only support them as the probable lesser of modernist evils. The vision articulated in this book will likely remain an agenda for future administrations no matter how the 1992 election turns out.

Some readers may suspect that the book would have been different had it taken into account the "Ross Perot phenomenon." No one, of course, would think that Perot gave promise of a postmodern presidency in our sense of the term. But someone might think that the response evoked by his offer to run, while verifying Frances Moore Lappé's assessment of the citizenry as angry, gives the lie to statements of others about its being passive and asleep. Perhaps. But—looking aside from the question of the values and motives of those who responded to Perot—it is one thing to get excited for a few months about someone who promises to "clean house" and, not incidentally, to finance his own campaign. It is something quite different to become really informed about the issues and to get politically involved in an ongoing way.

The first stage in the development of this book was a conference, which allowed the contributors to try out their ideas on each other and an audience of concerned citizens, then to revise their essays prior to publication, This conference, "Toward a Postmodern Presidency: Vision for a Planet in Crisis," was held at the University of California at Santa Barbara and sponsored by the Center for a Postmodern World and the Center for Process Studies. We wish to thank the many friends of the two centers whose financial contributions enabled the conference to break even. Special thanks in this respect go to that marvelous couple who have supported so many good causes, Maryanne Mott and Herman Warsh, without whom the conference would not have been possible, and to whom this book is dedicated.

We wish also to thank Clay Morgan of SUNY Press for the care he devoted to this book, with regard to both details and general conception, to Elizabeth Moore for efficiently guiding it through the production process, and to William Eastman, director of SUNY Press, for his continued support of the series in which it appears.

RICHARD FALK AND DAVID RAY GRIFFIN, AUGUST, 1992

INTRODUCTION TO SUNY SERIES IN CONSTRUCTIVE POSTMODERN THOUGHT

The rapid spread of the term *postmodern* in recent years bears witness to a growing dissatisfaction with modernity and to an increasing sense that the modern age not only had a beginning but can have an end as well. Whereas the word *modern* was almost always used until quite recently as a word of praise and as a synonym for *contemporary*, a growing sense is now evidenced that we can and should leave modernity behind—in fact, that we *must* if we are to avoid destroying ourselves and most of the life on our planet.

Modernity, rather than being regarded as the norm for human society toward which all history has been aiming and into which all societies should be ushered—forcibly if necessary—is instead increasingly seen as an aberration. A new respect for the wisdom of traditional societies is growing as we realize that they have endured for thousands of years and that, by contrast, the existence of modern society for even another century seems doubtful. Likewise, *modernism* as a worldview is less and less seen as The Final Truth, in comparison with which all divergent worldviews are automatically regarded as "superstitious." The modern worldview is increasingly relativized to the status of one among many, useful for some purposes, inadequate for others.

Although there have been antimodern movements before, beginning perhaps near the outset of the nineteenth century with the Romanticists and the Luddites, the rapidity with which the term *postmodern* has become widespread in our time suggests that the antimodern sentiment is more extensive and intense than before, and also that it includes the sense that modernity can be successfully overcome only by going beyond it, not by attempting to return to a premodern form of existence. Insofar as a common element is found in the various ways in which the term is used, *postmodernism* refers to a diffuse sentiment rather than to any common set of doctrines—the sentiment that humanity can and must go beyond the modern.

Beyond connoting this sentiment, the term *postmodern* is used in a confusing variety of ways, some of them contradictory to others. In artistic and literary circles, for example, postmodernism shares in this general sentiment but also involves a specific reaction against "modernism" in the narrow sense of a movement in artistic-literary circles in the late nineteenth and early twentieth centuries. Postmodern architecture is very different from postmodern literary criticism. In some circles, the term *postmodern* is used in reference to that potpourri of ideas and systems sometimes called *new age metaphysics*, although many of these ideas and systems are more premodern than postmodern. Even in philosophical and theological circles, the term *postmodern* refers to two quite different positions, one of which is reflected in this series. Each position seeks to transcend both *modernism* in the sense of the worldview that has developed out of the seventeenth-century Galilean-Cartesian-Baconian-Newtonian science, and *modernity* in the sense of the world order that both conditioned and was conditioned by this worldview. But the two positions seek to transcend the modern in different ways.

Closely related to literary-artistic postmodernism is a philosophical postmodernism inspired variously by pragmatism, physicalism, Ludwig Wittgenstein, Martin Heidegger, and Jacques Derrida and other recent French thinkers. By the use of terms that arise out of particular segments of this movement, it can be called *deconstructive* or *eliminative postmodernism*. It overcomes the modern worldview through an anti-worldview: it deconstructs or eliminates the ingredients necessary for a worldview, such as God, self, purpose, meaning, a real world, and truth as correspondence. While motivated in some cases by the ethical concern to forestall totalitarian systems, this type of postmodern thought issues in relativism, even nihilism. It could also be called *ultramodernism*, in that its eliminations result from carrying modern premises to their logical conclusions.

The postmodernism of this series can, by contrast, be called *constructive* or *revisionary*. It seeks to overcome the modern worldview not by eliminating the possibility of worldviews as such, but by constructing a postmodern worldview through a revision of modern premises and traditional concepts. This constructive or revisionary postmodernism involves a new unity of scientific, ethical, aesthetic, and religious intuitions. It rejects not science as such but only that scientism in which the data of the modern natural sciences are alone allowed to contribute to the construction of our worldview.

The constructive activity of this type of postmodern thought is not limited to a revised worldview; it is equally concerned with a postmodern world that will support and be supported by the new worldview. A postmodern world will involve postmodern persons, with a postmodern spirituality, on the one hand, and a postmodern society, ultimately a postmodern global order, on the other. Going beyond the modern world will involve transcending its individualism, anthropocentrism, patriarchy, mechanization, economism, consumerism, nationalism, and militarism. Constructive postmodern thought provides support for the ecology, peace, feminist, and other emancipatory movements of our time, while stressing that the inclusive emancipation must be from modernity itself. The term *postmodern*, however, by contrast with *premodern*, emphasizes that the modern world has produced unparalleled advances that must not be lost in a general revulsion against its negative features.

From the point of view of deconstructive postmodernists, this constructive postmodernism is still hopelessly wedded to outdated concepts, because it wishes to salvage a positive meaning not only for the notions of the human self, historical meaning, and truth as correspondence, which were central to modernity, but also for premodern notions of a divine reality, cosmic meaning, and an enchanted nature. From the point of view of its advocates, however, this revisionary postmodernism is not only more adequate to our experience but also more genuinely postmodern. It does not simply carry the premises of modernity through to their logical conclusions, but criticizes and revises those premises. Through its return to organicism and its acceptance of nonsensory perception, it opens itself to the recovery of truths and values from various forms of premodern thought and practice that had been dogmatically rejected by modernity. This constructive, revisionary postmodernism involves a creative synthesis of modern and premodern truths and values.

This series does not seek to create a movement so much as to help shape and support an already existing movement convinced that modernity can and must be transcended. But those antimodern movements which arose in the past failed to deflect or even retard the onslaught of modernity. What reasons can we have to expect the current movement to be more successful? First, the previous antimodern movements were primarily calls to return to a premodern form of life and thought rather than calls to advance, and the human spirit does not rally to calls to turn back. Second, the previous antimodern movements either rejected modern science, reduced it to a description of mere appearances, or assumed its adequacy in principle; therefore, they could base their calls only on the negative social and spiritual effects of modernity. The current movement draws on natural science itself as a witness against the adequacy of the modern worldview. In the third place, the present movement has even more evidence than did previous movements of the ways in which modernity and its worldview *are* socially and spiritually destructive. The fourth and probably most decisive difference is that the present movement is based on the awareness that *the continuation of modernity threatens the very survival of life on our planet.* This awareness, combined with the growing knowledge of the interdependence of the modern worldview and the militarism, nuclearism, and ecological devastation of the modern world, is providing an unprecedented impetus for people to see the evidence for a postmodern worldview and to envisage postmodern ways of relating to each other, the rest of nature, and the cosmos as a whole. For these reasons, the failure of the previous antimodern movements says little about the possible success of the current movement.

Advocates of this movement do not hold the naively utopian belief that the success of this movement would bring about a global society of universal and lasting peace, harmony, and happiness, in which all spiritual problems, social conflicts, ecological destruction, and hard choices would vanish. There is, after all, surely a deep truth in the testimony of the world's religions to the presence of a transcultural proclivity to evil deep within the human heart, which no new paradigm, combined with a new economic order, new child-rearing practices, or any other social arrangements, will suddenly eliminate. Furthermore, it has correctly been said that "life is robbery": a strong element of competition is inherent within finite existence, which no social-political-economic-ecological order can overcome. These two truths, especially when contemplated together, should caution us against unrealistic hopes.

However, no such appeal to "universal constants" should reconcile us to the present order, as if this order were thereby uniquely legitimated. The human proclivity to evil in general, and to conflictual competition and ecological destruction in particular, can be greatly exacerbated or greatly mitigated by a world order and its worldview. Modernity exacerbates it about as much as is imaginable. We can therefore envision, without being naively utopian, a far better world order, with a far less dangerous trajectory, than the one we now have.

This series, making no pretense of neutrality, is dedicated to the success of this movement toward a postmodern world.

DAVID RAY GRIFFIN,
SERIES EDITOR

INTRODUCTION: FROM MODERN TO POSTMODERN POLITICS

Richard Falk and David Ray Griffin

This book is based on three propositions, two that are obvious to most Americans today, and one that is less so.

The first obvious proposition is that our planet, in general, and our nation, in particular, are in crisis. This crisis has ecological, economic, social, and spiritual dimensions. Pollution is pervasive. Global warming and a growing hole in the ozone layer threaten unprecedented disasters. The human population, which required all of human history until 1800 to reach one billion, is now adding a billion every decade. At a time when starvation is already widespread, the amount of land available for growing food is rapidly diminishing. Nuclear holocaust remains a threat. The gap between rich and poor is greater than ever. In the 1980s the United States went from being the world's largest creditor nation to the world's largest debtor. Crime is increasing. The use of drugs has reached epidemic proportions. Cynicism and a sense of hopelessness are pervasive.

The second obvious proposition is that our political leadership, especially at the national level, is not proving adequate to the challenges we face. It is not even coming close. Political campaigns, run by image consultants, have become business ventures more than occasions for serious and imaginative discourse about problems of the day. Far

1

from being dealt with adequately by the executive and legislative branches of the federal government, the ecological crisis, for example, is hardly even mentioned in the election campaigns. And nothing close to comprehensive solutions for our economic problems, and the related challenges of crime and drugs, is offered. There is widespread agreement that our political process is not working. To be sure, it is working in one sense—to enrich a few. But it is not fashioning constructive responses to the interlocking national and global crises, and it is not building hope for the future among our young people.

The third proposition on which this book is based, the one that is not obvious yet to most people, is that these two crises—the global crisis and the crisis of political leadership—are due, at bottom, to the continued dominance of modernity at a time when its basic principles have become irrelevant and their application counterproductive. By "modernity" we mean that distinctive way of seeing the world and organizing human society that emerged in the sixteenth and seventeenth centuries (with important roots stretching back into the fifteenth and even the fourteenth centuries). There is much that was and is benign about modernity. But there is also much that has been problematic and is becoming more so. (This twofold nature of modernity has been articulated in previous books in this series, with *Spirituality and Society: Postmodern Visions* being most germane to the current volume.[1]) The present planetary crisis is, most fundamentally, a crisis of modernity itself.

The only way out, we believe, is through the emergence of a postmodern world, which would involve both a new vision of the very nature and purpose of life and a new way of organizing human society, as well as the political practices needed to get us from here to there. This will require a postmodern politics.[2] We title this volume, accordingly, *Postmodern Politics for a Planet in Crisis*.

In the subtitle, *Policy, Process, and Presidential Vision*, we indicate the dimensions of a postmodern politics that the book addresses. Most obviously, to solve our problems we will need new public policies—not refinements of modern policies to make them work a little better, but postmodern policies that will often amount to such drastic reversals of modern policies as to be considered unthinkable by those still captivated by the modern vision of the world. For example, it has been an article of faith in this nation for at least a hundred years, as William Appleman Williams has shown in *The Roots of the Modern American Empire*, that a healthy American economy, and thereby a contented populace, depends upon an ever-expanding market. But John Cobb proposes herein that we begin reversing this process, that we move instead toward local economies that are relatively self-sufficient, thereby reducing trade to the lowest level possible.

Leadership to formulate and enact such policies will, as already intimated, require a new vision, a postmodern vision that transcends the modern vision, which has increasingly guided policy during the modern period. The series in which this book appears is in large part devoted to the attempt to articulate aspects of such a vision.[3] The present book focuses in particular on the type of vision that is needed by political leaders, especially those who will occupy the office of the presidency in the coming decades. Given the symbolic power of the presidency and the vast persuasive impact a president has through this power and the mass media, there will be little hope that the kinds of changes needed in attitude and behavior will occur with sufficient rapidity to prevent unprecedented misery and death in the twenty-first century unless we have the vigorous leadership of postmodern presidents.[4]

Political vision, especially presidential vision, and public policy are related dialectically to the other dimension of the needed postmodern politics spoken of in our subtitle: political process. In a dyadic dialectical relationship, each dimension depends upon (and is in tension with) the other. On the one hand, the current political process is geared to producing the types of political leaders we have had. Without a radical change in the political process in this nation, we have little hope of electing presidents and other political leaders with a postmodern vision. On the other hand, such a radical change in the political process from the grassroots level on up will be difficult, if not impossible, without encouragement from the top. This dialectical relationship may, at first glance, make significant change seem impossible. But it is not, because the relationship of mutual dependence is only partial, and because not everything need be accomplished at once. The spread of new visions and priorities to a larger percentage of the electorate can lead to the election of new political leaders and can induce some older ones "to see the light." And the rhetoric and policy changes made by these politicians can lead in turn to still greater changes in the political process. Not a vicious cycle, but a benevolent spiral.

This dialectical relationship between process and leadership is not, however, the only reason to be concerned about a postmodern renewal of the political process at the grassroots level. The purpose of political activity in local settings should by no means be equated simply with the election, continuing education and prodding of political leaders at the state and federal levels. There is also much that can be done, and in fact can only be done, locally.

By a "postmodern politics," we mean, in most general terms, a politics based on the claims of wholeness upon our political imaginations. The wholeness involves both the whole human race, including future generations, and the life of the planet as a whole. Such claims depend upon the perceived possibility of a "new world order" that is genuinely new—one that is based on a sustainable relationship between the human species and the rest of the biosphere and on a concern for the human enterprise as a whole. And this new order must, we along with many others are convinced, come into being soon. The modernist fallacy is to suppose that the continuities of the last five hundred years can be maintained in face of the demographic and environmental pressures that have been building up in recent decades on the planetary life-support systems, and in face of the volatile mix of increasing populations, declining resources, and growing access in countries in all parts of the world to increasingly destructive weapons. The modernist fallacy supposes that technological reason and managerial adjustments, without any fundamental change in vision, values, and lifestyle, will lead us out of this labyrinth. We require a new style of leadership, grounded in a new vision of the world, for the approaching new millennium.

The presidency is both a metaphor for leadership and a focal point for struggle in this dynamic of challenge. Some of the questions within this challenge are these: Can we find the will and wisdom to fashion an appropriate idea of leadership to address the incipient needs of our citizenry, implying a better way to deal with the traditional concerns of security, resources, lifestyle, and the strangeness of "others" both within and without our borders? Can we bring the reality, not merely the rhetoric, of fairness and respect into political life, both domestically and internationally? Can we relearn how to use the land, water, air, and fire in a manner that benefits our children and their children? Can we show respect for the millions of other species that share this planet with us and express this in our human political economy? Can we inspire the sort of politics that begins to delimit and even to insist upon such a reorientation of basic perspective?

The essays in this book respond to this challenge. They share a commitment to the creation of another America, one in which the promises of the U.S. Constitution will finally be realized for all our citizens, one that actualizes the increasingly appreciated necessity of establishing harmonies between society and nature, and one that honors transnational norms of legality and fairness.

The imperatives directed at America are elements of a far larger global drama, but the American response is crucial. Not only is America more responsible than any other nation for the present condition of the planet, both geopolitically and ecologically; it is also the main symbol and embodiment of modernity. The shaping imagery of the modern experience is stamped indelibly "made in the USA." This acknowledgment can lead either to triumphal arrogance of the "end of history" variety (a shortcut to disaster, given the global situation) or to an exemplary acceptance of responsibility and accountability. We are committed to changing the response soon from the former to the latter.

The term *postmodern* is used today in a wide variety of ways: some of these we affirm, some we only partly associate ourselves with, and others we reject completely. We have already briefly indicated how we intend the term and what we would mean, therefore, by "postmodern politics" and "postmodern presidential vision and leadership." Other dimensions of our meaning are given in the various essays in this volume, a brief preview of which, with special emphasis on identifying the domain of the postmodern, may be helpful here.

For John Cobb, at the core of modernity is the conviction that economic growth is always good, both in itself and as the precondition for solving other problems. This conviction has led to an ever-expanding market and thus to the global market of today. Cobb argues, in opposition to this disposition, that continued economic growth will not enable us to deal with our other problems, such as poverty and environmental degradation, but will continue to exacerbate them. Most startlingly, he argues that "even in strictly economic terms, continued growth does not contribute to well-being." Having concluded that "the scope of the dominant market is the issue," he suggests that a postmodern president would urge us to reverse directions, to move toward a system of relatively self-sufficient local communities. This move to *economic* decentralization would be the most important step we could take to promote *political* decentralization, to protect the biosphere, to decrease militarization, and to improve the lot of the poor in third world countries as well as our own. One reason for putting Cobb's essay first is that, besides presenting its own distinctive proposal, it touches on many of the concerns that are treated more extensively in the other essays.

Joanna Macy focuses on the unprecedented sense of time of late-modern experience, which she describes as a "pathological denial of the reality and ongoingness of time." The presidency of Ronald Reagan symbolized this cancellation of the future. Making this analysis concrete, she considers the way we have produced and disposed of nuclear wastes to be "the most appalling display of our denial of the future." Breaking out of this "temporal prison" is the precondition for any realistic prospect of coping with the ecological crisis. Rather than retreating to premodern spiritualities of escape from time as enemy, we need to "become friendly with time and reinhabit time." Spiritually, this means an orientation based on cosmic stories that nourish "a time-developmental consciousness." Politically, this means a "postmodern politics of time." Some concrete examples in structures of governance would be Nuclear Guardian Sites, representatives in Congress for the people of the future, and a House of Spokespersons for the future.

Wes Jackson emphasizes the interdependence of agriculture and rural community. They are being destroyed by the deadly combination of two central aspects of modernity: the drive to subdue nature and the profit-making ethos. Like Macy, Jackson sees as a precondition for any effective response to our crises a "mental shift in how we see the world," and for him, likewise, this involves a vision of the interconnectedness of all things. With reference to agriculture in particular, this new perception means that ecology becomes the primary discipline in the postmodern world. This change entails replacing the idea of "subduing nature" with the new-old idea of "nature as the measure." Macy's concern with the long-term future is echoed in Jackson's call to "just say no" to extractive agriculture in favor of a sustainable agriculture. The call of many for a change from an anthropocentric to an ecological attitude is reflected in his moving conviction that all agricultural plants and animals should be treated as valued relatives of wild things, rather than as human property without intrinsic value. The postmodern recovery of older values and practices in response to new conditions is reflected in Jackson's central claim, which is that "the Jeffersonian ideal of the family farm and strong rural community [is] a practical necessity in a world of declining energy and material resources." Jackson's essay indicates, by implication, the kind of people we need as secretaries of agriculture, at both the federal and state levels, if we are to develop a postmodern, sustainable agriculture.

David Griffin, focusing on the global ecological crisis, portrays modernity, as does Jackson, in terms of the drive to dominate nature for human benefit, a drive that found justification in the anthropocentric dualism of the early modern worldview and found expression in modern economics and technology. A political leader with a postmodern vision would be one who has broken free from this self-destructive outlook, who has come to see humanity as one among millions of species that have a right to flourish, and who sees that the human economy must, for the sake of the human race as well as other species, fit harmoniously within nature's economy. A postmodern president would lead America and thereby the world to realize that the ecological crisis is the greatest challenge ever faced by the human race, and would, accordingly, lead us in response to develop the biggest "crash program" of all time. (Griffin's essay is longer than the others because it is in a sense two articles in one. The book was originally to have an essay by Amory and Hunter Lovins. When that became impossible, Griffin's essay was expanded so as to include some of the kind of factual information about energy and other matters that the Lovinses essay would have provided.)

Jim Wallis believes that the modern world has generated "a global economic, social, and spiritual crisis that has yet to be named." This is no abstract issue for him, as he writes from "the most murderous neighborhood in the most murderous city in the most murderous nation in the world." While others are speaking of the decay of the physical infrastructure of our country, a more basic type of decay is that of our *moral* infrastructure. At the root of this crisis is a set of twisted values reflecting "a system whose primary reality is economic." The modern presidency, being "utterly bereft of political and spiritual vision," serves merely to protect this system. A postmodern presidency will challenge this system on the basis of values arising from the grassroots and, ultimately, from a religiously based moral vision. This vision will be distinctively postmodern in its understanding that all our destinies—those of all peoples and of the earth—are tied together.

Douglas Sloan, writing about a postmodern education, believes that even more basic for addressing our global crisis than moral commitment and political action is "a transformation of the ways we think about the world and come to know her." At the root of our crisis lies a late-modern, far-too-narrow conception of education, which is preoccupied with quantitative abstractions, leaving out the qualitative dimensions of experience. In response to the back-to-the-basics movement, Sloan argues that the real basics are not the three R's but wonder, interest, confidence, compassion, courage, social feeling, a sense for beauty, and reverence for life. An education that overlooks these dimensions of reality not only will produce inner poverty in the lives of students, but also will be "a disaster for the society in which these children will be the leaders." Our present inclination to rely upon purely technical solutions for societal problems "bespeaks a deep deficiency in our political, moral, and intellectual imagination." In contrast with the current educational emphasis on thinking that stresses quantitative abstractions and that is detached from feeling, willing, and valuing, we need a postmodern education in which all these dimensions of the mind are fully developed. One thing a postmodern president could do would be to help us overcome our narrow conception of national interest, understood in purely economic and military terms, which reinforces our narrow conception of education. Sloan's essay has implications as well, of course, for the kinds of secretaries of education we need in the coming decades to guide the development of a postmodern educational system.

For Roger Wilkins the postmodern world is in one sense already here. He believes that the postmodern era began for our nation when we developed atomic weapons. This weaponry, and its use, destroyed the old U.S. certainties. But we have not yet, in response, evolved a postmodern presidency. We have instead had a series of "mostmodern" presidents, whose sense of their office has been paradoxically puffed up by the annihilatory power at their disposal and who have sought to deal with postmodern problems by pushing the values, goals, and means of the modern presidency to the hilt. Americans have been characterized not only by certainty and self-confidence, but by violence, by habits of mastery and control used to dominate both nature and other peoples. A genuinely postmodern president would lead us convincingly away from this long experience of domination. Wilkins, like Jackson, refers back to Jefferson and sees our last, best hope in finally learning to take democracy seriously. Like Sloan, he believes that education must lie at the heart of this transformation. We must educate our children to be true citizens of their nation and their planet, citizens for whom the "general welfare" will be at least as important as the "common defense."

Frances Moore Lappé is concerned primarily with the political process. She sees at the root of our present inability to deal with the crises of our troubled planet a set of modern assumptions. These assumptions have made politics seem suspect, economics seem beyond human guidance on the basis of norms of fairness and empathy, and freedom seem to be little more than freedom for unlimited accumulation. Repudiating these assumptions is a precondition for a "deep democratic renewal" that will replace the thin, passive democracy of today with a robust and participatory democracy of the sort needed to deal with the threats we face. Even more explicitly than our other contributors, she calls for a retrieval of the best elements in the American tradition—in particular, the values of freedom, democracy, and fairness: "these beautiful words we must reclaim for a postmodern vision." With a postmodern vision of "human nature as socially constituted, not atomistic," we will come to appreciate the political process as an expression of our nature. With a "postmodern vision of our interrelatedness and mutual interests," our sense of self-interest will expand, and we will take a longer-term approach to government planning and budgeting. The postmodern vision will also enable us to move beyond modern trade-offs, such as those between government responsibility and individual responsibility, and between market and government. With regard to the latter, we need a public exploration of how to extend the democratic principle of accountability to the various facets of economic life.

Richard Falk, like the other authors, stresses the priority of a new way of thinking, speaking of "a mind-set that transcends modernism by reconceiving the character of reality itself." He, like Wallis, understands modernism in terms of an emphasis on "materialist satisfactions" but adds to this a preoccupation with territorial sovereignty. Like Wilkins, he sees the postmodern situation in terms of the emergence of various factors, such as nuclear weapons and global pollution, that render modernist notions of national security increasingly obsolete. A postmodern president will realize that "the only way to protect the well-being of Americans is to uphold the global commons." He sets forth several illustrative proposals to implement postmodern policies: adding a House of Overseas Delegates to Congress, extending democratic accountability to foreign policy, and making the Nuremberg Principles apply to the activities of U.S. politicians so that these principles take precedence over unconditional claims of national sovereignty. With regard to obtaining postmodern presidents, Falk believes, as do Wilkins and Lappé, in the importance of reconstituting a genuine democratic process. "If we want a more responsive presidency, we must begin by awakening the citizenry from its long sleep."

Frank Kelly's concluding essay is concerned with precisely this issue: how we might obtain postmodern presidents. His proposal is based in part on the complaint voiced by Wallis, Griffin, Lappé, and Falk that the real issues facing us today are not even discussed in presidential campaigns as now structured. It is also based in part on a postmodern perception of citizenship shared with Wilkins and Falk: "All human beings are more than citizens of nations. We are inhabitants of a small planet now endangered by nuclear weapons and the threat of environmental destruction" (which implies that other nations have a rightful voice in the discussion of who is suitable to be president of America, given the projection of its vast economic and military power to all corners of the globe). Finally, Kelly takes seriously Harry Truman's advice that "we should find the best candidates and get them to run." On these bases, Kelly suggests a new way to prepare for a presidential election that centers upon "a systematic search for extraordinary candidates." Kelly thus offers us a concrete proposal for the kind of active "citizen democracy" that Lappé, Wilkins, and Falk have urged upon us as a political necessity.

Kelly's essay brings us back to a central issue of the book, broached earlier: the relative importance of the political process in general, especially at the grassroots level, on the one hand, and presidential vision and leadership in establishing new policies, on the other.

Some who are concerned with the development of a genuine democracy, one that involves strong grassroots participation, dismiss presidential politics altogether, considering the presidency either irrelevant or a lost cause. Although we share some of the frustrations that give rise to this attitude, we consider it misguided. Given the vast powers of the White House to shape foreign policy, initiate or veto domestic legislation, make appointments, and shape public debate and perceptions, it is naive to consider the presidency irrelevant to the real issues of today. And it is prematurely defeatist to consider the presidency beyond change and thereby to allow modernist forces to maintain control without even facing a challenge. For the budding postmodern movement to give up on the presidency is to play into the hands of destructive forces and to lose by default the office that could become one of the greatest powers in the world today for positive change.

Instead of thinking in oppositional terms between grassroots activism and presidential politics, we think in "both/and" terms. One aspect of this both/and position between the political process and the presidency, expressed by Griffin with regard to the ecological crisis, is that our various crises need to be addressed at several levels at once. Some aspects need to be dealt with at the local level; others must be handled at the state level; still others can only be solved at the national level; and still others need solutions coming from global authorities. (And perhaps political regions and bioregions have their roles to play as well.) The need for postmodern political leaders, especially in the White House, is a necessary condition for solving our problems, but it is far from a sufficient condition. This both/and position is also expressed by Lappé, despite her emphasis on the development of a "democratic culture" and her reluctance to rely upon "experts" to find the solutions for our planetary problems. For these reasons, she might seem to be discounting the importance of the presidency in favor of grassroots organization. But she expressly rejects the notion of a trade-off between government responsibility and individual responsibility and points out that government, by its policies, can either foster or stifle individual responsibility. The both/and position is also implicit in Macy's essay: Her observation that Reagan as president helped diminish our sense of responsibility for the future implies that a different president, one more nearly embodying Macy's postmodern sense of time, could help American citizens develop an enlarged feeling of responsibility for the future.

Another feature of the both/and position is that citizens with postmodern values need to become more actively involved even in those issues that are appropriately decided, finally, by the executive and legislative branches of the federal government. In this vein, as Lappé and Falk stress, the principle of democratic accountability must be expanded to include economics and foreign policy. Again, to argue, as this book does, that postmodern political leadership, especially at the presidential level, is urgent—indeed, that we will probably not long survive without it—is quite consistent with the insistence on an activist citizenry. Far from being in opposition, postmodern political leadership and postmodern activism, even militancy, are symbiotically linked.

One example of a postmodern relation between a president and the national political process is suggested by Cobb. Reflecting a style of leadership that Cobb has elsewhere called "leadership by proposal," his president would not try to use the power of the office to force a change of direction upon the American economy, but would instead seek to engender a "great national debate" about the merits of his proposal. This proposal exemplifies a theme running throughout the book, namely, that a postmodern politics will focus not simply on ends but also on means, with the desired means being a participatory process that helps revitalize democracy in our country. We place our hopes neither on one or more political leaders alone, nor solely on an aroused citizenry animated by postmodern priorities, but on the beneficial and organic confluence of the two.

One other feature of postmodern politics as conceived in this book involves the relations among ecological issues, poor people in this country, and the poor in third-world countries. In most modern discussions, each of these interests is portrayed as in tension with the other two. Policies designed to avoid further environmental degradation, for example, were thought to work against the welfare of poor people, both at home and abroad. And policies designed to aid the poor in America would, it was supposed, generally work against the poor in other countries, and vice versa. But the present book is based in part on the perception that this image of zero-sum trade-offs is not only demoralizing, discouraging any joint commitment to ecological and equity values, but also fallacious. In general, precisely the same policies that hurt the environment also hurt the poor, both here and elsewhere. For instance, global warming is likely to flood densely populated coastal regions in such third-world countries as Bangladesh; and it is the poor in the inner city who suffer most directly from pollution and toxic wastes. Accordingly, policies that will lead to the preservation of the nonhuman portions of nature can also be the best policies for helping the poor, both here and abroad, and for overcoming the increasing gap between rich and poor countries, and between rich and poor people within various countries, including our own.

The most significant event with regard to these issues in recent times is, of course, the much-heralded "collapse of communism" in the former Soviet Union and its satellites and the resulting "end of the cold war." In spite of the many grounds for relief, this development is fraught with ambiguity for the overall global situation. The result could be simply a speeding up of the global collapse. Although they differed significantly in some respects, industrial capitalism and industrial socialism were at one in their goal, which was the domination of nature for (short-term) human welfare, and they assumed a direct correlation between this welfare and material output. What the competition between them has proved is that capitalism is more efficient at mobilizing resources for material output than is centrally planned socialism. Both systems sought to achieve their shared goal in such a way that, roughly speaking, the gross national product has been a measure of how much of nature was destroyed that year. The collapse of state-centric socialism in the former Soviet Union and in Eastern Europe could mean, accordingly, primarily the incorporation of several hundred millions more people into a system that is much more efficient in destroying nature. (The Soviet Union was in general more polluting *locally* than the United States; but the United States has used up far more natural resources per capita and has been much more responsible for the emission of greenhouse gases and ozone-layer-depleting substances.) Furthermore, a new relationship of cooperation between Russia and the United States and their allies could mean, as many third-world thinkers fear, both neglect and an intensified exploitation of the poorer and weaker countries.

The collapse of the cold war could, by contrast, open the way to developing policies that would serve to reduce the gap between rich and poor nations, and between the rich and poor within each nation, and that would simultaneously be ecologically sustainable and protective of the other species of life with which we share this planet. Enormous economic resources that were previously devoted to military budgets could be redirected. The same is true of many of our best scientific and technological minds. Also, with the collapse of communism at its center, indigenous movements for economic justice in various countries can no longer be subverted and opposed on the alleged grounds that they are part of an international communist movement. And, indeed, with that fear gone—insofar as it ever was a genuine fear—energy and intelligence can be redirected wholeheartedly to more serious security issues facing us, such as the threat of ecological deterioration and the possibility that economic desperation and bitterness may lead some nation or group to use nuclear weapons. The end of the cold war could, in short, make the development of a postmodern world order more quickly realizable. The end of the cold war presents us with a choice between a mostmodern and a genuinely postmodern world, which we regard, in its essence, as the choice between death and life.

The decline in the quality of political leadership that we see in our country today is part of a worldwide phenomenon. We believe that this development is due not simply to the fact that people with lesser abilities are being put into leadership positions, and not simply to the fact that political problems have been increasingly difficult. We believe that it signifies primarily a crisis of the modernist imagination. The reason the problems seem increasingly intractable is that the modernist vision is increasingly less relevant to global realities. That is, we can distinguish between a postmodern condition, on the one hand, and a postmodern vision and agenda, on the other.[5] The postmodern condition is, as argued most clearly by Wilkins and Falk, already upon us; a postmodern vision and agenda have been emerging for some time, but political processes remain firmly in control of individuals and institutions locked into the modernist vision and agenda. What passes as political debate involves mainly tactical differences within this larger consensus. We believe that the much-remarked decline in the quality of leadership will not be reversed until we have political leaders who understand the postmodern condition and have a commensurate postmodern vision and agenda.

We should perhaps add here that, just as there has been a wide range of leadership possibilities—in style, tactics, and quality—within the modernist political vision, the same will be true within a postmodern vision. In proposing a postmodern politics, we have no blueprint in mind and look forward to no monolithic movement (as illustrated by the fact that the present volume is far from monolithic). To the contrary, we envisage a release from the straightjackets with which political life has been increasingly constrained by the forces of modernity. In speaking of a postmodern politics, we have in mind as common denominators only the general matters of vision, policy, and process that we have addressed.

Given this caveat, we are convinced that postmodern politics, including postmodern presidential vision and leadership, are necessary if we are to survive without unspeakable horrors in the coming century. To suggest that the far-reaching changes implied by a transition from modern to postmodern politics could occur in the near future, as is necessary, will seem naively optimistic to some. And yet, the same would have been said just a few years ago about predictions of radical change in the Soviet Union and Eastern Europe. To be sure, the changes for which we hope are even more extensive and cut deeper into the sinews of societal practice. But extraordinary situations can evoke extraordinary responses.

Part of the reason we have hope, in spite of the overwhelming character of the crises that face us, is the importance we attribute to vision. Those who see no realistic possibility for change often stress, instead, the supposedly autonomous nature of various forces that are embedded in the modern world, such as modern technology and market economics. It is true that these forces are deeply embedded and that changing course will not be easy. But we do not agree that these forces are autonomous. Modern capitalism and technology came into being as a result of decisions based on a new vision, a vision that challenged premodern ideas about both what is important and what is possible. And the impact of this modern vision has been sustained by the continuation and dissemination of a supportive cultural consensus. With the emergence of a new vision, one that shows that the unconditional continuation of modern capitalism and technology is neither desirable nor possible, and that the development of a postmodern economics and technology is both necessary and possible, these seemingly autonomous trajectories can be altered, hopefully before they bring about irreversible collapses of human civilization and the wider ecological system of which it is a part.

It is not, to be sure, merely the supposedly autonomous nature of modern economics and technology that lead many commentators to be pessimistic. Besides the "momentum" of these forces—a metaphor that stresses their impersonal nature—they are backed by extremely powerful interests, by people and institutions who will stop at little to destroy, in one way or another, those who advocate and act upon a postmodern vision. (Oliver Stone's movie "JFK" has raised for many people the intramodernist possibility that parts of the CIA, the FBI, and other branches of the government may have actually participated in the planning and cover-up of the assassination of President Kennedy out of fear that he was about to change course in a manner threatening to elite members of the military-industrial-intelligence complex.) But to acknowledge that changing course will not be easy—courageous and often self-sacrificial leadership will be needed—is insistently not to concede that it is impossible. We would far rather risk the charge of being naive than succumb to cynicism. Placing our faith in the viability of a form of postmodernism at least offers the possibility of ways out of our seeming civilizational impasse. Beyond offering some basis for hope about the future, we believe that a postmodern perspective helps us to discover a relevant realism, thereby avoiding both a naive optimism and a paralyzing pessimism. It is in this spirit that we present these essays.

NOTES

1. David Ray Griffin, ed., *Spirituality and Society: Postmodern Visions* (Albany, N.Y.: State University of New York Press, 1988).

2. In speaking of "postmodern politics," we have in mind something quite different from the concerns articulated in a volume entitled *Postmodernism and Politics*, edited by Jonathan Arac (Minneapolis: University of Minnesota Press, 1986). The postmodernism of that volume is primarily postmodern literary criticism, is mainly deconstructive, and arises out of the world of postmodern Marxist reflection (ix, xxxv). Also, as Arac indicates, the contributors to that volume have no hopes for a postmodern politics that will transform the world or even American society in general ("We will not transform American life today, or tomorrow"), but at most hope to transform academic habits and disciplines (xxxix). For those interested in examining that kind of postmodernism and its relation to politics, Arac's introduction (ix–xliii) is to be highly recommended.

3. Besides the book mentioned in note 1, the other volumes in the series most directly related to the current book are *Sacred Interconnections: Postmodern Spirituality, Political Economy, and Art* (1990), edited by Griffin; *The Ignorant Perfection of Ordinary People* (1991), by Robert Inchausti; and *Ecological Literacy: Education and the Transition to a Postmodern World* (1992), by David W. Orr. The shift of overall worldview is addressed with respect to science in *The Reenchantment of Science: Postmodern Proposals* (1988), edited by Griffin. It is addressed with respect to philosophy and theology in *God and Religion in the Postmodern World* (1989), by Griffin; *Primordial Truth and Postmodern Theology* (1990), by Griffin and Huston Smith; and *Varieties of Postmodern Theology* (1989), by Griffin, William A. Beardslee, and Joe Holland. The latter volume deals most explicitly with the contrast between the constructive postmodernism of this series and the more deconstructive movement that is usually in mind when the term "postmodernism" is used. The philosophical roots of the constructive postmodernism of this series are explored in *Founders of Constructive Postmodern Philosophy: Peirce, James, Bergson, Whitehead, and*

Hartshorne (1992), by Griffin, John B. Cobb, Jr., Marcus P. Ford, Pete A. Y. Gunter, and Peter Ochs.

4. In 1988, Richard Rose published a book entitled *The Postmodern President* (Chatham, N.J.: Chatham House). The meaning he gives to the term, however, is quite different from ours. He distinguishes three phases of the presidency: the traditional, the modern, and the postmodern. The traditional president had little to do. The modern presidency was initiated in 1933 by Franklin Roosevelt, who was the first to be an active leader in peacetime; it came to full flowering after World War II, when the United States, being both an economic and a military superpower, had hegemony around the globe. The modern president had much to do, and the power to do it. The postmodern presidency, by contrast, does not have the resources to do all that is expected of it. The postmodern world is "a posthegemonic world" (11): "The United States can no longer dominate the world economy or use force to impose its will on every continent" (26). Whereas the postmodern presidency began with the Vietnam War, Jimmy Carter was the first fully postmodern president (26). Because the United States no longer has economic hegemony, to govern now requires cooperation with other nations (4, 25).

While Rose's book is excellent within its own framework, it can be seen from this brief summary that his distinction between the modern and postmodern presidencies differs from ours in at least two respects. First, for him the modern presidency ran only from the 1930s to the early 1960s (with the period from the early 1960s until 1976 being transitional), whereas for us all of our presidents thus far have been firmly, although variously, modern. This is related to the second difference, which is that for Rose the distinction between modern and postmodern presidents has to do with the status of the United States and thus the power of the presidents vis-à-vis other nations (hence his subtitle: *The White House Meets the World*), whereas for us the distinction has to do primarily with worldview and values. From our viewpoint, Rose's postmodern presidents are still modern in that they still assume that the task of the president is to promote American interests in the narrow and largely material sense, rather than to promote American security by working for a more equitable and sustainable economic order and increasing the security of all nations. Rose's interpretation of a postmodern presidency does approach ours in his stress on the fact that leadership now involves cooperation, and that this requires learning to understand the values and concerns of other peoples. But in Rose's book this approach is a practical adjustment to the loss of American power. It is now necessary because of the decline of American hegemony, not because it is inherently good (although Rose may personally believe that it is) or mandated by the ecological agenda. Rose's position thus remains aligned with what we designate as "modernism."

5. We are indebted to Charles Jencks for this way of phrasing the distinction; see his introduction to *The Post-Modern Reader* (London: Academy Editions/New York: St. Martin's Press, 1992).

PART I

POLITICAL VISION AND POLICY FOR A POSTMODERN AMERICA

1

A PRESIDENTIAL ADDRESS ON THE ECONOMY

John B. Cobb, Jr.

My friends, what I have to say to you today may sound strange indeed, coming from one whom you have only recently elected to the presidency of the United States. In this period, as I have felt the responsibility of this office, my perception of our national situation has changed. The conventional wisdom by which I have operated in the past, and which shaped my campaign speeches, no longer satisfies me. I have been groping my way into a quite different vision—one that is, for me, truly new. Some of you have long seen what I am just beginning to see, but many of you will find what I have to say to you today both odd and disturbing.

The recent campaign, like most campaigns, emphasized economic issues. As the challenger, it was my role to highlight the weaknesses in the economy. These are many. I emphasized the unfavorable balance of trade, the growing dependence of our economy on foreign investments and borrowing, the national insecurity that results from our increasing dependence on imports even for national defense, and the growing gap in income between the rich and the poor. I criticized also the destruction of human communities that results from the closing of factories, and I called for more vigorous action with regard to acid rain, depletion of the ozone layer, and the greenhouse effect.

I continue to see all of these as problems. In that regard I have not changed my mind. But my campaign speeches suggested that by stimulating the growth of the economy, by breaking down barriers against our goods in foreign markets, by renegotiating the debts of third world countries so that they could again buy our products, and by increasing the productivity of our workers, all our economic problems could be solved. In truth, the difference between my proposals and those of my opponents were not great. Mainly I put myself forward as better able to bring to Washington the sort of team that could make the system work more effectively and humanely.

I have, in fact, brought together a fine group of women and men to give leadership to our nation. I am proud of them. We have struggled to find a way to make good on the claims I made in the campaign. We have generated some excellent ideas on particular issues, which we will implement soon. But overall the results of our reflection have been discouraging.

There seem to be contradictions built into the system. Policies designed to speed up economic growth can be expected to increase the gap between the rich and the poor. This is because lower labor costs are needed to make our products more competitive. We want to protect workers and communities from the effects of plant closings, but we have been forced to acknowledge that rapid economic growth depends on the free movement of capital to those places where it can be most efficiently, that is, most profitably, employed. The economic system depends on the free flow of capital and on labor mobility. Any effort on our part to protect the communities that are weakened or destroyed by the closing of plants would work against the growth of the whole economy.

We also came to see that there is a tension between stimulating economic growth and responding to your demand that we stop the degradation of the environment. The conventional wisdom has been that with a healthy economy the nation can afford the costs of environmental cleanup. But especially as we face the prospect of global warming, this conventional wisdom breaks down. To slow the greenhouse effect, we need to reduce the use of fossil fuels, but policies designed to stimulate growth and competitiveness seem to require increased use of these fuels.

We toyed with the idea of economic planning. We thought that the government might steer economic growth into channels that were not damaging to the environment. But we did not pursue this far. Central planning of the economy has had a dismal record all over the world, and we had hardly any ideas of how the economy could grow and become more competitive globally without increased use of fossil fuels.

We considered a massive move to nuclear energy, but we gave that up too. The amount of fossil fuel required for a massive buildup of nuclear energy production is staggering! More important, the dangers involved in nuclear energy are no less disturbing than the consequences of burning fossil fuels. Many people are most concerned about accidents, and these will inevitably occur. But there are other, equally important, concerns. The problem of decommissioning old plants has not yet been recognized in its full seriousness. And there is the appalling problem of disposing of wastes that remain poisonous for tens of thousands of years. A world covered with ever increasing quantities of deadly poison is not the legacy we want to leave.

The final straw that tilted our thinking away from conventional wisdom was finding a statistical evaluation of how the national economy has done since 1951. Conventionally, we have been taught to judge the success of the economy by the growth of per-capita gross national product. We knew this had been questioned occasionally, but we had not seriously considered an alternative. Now we found a proposal of an Index of Sustainable Economic Welfare (ISEW)[1] that could serve as an alternative basis for evaluation. When it is employed, perceptions of the performance of the economy in the past few decades are startlingly different. Let me give you an example. Remember that all figures are adjusted for inflation.

The per-capita GNP in 1969 was $5,366, and in 1986 it was $7,226. This is an increase of 35 percent. But during the same period there was no significant improvement in sustainable economic welfare as measured by the new index. The per-capita figure was $4,700 in 1969 and $4,732 in 1986, a gain of less than 1 percent. Indeed, when long-term environmental effects were factored in, the per-capita ISEW *dropped* from $3,777 in 1969 to $3,403 in 1986, or almost 10 percent! In short, the economic growth of that seventeen-year period was accompanied by a substantial loss in sustainable economic welfare.

Of course, the ISEW figures, like any such figures, depend on many somewhat arbitrary decisions. What counts as economic welfare? How do we judge its sustainability? None of us agreed in detail with all the judgments expressed in the ISEW, and we are sure that much more refined and accurate calculations can be made. Yet in a general way the ISEW makes sense. This index begins with personal consumption as the basic positive contribution to welfare. Because this is the largest element in the GNP as well, there is a bias in the two indexes toward conformity. One could easily argue that much personal consumption—of alcohol, tobacco, and junk foods, for example—does not contribute to real economic well-being. To make such a judgment would tend to increase the disparity between GNP and ISEW. But it is too hard to draw a line between beneficial personal consumption and that which is either harmful or worthless. We therefore decided that a measure of welfare has to accept the convention of economists that individuals are the final judges of what is good and that they express that judgment in their purchases.

As one who has been concerned about the growing gap between rich and poor, I was pleased to see that the ISEW factored income distribution into its calculations. I have also been concerned about growing national indebtedness, which certainly does not seem sustainable over the long haul without damage to our economic welfare. The ISEW takes account of that.

There has been a lot of talk among economists about the contribution of unpaid labor, especially housework, to the economy. ISEW includes that. Also, few doubt that there are costs of pollution or that, when wetlands and topsoils are lost, nature's services to the economy are reduced. The ISEW considers matters of this sort.

Finally, although the authors recognize that the discipline of economics provides little basis for calculating the costs to the future involved in resource exhaustion and in such massive environmental changes as reduction of the ozone layer and the greenhouse effect, they have introduced these, too, in the second set of figures I quoted—those that show a 10 percent decline in sustainable economic welfare from 1969 to 1986. Surely these are relevant considerations, even if no one knows how to measure them.

Our conclusion has been that the detailed figures are not reliable, but that the general implications are inescapable. *Growth of per-capita GNP can accompany decline in sustainable economic welfare.* Indeed, it may now be doing so.

I emphasize that only *economic* welfare is under consideration here. The argument in favor of growth of GNP is further weakened when one thinks of other changes in our society that have accompanied economic growth. These are phenomena that have often in history been associated with urbanization and thus, at least indirectly, with economic growth. I refer to the increase of crime, the breakdown of family life, the increased use of drugs, and the deterioration of public education. Perhaps we can summarize all of this under the heading *breakdown of community.* As we thought about this, we saw that most of the policies designed to stimulate economic growth also work toward this breakdown of human community.

The conclusion to which we have come is that the *economic policies of the United States should no longer be directed primarily to the increase of market activity that is measured by the gross national product.* They should rather be directed to contributing to the *total well-being of all our citizens now and in the future.* The great question, then, is this: What does that mean? In what direction should the economy be channeled?

We are clear about some of our goals. We want to reduce the gap between the rich and the poor, ensuring all citizens a decent life. We want to reduce the use of fossil and nuclear fuels. We want to encourage the development of strong community life all over the nation. And we want to maintain and even increase the economic freedom of our citizens.

If we know in general where we want to go, why does it seem so difficult to find policies that will take us there? We certainly have the resources to meet the needs, and even many of the more reasonable desires, of all our citizens. Community is something that develops of itself when people are given a favorable context. And within a healthy community, individuals can make a great many decisions about their work and their purchases.

One problem, of course, is that we want to continue to produce a great deal while using less fuel, both fossil and nuclear. But that need not pose an insuperable obstacle. Amory and Hunter Lovins have shown us many ways in which we can continue to get all the use we now have from these energy sources with far less input of fuel.[2] We can build houses that require little or no fuel and that still have year-round comfort. We can light them well with far less use of electricity. Our toilets can function well with far less water. Cars and other forms of transportation can be far more efficient than they now are. And so it goes. Once we recognize that the need is to have more efficient use of energy and other resources, and once our technology is directed to that end, enormous improvements are possible.

I will be proposing some steps in the direction of energy efficiency in the near future. Even this emphasis cuts against deeply entrenched habits of mind that see expansion of energy production as the natural preparation for further growth. But because the focus on efficiency is both profitable to industry and beneficial to consumers as well as to the environment, I hope to persuade Congress to enact legislation that will accelerate already existing trends in this direction. By concentrating efforts now on more efficient use of energy and other scarce resources, we can buy time for jointly considering other changes that go deeper and cut more sharply against the conventional wisdom.

For example, certain lifestyle changes could reduce use of energy while improving the quality of life at the same time. We could build our cities in ways that would require far less commuting. Paolo Soleri has shown how the need for private transportation within the city could be done away with altogether, with great gains in space, quiet, and beauty.[3] Citizens could get to any part of the city in ten or fifteen minutes by elevator, escalator, moving sidewalk, and walking. Genuine countryside would begin immediately at the city's edge.

A simple and healthful change in the national diet would drastically reduce the amount of land needed to produce food. At present 80 percent of our cropland grows grains to be fed to livestock. This not only uses a great deal of fossil fuel; it also puts pressure on marginal land that could recover if it were instead used for grazing or allowed to return to wilderness. A reduction of meat consumption by one-third would largely eliminate the need to feed grain to cattle. We could begin to regenerate the land and also share it with the wild animals that we have so extensively displaced.

Agricultural policy raises still more fundamental questions. According to the conventional wisdom, agriculture in this country, since the Second World War, has been a great success story. Productivity as measured by production per hour of labor has greatly increased. Far fewer people produce more crops than ever before. Agriculture provides a huge surplus for export, enabling us to buy oil, minerals, and industrial goods from our trading partners. We can also use our food surplus as a diplomatic weapon.

But we are impressed by the other side of this progress. Our policies have led to monocultures heavily dependent on fertilizers, insecticides, and herbicides. The natural fertility of the soil is depleted. Mass production is associated with practices that lead to erosion at altogether unsustainable levels. In reality, we are exporting our legacy of fertile soils.

Meanwhile, the small family farm and rural community, once the backbone of the nation, have become endangered species. They are replaced by agribusiness, which applies to the land the same policies that mining interests apply to minerals, those of an extractive economy. This economy not only mines the soil; it also drains off the economic resources of rural people into the urban sector.

If agriculture is to serve the people, we need a resettling of rural America and a renewal of rural community. American agriculture should be reoriented to local and regional markets, providing them with the diversity of products needed. Food should be grown near where it is consumed, thus drastically shortening supply lines and reducing the need for elaborate packaging. Of course, surpluses should be exchanged and sold abroad, but these should be true surpluses, grown in sustainable ways without undue use of fossil fuels. All of this means that we need to move *toward relatively self-sufficient local communities and away from primary orientation to the global market.*

Viewing our goals in this way has led us to change our thinking about national security. Conventional wisdom sees us as needing to police and control the global trade routes, the sources of supply, and the markets on which we all depend. But if we and other peoples move toward local self-sufficiency, these trade routes lose some of their importance. We will not need a military power capable of fighting wars halfway around the globe.

Indeed, as we have thought about these matters, we have come more and more to the conclusion that the scope of the dominant market is *the* issue. For two centuries we have aimed to extend the market to include larger and larger areas, so that more and more goods can be produced. We have been brilliantly successful, and all of us enjoy many of the fruits of this process. Now we find that the price has been high all along and that it is becoming disastrous. Many of our military conflicts and much of our need for huge armaments even in peacetime have resulted from the desire to control distant resources and markets. Meanwhile, the market has become so large that the biosphere is threatened. The assault on stable communities has become so powerful that the quality of personal life and character is deteriorating. Indeed, the workers produced by a society in which communities are so weak do not have the motivation and the discipline that make for a successful economy. The market is undercutting its own base.

As a nation we have been fully committed to a global economy. We have been taught that large markets are crucial to growth. The larger the market, the greater the possibility of specialization; the greater the specialization, the higher the productivity of labor; the higher the productivity of labor, the larger the per-capita gross product; the higher the gross product, the better off everyone is. The argument is a strong one. Indeed, with important qualifications, we accept all of it except the final step. This step may have been correct until fairly recently, at least if we limit our consideration to strictly economic welfare. But now we are convinced that, *even in strictly economic terms, continued growth does not contribute to well-being.* Hence, while the rest of the argument may be largely accurate, there is no reason for us to follow its prescriptions. The larger market, that is, the global market, needs to be evaluated on other grounds. Are there reasons for favoring the global market, other than its contribution to the increase of global production?

There are many consequences of the global market that appear good and desirable. It makes the whole world interdependent. It encourages the flow of international capital to countries where the workers are very poor and unemployment is very extensive. Technology accompanies capital, so that the transfer of advanced technology to the third world is facilitated. Meanwhile the U.S. consumer finds prices low and goods varied and abundant. It seems that everyone gains.

But if we look a bit more closely, we see another side. Interdependence based on specialization means for many countries total dependence on international markets controlled, and even manipulated, by financiers on whom they have no influence. In many instances these countries have lost the power to make basic decisions about their own lives. To many, "interdependence" is just another name for dependence. It is experienced as virtual slavery. Eventually, even the United States, if present trends continue, will find its freedom severely circumscribed by international finance. A world in which the economy is global, while political power is local, does not promise opportunity for popular participation in making the decisions that are most important to human well-being. In that kind of world, the most important decisions are made by the leaders of international finance, and their goals have little to do with the welfare of the people affected.

The alternative to global markets is national, regional, and local markets. What would it mean to reverse the long trend toward larger and larger markets and to work for smaller markets instead? Would that entail a drastic lowering of living standards?

Not necessarily. Kirkpatrick Sale has shown that a town of only ten thousand people could be largely self-sufficient in industrial production, with several competitive companies in each category. Local economies can take advantage of most of the technological advances of recent times. And most localities can also be self-sufficient in food production.[4]

Why propose such a vision? What advantages would it have? First, a community that was largely self-sufficient economically would be likely to be far more stable. Its people could participate in the decisions governing their lives. They could establish standards for pay, health, safety, and pollution for the benefit of the community, without fear that other companies, not so regulated, would undercut the local ones with lower prices.

Second, pressure on the environment could also be eased. Short supply lines would reduce transportation, with its heavy demands on energy. Smaller, diversified family farms could replace agribusiness, with human and animal labor reducing dependence on oil products. Passive solar energy could be used much more extensively and efficiently.

I have pictured the extreme and hypothetical case of truly local economies over against the other extreme, but increasingly real, case of a global economy. There are many options in between. The first choice, in fact, is between the global economy and a relatively self-sufficient national one. If we chose the national market, then we could move on to considering further steps in decentralization. The vision that would guide us would be one of a community of communities of communities. Quite small communities would be more self-sufficient than at present. They would be grouped into communities of communities that would be considerably more self-sufficient. And at the national level this self-sufficiency would be quite high. It would take a lot of thought and experimentation to determine just how much self-sufficiency is possible and desirable at each level. My point is that giving thought to these questions would engage our economists, as well as our sociologists and other specialists, in reflection quite different from what has been called for by the assumption that larger markets and more production are inherently desirable.

Our nation has tried at times a certain amount of political decentralization. We favor that, too. But when *political decentralization* is accompanied by *economic centralization*, it does not work well. It only serves to make the economic forces dominant over the political ones. For example, because the states do not have self-sufficient economies, they need investments from sources that are national and international. Hence, governors must compete with one another in trying to get factories to locate in their states. State legislatures must pass laws to make their states attractive to industry, even when in other respects this works against the public welfare. Thus political decentralization, rather than empowering people to make the decisions that most affect them, often weakens their ability to do so. If we want genuine local autonomy, political decentralization must be accompanied by economic decentralization. A state that was relatively self-sufficient economically could make many of the decisions that its citizens want. This is a third reason for moving toward regional self-sufficiency.

Moving toward national markets does not entail isolationism. Many of the problems we face today are global, and it is fruitless to deal with them only on a national level. We *are* interdependent. We need a forum in which global development can be discussed. Indeed, we need to have more rather than less power exercised at the global level. The urgency of dealing with the greenhouse effect and the depletion of the ozone layer should make that apparent to all. But increasing the political power of the United Nations and the World Court, so that they may be able to implement the actions required everywhere, does not count against the decentralization of the economy.

For the United States to move rapidly in the direction of national, regional, and local self-sufficiency would be profoundly disruptive of the economies of many other nations. Exports to us constitute a critical element for many of them. A few, such as Japan, Taiwan, Singapore, and now South Korea, have become prosperous through participation in the global economy. Others are trying hard to emulate them. For the United States to withdraw from the global market, after having for so long encouraged other nations to enter it, would seem a betrayal of their efforts and hopes. The proposal to move toward self-sufficiency confronts a profound moral challenge. Whatever we do, we must be sensitive to the consequences for these other people as well as for ourselves.

But however great our concern for them, we cannot continue current practices indefinitely. At present, the prosperity of some of these other countries and the hopes of others depend on our running a very unfavorable balance of trade. By exporting much more to us than they import from us, they accumulate dollars. In this way, wealth is transferred from this country to others. But how far can this go? Surely there is a limit. At some point trade must come into balance. At present, we can avoid this by borrowing money from our trading partners and selling them our assets. But are we willing as a people to pursue this policy indefinitely? Do we not want to leave to our children a nation in which they exercise ownership of most of its land and productive resources? This desire provides a fourth reason for moving toward economic decentralization.

There is yet a fifth reason for not wanting to continue present policies. In most of the countries that have profited from them, the profit has gone to a very small part of the population. The shift from subsistence farming on the part of the many to agribusiness for export to us, for example, has been very costly to most of the small farmers. They have lost their independence and are forced to work for large agricultural concerns, many of them foreign owned, under conditions that are dehumanizing. One reason military governments have been so prevalent in so-called developing countries has been that the methods employed in the shift to export-oriented economies have been brutal in relation to so many of the poor. An abrupt shift in U.S. policy away from openness to unlimited import would be disruptive, but if it led to the development of more self-sufficient local and regional economies in Latin America, Africa, and Asia, those people would in the long run be better off too. Hence, even the moral concern for third world peoples turns out to be a reason for moving, carefully and responsibly, to self-sufficient economies.

An extreme instance of the negative effect of our openness to imports from other countries is found in Amazonia. A few Brazilian capitalists have found that it is profitable to cut down the forests and raise cattle. They export the beef to us. They do in this way increase the gross national product of Brazil, earn dollars with which to service Brazilian debts, and themselves become richer. But the Brazilian people as a whole do not profit. Certainly the inhabitants of Amazonia, who are displaced from their ancestral homes, do not benefit. Their fate is much like that of many of the native Americans in this country during the nineteenth century. The Brazilian people as a whole are losing a very precious national asset—the world's largest tropical forest. Furthermore, the pasture land they are getting in exchange is often productive for only a few years. And finally, the people of the whole world are losing, as the capacity of the Amazonian forest to slow the greenhouse effect is being lost and, instead, the burning of the trees adds to the carbon dioxide in the atmosphere. So great are the costs of this operation, in comparison with what is gained, that among the measures we will soon propose to Congress will be the banning of the importation of beef raised in the Amazon region until our investigations can assure us that no further destruction of the forests for the purpose of raising cattle is being allowed.

As president, I cannot redirect economic policies at will. I am no match for the enormous vested interests that depend on and support the current policies. The moves toward national self-sufficiency and further decentralization would be opposed at every turn. This opposition would be supported by all the conventional wisdom. Again and again we would be told that the proposed policies would carry us back to the Dark Ages and put an end to all the hopes and aspirations of third–world peoples. Plenty of representatives of the elites of the third world would echo these sentiments. Idealists concerned for the world's poor would join their voices with the managers of international finance.

Even if I had the power to reorder the economy in the face of all this opposition, I would not want to exercise it. The world we want is one in which people participate in making the basic decisions about their lives and communities. We can only move toward such a world as we participate in envisioning and wanting it. My hope today is to engage your interest in a great national debate. Do we as a people want to continue our present course, responding as best we can to the inevitable crises we will face? Or do we want to change course? If so, in what direction shall we go?

On the other hand, there are immediate decisions that must be made. The Uruguay Round of proposals for revision of the General Agreement on Tariffs and Trade (GATT) confronts us with far-reaching decisions. These proposals have been strongly supported by the government of the United States. As I now see it, they carry us very far in just the direction that now seems to me wrong.

To adopt these proposals now, before the national debate has occurred, would render that debate in many ways useless. While we debated which way we wanted to go, we would have gone so far in one of the directions that a change would become almost impossible without massive disruption and suffering. Accordingly, I will throw the weight of this administration against the implementation of the new proposals. I need your understanding, if not your full support, for this reversal of U.S. policy. Hence I want to explain what these new proposals involve.

The ideal of a global market calls not only for the abolition of all tariffs, but also for the removal of all other restrictions on the free flow of capital and goods around the world. The ideal is "a level playing field." That means that no nation can set standards for imports that are not global standards. For example, if the United States refuses to import agricultural products that we judge carcinogenic when other countries do not have such high standards, that is viewed as an act in restraint of trade. U.S. producers can be held to higher standards, but they must compete with producers elsewhere who can export their goods to us without measuring up to these standards. Obviously, we will be under pressure to lower standards for our own producers as well.

More generally, much of our present agricultural policy will be set aside if we move ahead with the new proposals for GATT. These envision a world in which governmental involvement in supporting agriculture will cease. Many analysts judge that the result will be the end of small-scale farming not only in the United States but throughout the world. Such farming could compete successfully only if conservation of soil were a factor in price. But governmental interference in the market to introduce such calculations would become even more difficult, if not impossible. Producers in one country who tried to develop sustainable agricultural practices would have to compete with producers elsewhere who did not. Global agriculture would become still more dependent on fossil fuels, until these became, rather abruptly, unavailable.

Those of us who are concerned at the extent to which U.S. industry has already succumbed to international pressure and U.S. capital is invested elsewhere cannot be pleased by the extension of the policies that have already had such massive effects on our economy. Until the costs of labor and of meeting government regulations pertaining to health and environment fall to Mexican levels, for example, industry will continue to move across the border. What few restrictions we now have would be gone.

One argument for the level playing field is that it will lead to movement of capital to the poorest countries. This is a mixed argument, since it means that capital will continue to flow out of our own country and further reduce the wages of labor here. But even if we are willing to sacrifice our economic interests so that the poorest of the poor may benefit, we are brought up short. The new proposals make it even more difficult for third-world nations to safeguard their natural resources or protect their people from the abrupt changes involved when capital is moved in and out of their countries. They will no longer be able to insist that businesses in their countries are owned primarily by their own citizens. Efforts of their citizens to establish productive enterprises will have to compete immediately with long-established transnational producers.

Indeed, the major opposition to the new proposals has come from the third world. The Third World Network has published a book expressing this opposition, *Recolonization: GATT, the Uruguay Round and the Third World.*[5] Its title indicates how it understands the effect of these proposals. Even though certain elites in these countries might gain, it would be a serious mistake to suppose that these proposals will benefit the people as a whole.

Actually, it has been in part the study of these proposals as they implement the ideal of a unified global economy that has led my advisors and me to decide that this is the wrong direction. In a unified global economy, standards for labor, health, and environmental protection would all fall toward levels set by the global economy. Nothing in the proposals suggests that these would be anything but very low .

These proposals make the meaning of "free trade" very clear. Those who are free are the multinational corporations, especially the great transnational financial institutions. They are free to move capital around the world to whatever place it can be most profitably invested, and they are free to move the products of their investments also. What and who are they free from? They are free from interference by concerns that may restrict profit or complicate doing business in diverse countries. These concerns include the desire of people to have some control over their own lives and to participate in establishing the conditions and standards of labor, the health of the public, and the protection of the environment. The transnational corporations will be free from these because governments, which have in the past been able to set standards and implement programs in these areas, will be greatly restricted in all these respects. Although governments may not have good records, in most places they are the only agencies through which the will of communities can be expressed. I do not believe that we should disempower them further.

Because my own reflection has led me to the conviction that hope lies in moving toward a decentralized economy—toward communities that are relatively self-sufficient economically—I believe that many of you, when you consider the real alternatives, will come to agree with me. The next presidential election can be a referendum. By then the specific policies required will be clearer. I hope that many people who agree with me will run for Congress. Votes for them and for me then will be support for a major shift of direction. If all this happens, the people of this nation will have a momentous opportunity to choose—I am sure I can count on opponents vigorously opposed to all that I propose! If, confronted by clear alternatives, you choose the changes I advocate, I will do all in my power to implement them. If you choose to continue to follow the conventional wisdom and support a global economy designed to generate an ever-increasing gross world product, I will step aside and hope that others can find a way to avoid the catastrophes to which I now believe that course inevitably leads.

NOTES

1. Herman E. Daly and John B. Cobb, Jr., *For the Common Good: Redirecting the Economy toward Community, the Environment, and a Sustainable Future* (Boston: Beacon Press, 1989), 373, 401–55. [Lester Brown of Worldwatch Institute has said that "the Daly-Cobb Index of Sustainable Economic Welfare is the most comprehensive indicator of well-being available "(*State of the World 1991* [New York: Norton, 1991], 10).—Eds.]

2. Amory B. Lovins and L. Hunter Lovins, *Brittle Power: Energy Strategy for National Security* (Andover, Mass.: Brink House, 1982).

3. Paolo Soleri, *Arcology: The City in the Image of Man* (Cambridge, Mass.: MIT Press, 1969).

4. Kirkpatrick Sale, *Human Scale* (New York: Cowan, McCown, & Gesgheyon, 1986).

5. Chakravarthi Raghavan, *Recolonization: GATT, the Uruguay Round and the Third World* (Penang, Malaysia: The Third World Network, 1990).

2

THE FULL MEASURE OF OUR DAYS: TIME AND PUBLIC POLICY IN A POSTMODERN WORLD

Joanna Macy

Our progressive destruction of our natural support system, as well as our capacity to slow and stop that destruction, can be understood as a function of our experience of time. The present generation has an idiosyncratic and probably unprecedented experience of time. It can be likened to an ever-shrinking box or ever-tighter compartment of time, in which we race on a treadmill at increasingly frenetic speeds. Cutting us off from other rhythms of life, this box cuts us off from the past and future as well. It preempts or blocks our perceptual field of time while allowing only the briefest experience of time.

Until we break out of this temporal trap we will be unable fully to perceive or to adequately address the crisis we have created for ourselves and the generations to come. Current reflections on our relation to time and new approaches for changing it give promise that we may be able to inhabit time in a healthier, saner fashion. By opening up our experience of time and engendering a politics of time, we can take the full measure of our days—in organic, ecological, and even geological terms and in revitalizing relationship with other species—so that life and time itself may continue on this earth.

I. The Beings of the Three Times

Before proceeding with my reflections and proposals, let me begin as I often begin my workshops on empowerment for social action: with an invocation of the beings of the three times. We invoke them because, at this brink of time, we need them.

We call first on the beings of the past: Be with us now all you who have gone before, you our ancestors and teachers. You who walked and loved and faithfully tended this land, be present to us now that we may carry on the legacy you left us. Silently in our hearts we say your names and see your faces.

We call also on the beings of the present: All you with whom we live and work on this endangered planet, all you with whom we share this awesome turning point in our journey together, be with us now. Fellow humans and brothers and sisters of other species, help us open to our collective will and wisdom. Silently we say your names and picture your faces.

Lastly we call on the beings of the future: All you who will come after us on this earth, be with us now. All you who are waiting to be born, it is for your sakes, too, that we are working in our different ways, for your sakes that we meet at this conference. We cannot picture your faces or say your names—you have none yet—but we ask for your presence. Help us to be faithful in the task that must be done—so that there will be for you, too, and for your children, this blue sky, this fruitful land, these running waters.

II. The Reading of the Will

In contrast to this prayer, our generation's true regard for the beings of the future is portrayed in a recent cartoon by Toles of the Buffalo News. To a group sitting before him expectantly, a lawyer is reading a will. It says:

Dear kids, We, the generation in power since World War II, seem to have used up pretty much everything ourselves. We kind of drained all the resources out of our manufacturing industries, so there's not much left there. The beautiful old buildings that were built to last for centuries, we tore down and replaced with characterless but inexpensive structures, and you can have them. Except everything we built has a lifespan about the same as ours, so, like the interstate highway system we built, they're all falling apart now and you'll have to deal with that. We used up as much of our natural resources as we could, without providing for renewable ones, so you're probably only good until about a week from Thursday. We did build a generous Social Security and pension system, but that was just for us. In fact, the only really durable thing we built was toxic dumps. You can have those. So think of your inheritance as a challenge. The challenge of starting from scratch. You can begin as soon as—oh, one last thing—as soon as you pay off the two trillion dollar debt we left you.

Signed, Your Parents.

From the assembled listeners comes a single comment: "Gee Thanks."

What is staggering about this cartoon, to the point of being funny, is not any exaggeration, for there is none, but the sheer enormity of the reality it portrays and our apparent insouciance in the face of it. This state of affairs can be approached, of course, from a moral perspective, in terms of the selfishness of our generation. But I find it more helpful to understand it in terms of our experience of time; for it reveals a blindness, a pathetically shrunken sense of time, that amounts to a pathological denial of the reality and ongoingness of time.

This disregard for the future is all the more amazing in that it runs counter to our nature as biological systems. Living organisms are built to propagate and to invest a great deal of time and energy in the complex set of behaviors that that requires. Through these behaviors, which usually have no direct survival value to the individual, the future is wired in. There is, as systems-thinker Tyrone Cashman points out,

this spilling out into the future that is the entire essence of organisms. Any plant or animal for whom, throughout its species history, this was not its most essential characteristic would not exist at all. This wired-in relationship to time is alterable only at the price of extinction. Of course, this time-thrust, this into-the-future-ness of all living beings can be lost by a species. But then, immediately, the species itself disappears, forever.[1]

III. THE BROKEN CONNECTION

This system design common to all organisms is clearly evident through-out human history, as men and women have labored and created works to endure through time. It makes our present generation's disregard for the future appear amazing, indeed. What developments can account for it? What has happened to our relationship to time?

For one thing, the bomb has happened. The advent of nuclear weapons has ruptured our sense of biological continuity and our felt connections with both past and future. Robert J. Lifton says:

> One need not enter the debate as to whether nuclear war would or would not eliminate *all* human life. The fact that there is such a debate in itself confirms the importance of *imagery* of total bio-logical destruction, or radically impaired imagination of human continuity.

This impaired imagination reaches backward as well as forward because

> our sense of connection with prior generations . . . depends on feeling part of a continuing sequence of generations. . . . The image of a destructive force of unlimited dimensions . . . enters into every relationship involving parents, children, grandparents, and imagined great-grandparents and great-grandchildren. . . . We are thus among the first to live with a recurrent sense of bio-logical severance.[2]

From the despair work I have facilitated with thousands of people in workshops designed to overcome psychic numbing and feelings of powerlessness, I know this to be true. When they feel safe to express their inner responses to the nuclear and ecological crises, it is the threatened death of all life that surfaces as their deepest and most per-vasive anguish. It is an anguish far deeper than their fears for their per-sonal, individual well-being.

IV. THE FUTURE CANCELED

The sense of biological severance of which Lifton speaks found form and reinforcement in the Reagan era. It was reinforced not only by

Reagan's years of saber rattling, but also and perhaps even more by the frontier mentality that he and his administration represented. This mentality exhibits a habitual lack of any need to husband the earth for the future, because there is always fresh, unlimited land to move on to. Tyrone Cashman in a current work explains the connection.

> When the frontier was over, when there was no more empty land, no more unexplored territory, the engine of American ambition had no place to go. What we have done, and elected Ronald Reagan to stand as symbol for, is to cancel the future.
>
> Reagan essentially assured us, through his personal lack of concern for the future, his escalation of nuclear weapons production, and his own public comments about Armageddon and the end of history, that the future was cancelled, that we needn't concern ourselves about it any more. Thus, it became morally permissible to treat the lands we live in and the rivers and the soils and the forests much as we had treated them when we knew there was an unlimited open frontier in the West there for us to move to when the lands we were exploiting were exhausted, destroyed and befouled.
>
> When the future is cancelled, there is no need to care for the lands we live on. As James Watt so clearly stated, we can use it all up now because we are the last generation. The great feeding frenzy of the 80's when the economic system was partly deregulated and the leveraged buy-outs and hostile take-overs were a daily occurrence, resulted in part from the sense of the end of the era, and those who had the power to salt the stuff away before the whole thing went to hell, were out to do that.[3]

V. THE TIME SQUEEZE

These developments are embedded in and aggravated by a contemporary lifestyle of increasing speed. We suffer ever more chronically from the loss not only of past and future, but of the present as well. We hurry. We complain about crowded schedules and pressure of commitments, then check our watches and rush on. We experience "burnout" and work hard to earn moments where time can cease and we can relax—then take our laptop along on vacation. For we cannot waste the most precious commodity of all.

Time itself, both as a commodity and an experience, has become a scarcity; and many voices now are pointing out the irony that we who have more time-saving devices than any culture at any other period appear the most time-harried and driven. The paradox is only apparent, however, for our time-scarcity is linked to the very time-efficiency of our technology. As Jeremy Rifkin chronicles in *Time Wars*, our measure of time that once was based on the changing seasons, then the wheeling stars, and then the ticking of the clock, is now parceled out in the nanoseconds of the computer—and we have lost time as an organically measurable experience.[4]

The hurry in which we live invades our thought processes, our bodies, our relationships. In the present economy of time, says Alfred Herehausen, chairman of the board of the Deutsche Bank, "we suffer from a remarkable illness, a hectic fever. We don't take time to ponder things, to think them through to the end." Larry Dossey, physician and author of *Space, Time and Medicine*, points out that this causes *hurry sickness*. "Our perceptions of speeding clocks and vanishing time cause our own biological clocks to speed. The end result is frequently some form of hurry sickness—expressed as heart disease, high blood pressure or depression of our immune function, leading to an increased susceptibility to infection and cancer."[5] We find ourselves moving too fast for the cultivation of friendship, which has its own tempo and is not always time-efficient and time-predictable in the unfolding of trust and self-disclosure. Even classroom relationships suffer, the age-old relationships between student and teacher. "My teachers talk slower than my Atari," complains a nine-year-old; "so slow they make me mad sometimes. I think: come on, enough of this, let me go home to my Atari. It tells me things faster."[6]

Perhaps we are in the Kali Yuga—the "age of iron"—ancient India's name for the final degenerative, preapocalypse era of the world's cycles. One meaning of Kali Yuga is "the dregs of time": a temporal density, as gritty and bitter as used coffee grounds. In this endtime, time gets extreme, speeding up, clogging our pores.

My second visit to my son on a wilderness farm in Northern British Columbia was only one year after the first. As I jeeped in and then trekked the twenty-five miles from the nearest public road, I looked up at the surrounding mountains and saw changes so startling they stopped me in my tracks. The once beautiful, wild, unbroken slopes and ridges of cedar and Douglas fir were now defaced by huge square areas of clear-cut. It was shaven, unsightly. "Pampers," said my son, when I asked. "It's a company that makes paper diapers."

All week, as I helped with the haying and the milking of the goats, I would look up at those slopes in anger and grief. "I never put paper diapers on *my* children," I muttered. Actually, there weren't any being mass-produced, so as a matter of course I used cloth ones, soaking and washing them, as my mother had before me. To be honest, I have to admit that, if I were a young mother today, I'd be tempted to use the disposable ones, because, of course, I would be in a hurry. To save ten or twenty minutes, we cut down an old-growth forest.

Speed and haste, as many a wise one has pointed out, are inherently violent. The violence they inflict on our environment is not only because of our appetite for time-saving devices and materials, but also because they put us out of sync with the ecosystem. The natural systems around us, and off of which we feed, move at slower rhythms than we do. The feedback loop is longer, takes more time, than interactions with our machines. We are like the hummingbird that moves so fast, with a metabolic rate so rapid, that it cannot see the movements of the bear coming slowly out of hibernation. To it, the bear appears as stationary as a glacier does to us. Our own accelerating speed puts us out of sync with more and more of the natural world and blinds us to many of our effects upon it.

By speed we strive to conquer time, imagining that we can escape the pressures of time. It doesn't take much subtlety to see that we get caught thereby in a vicious circle. The time pressures we create in our computerized world, and the time pressures we consequently experience, further inflame our desire to escape from time. This is a classical positive (or deviation-amplifying) feedback loop, and we are all victims of it. No matter how we writhe and turn to free ourselves from time, we twist ourselves more tightly in it. We become enslaved by what we would master, devoured by what we would consume, and increasingly view it—yes, view time itself—as enemy.

VI. SPIRITUALITY AS ESCAPE FROM TIME

Increasing numbers of us turn to spiritual practices, such as meditation, to find release from this rat race. Closing our eyes, breathing deeply and slowly, we seek to rise above the pressures of our days into a timeless calm. This behavior can be helpful in slowing us down a bit, but it often perpetuates the notion of time as an enemy to be conquered or outwitted.

In many Hindu practices, time is considered to be unreal, a trap of illusion, a form of *maya* from which to escape into the greater reality of timelessness. In Buddhism, in which more reality is accorded to change, teachers often use the central notion of impermanence, *anicca*, to arouse revulsion or an awareness of the general unsatisfactoriness of life, as a prod to practice. See, what you prize soon passes. Flowers wilt, paint peels, lovers leave, your own body sags, wrinkles, decays. Ah woe! Better fix your gaze on what is free from the ravages of time.

Western religions as well reveal this animosity to time. Reach for eternity. Keep your eyes on the pie in the sky. New Age spiritualities with their oft-repeated admonitions to "Be Here Now" also serve to devalue chronological time and tend to encourage disregard for past and future.

This mind-set among people of different religious backgrounds was evident at a workshop where we discussed our experience of time. All the participants spoke feelingly about the frenzied and fragmented pace of their daily lives. When I invited them to hypothesize alternatives to the pace and pressure, only one alternative was voiced: escape into timelessness, into the mystic moment. The only way out that they saw was a search for cessation through spiritual practice, aloof from chronological time.

This bothered me a lot, because I was working hard on the issue of nuclear wastes, looking for ways to relate to time that could help us face up to the challenge of their incredibly long-lived radioactivity. I wanted us to find the ability to inhabit time, longer stretches of time, not escape from time altogether.

It occurred to me then that our fear of time, like our fear of matter, is a legacy of the hierarchical, indeed patriarchal, mind-set. As many, from James Hillman to Susan Griffin to the many new voices of ecofeminism, have pointed out, this essentially dualistic mind-set has viewed the spiritual journey as an extrication of spirit from the coils of matter. Setting one at odds with the very element on which one depends, it engenders a love-hate relationship with matter, in which one seeks to conquer that which one fears. Has this mentality devalued chronological time in the same manner, perceiving it as the enemy, fostering a love-hate relationship that enslaves us to futile efforts to conquer and escape from time? Can we not see an equation here? The equation would be this: As spirit is to matter, so is eternity to time.

$$\frac{\text{SPIRIT}}{\text{MATTER}} = \frac{\text{ETERNITY}}{\text{TIME}}$$

Each side of this equation represents that which we seek to escape *from* in relation to that which we seek to escape *to*, imagining it to be more valuable.

That equation triggers other reflections. If in our fear of time we strive to conquer time, we are, thanks to our technology, in great danger of succeeding. A distinctive feature of our nuclear-war-making capacity is speed. The thrust of technological design is ever to shorten the time of response to attack, and to make launch-on-warning as instantaneous as possible. The time allowed for human appraisal and intervention—to see, for example, if the attack is real or the result of a computer misreading—is continually reduced. It is now to the point where computer scientists at Stanford University have concluded from their models that the risk of an accidental nuclear war, caused by computer malfunction, will rise to 50 percent in ten years. Our nuclear missiles, poised on hair-trigger alert, may be the logical unfolding of our "spiritual" desire to escape from time—and the final, time-stopping blast, the ultimate expression of that desire.

So we ask, How can we now break free of our fear of time so that time may continue? Can we become friendly with time and reinhabit time, that our days on this earth may be long?

VII. To Reclaim Time, Reclaim Story

To fall in love again with time, we need narrative. "It's all a question of story," says Thomas Berry. "We are in trouble just now because we do not have a good story." Although they are ineffective for us now, we had some good stories of our world in the past. "They did not necessarily make people good, nor did they take away the pains and stupidities of life or make for unfailing warmth in human association. They did provide a context in which life could function in a meaningful manner."[7] And that is all we ask right now, that life function in a meaningful manner.

Berry holds that the new story we need to guide us through the perils of this era must include the whole universe and all its beings. Only in that context can we perceive the long panorama and web of kinship that is basic to the creative commitment we are called now to make. Story nourishes, as he points out, a "time-developmental consciousness." And our particular story, Earth's and ours, has, of necessity, both grandeur and pain.

> Perhaps only by seeing the permanent destruction we have inflicted upon the Earth Community can we come to the realization that the Earth Community is in fact a dimension of ourselves. Perhaps only when that loss is felt personally, can the human realize that the grandeur of the human is the grandeur of the Earth. Perhaps only by feeling directly the folly of destroying Earth's beauty can we awaken to the simple truth that we are destroying our macrophase self.[8]

To appropriate the story of the evolving Earth as our own can radically expand our consciousness of time and our felt continuity with past and future. In Deep Ecology workshops we set about this deliberately and experientially. Our purpose is to deepen our sense of what is personally at stake for us in issues of planetary distress, and also to strengthen our sense of authority when we act in defense of life on Earth. We are then acting not out of personal whim or private nobility, we remind ourselves, but clothed in the full authority of our five billion years.

I would like to give the flavor of some of this Deep Ecology work, as it seeks to widen the experience of time. Here are some passages transcribed from a narrative of our planetary biography that I offered at a women's encampment and recounted to a heartbeat rhythm on a drum:

> Come back with me into a story we all share, a story whose rhythm beats in us still. The story belongs to each of us and to all of us, like the heartbeat of our living universe. . . . Right now on our planet we need to remember that story, for we are in a hard and fearful time. And it is the knowledge of the bigger story that is going to carry us through. . . .
>
> Let us imagine that our life as our planet could be condensed into twenty-four hours, beginning at midnight. Until five o'clock the following afternoon all our adventures were geological—volcanic flamings then steaming rains washing over the shifting bones of the continents into shifting seas. . . . The fire of those early volcanoes, the strength of those tectonic plates, is in us still. . . .
>
> And in these bodies of ours, we carry traces of Gaia's story as organic life. We were aquatic first, as we remember in our mother's womb, growing vestigial gills and fins. The salt from those early seas flows still in our sweat and tears. The age of dinosaurs we carry with us, too, in our reptilian brain. Complex organic life was learning to protect itself and it is all right there in our neurological system, in the rush of instinct to flee or fight.
>
> When did we appear as mammals? In those 24 hours of Gaia's life, it was at 11:30 PM! And when did we become human? One second to midnight.
>
> Now let us take that second to midnight that is our chapter as humans and reckon that, in turn, as 24 hours. Let's look back at the 24 hours that we have been human. Beginning at midnight and up to two o'clock in the afternoon we live in small groups in Africa. Can you imagine you remember?[9]

Here follow impressionistic cues as to how we lived then and changed.

Then in small bands we begin branching out. We move across the face of Gaia; we learn to face the cold and hunt the mammoth and name the trees of the northern forests, the flowers and seasons of the tundra. We know it is Gaia by whom we live and we carve her in awe and fear and gratitude, giving her our breasts and hips. When we settle into agriculture, when we begin domesticating animals and fencing off croplands and deciding that they could be owned as private property, when we built great cities with granaries and temples and observatories, the time is eleven fifty-eight. Two minutes to midnight.

At eleven fifty-nine comes a time of quickening change: we want to chart the stars within as well as those we see in the skies; we seek the authority of inner experience. To free the questing mind we set it apart from Gaia. . . . The great religions of our present planet-time arise. At six seconds to midnight comes a man called the Buddha and a pulse beat thereafter another called Jesus.

What now shapes our world—our industrial society with its bombs and bulldozers—has taken place in the last few microseconds of the day we have known as humans. Yet those few microseconds bring us right to the brink of time. We are now at a point unlike any other in our story. We have opted to be alive when the stakes are high, to test everything we have ever learned about interconnectedness, about courage. We are alive right now when it could be curtains for conscious life on this beautiful water planet.

When you go out from here, please keep listening to the drumbeat. You will hear it in your heart. Remember that it is the heartbeat of the universe as well, and of Gaia your planet and your larger self. When you return to your communities to organize, to say no to the machinery of death and yes to life, remember your true identity, your true lifespan. Remember your story, our story. Clothe yourself in your true authority. You speak not only as yourself or for yourself. You were not born yesterday. You have been through many forms, many dyings and know in your heartbeat the precarious, exquisite balance of life. Out of that knowledge you can speak and act. You will speak and act with the courage and endurance that has been yours through the long eons of your lifestory as Gaia.[10]

VIII. NUCLEAR WASTE: BRIDGE TO THE FAR FUTURE

Just as this kind of "evolutionary remembering" can expand our awareness of the past, there is a variety of analogous paths to heightened
consciousness of the future. Ecological restoration work brings a sense
of connection with coming generations; to plant a tree extends one's
sense of tenure on this earth. Careful, compelling novels, such as *Ridley
Walker* by Paul Hoban or *Always Coming Home* by Ursula LeGuin,
can make far distant generations and their claim on life seem more real
to us. For me, the most lively link to beings of the future centuries and
millennia comes from a surprising source: nuclear wastes. I have been
involved with this issue for some fifteen years and know that it has
altered my experience of time.

Let it first be said that the way we and other countries have produced and disposed of nuclear wastes is probably, of all our behaviors,
the most appalling display of our denial of the future. For not only does
their radioactivity produce disease, death, and sterility; it affects the
genetic code itself. Likened to a madman in a library, it can scramble
and lose forever the blueprints for life crafted by our long evolutionary
journey. Yet, knowing this, we have dumped hundreds of thousand of
metric tons of this waste, dangerous for up to a quarter million years,
into open unlined trenches, into the sea, into cardboard boxes, into
tanks that crack and corrode within a decade or two.

The only permanent solution for high-level waste that our government will provide is to hide it, out of sight and out of mind, in mammoth, deep, geological repositories—although this strategy makes the
leaking containers inaccessible for repair. The posture taken by many
antinuclear citizens who protest the presence of this waste is in some
ways analogous: The NIMBY (Not-In-My-Backyard) syndrome often
involves a reluctance to acknowledge that our generation has really
produced this material. This is a denial of the brute fact that it is piling
up in countless sites and will wreak havoc on our descendants if not
housed with devoted care and guarded with vigilance.

To see if we can come up with an alternative response to nuclear
waste, I have experimented with ways that would help people experience on an immediate, intuitive, gut level its ongoingness through time.
On one memorable occasion at an *ad hoc* "people's council" near Los
Alamos, when discussion about the waste was limited to wishing it
away, I pulled out a small tape recorder. "Let's assume," I said, "if we
can't stop the waste from going into the Carlsbad repository, that we
can at least place this cassette there on the surface for future generations to find and listen to. What do we want to say to them?"

Passing the recorder among them, the men and women began to speak into it. "My name is George. I'm back in 1988 and trying to stop them from burying this radioactive waste. If they do and if you hear this, listen. This stuff is dangerous, stay away, don't drill here. You may think it's some old superstition, but it's not; it's really deadly, take care."

As the words came, the distant, unborn ones to whom they were addressed became vividly real and present to us. We were inhabiting large stretches of time. Soon the group was entertaining alternative possibilities, strategies that involved visible, above-ground enshrinement of the waste and monastic disciplines for monitoring and guarding it. The NIMBY response evaporated and was replaced by a willingness to care for the waste in order to protect future generations. "It's gotta be done or at least overseen by us the people; government and industry don't have the motivation." Several young citizens even volunteered to go live and work at such a "guardian site."

Another experiment with time has involved an enactment on the same theme, in which we play the roles of the future ones, speaking *for* them instead of *to* them. At presentations in the United States and Europe, I have invited people on a fantasy journey to a nuclear guardian site a century or two from now. From that vantage point, we look back at the generation that left the legacy of radioactive waste and seek to understand our own (future) task in relation to it. At each event, participants have been deeply stirred. With this fresh perspective on what our post-World War II generations have done, horror has arisen, and shame; but the predominant response has been one of hope. This hope comes from the glimpsed possibility that humans may build institutions to enshrine and guard the waste, and that they may have the capacity to be faithful. It also comes from simply experiencing the possibility that there may actually *be* a future.

The point I wish to make here does not concern any particular mode of dealing with radioactive waste, so much as our capacity to break out of our temporal prison and let longer expanses of time become real to us. We can do it, we are good at it, and we like it.

Our radioactive legacy has had another and peculiar effect on my experience of time. For me, suffering from the big squeeze as much as anyone, time's main meaning was scarcity and haste. Especially in social action, the clock was always ticking. Hurry, hurry to stop the next escalation of the arms race, to block the B-1 bomber or the Trident II. Make those calls, circulate those petitions, hurry to keep the world from blowing up, the countdown has started. When I began to focus on nuclear waste, when the longevity of its terrible toxicity dawned on me, when I glimpsed what this would mean in terms of duration of human attention, the demands of time reversed themselves. The question of how fast one could get something done was replaced with the question of how long—how lo-o-n-n-ng—a period one could do it in. Will we actually be able to remember the danger of these wastes and protect ourselves for a hundred years? A thousand? Many millennia? As I pondered the likelihood of this, the challenge became duration, not speed, the long haul, not the quick move. My breath slowed, the rib cage eased. The horror of the waste was helping me inhabit time.

IX. POSTMODERN POLITICS OF TIME

If, for a livable world, we must learn to reinhabit time, what changes are required in our system of self-governance? What political practices would reflect and encourage our sensitivity and responsibility to coming generations?

Responses to these questions cover a wide range of proposals. They include the length of terms of legislative office, and the need to relieve harried representatives from the pressures of biannual electoral campaigns and allow them time to think. They feature the alterations in executive budgetary requirements, freeing disbursements from having to be hastily made in a given fiscal year.

Of particular interest to me is the institution of structures that can help us to be responsible to future generations by giving them a voice. Such innovations are totally in keeping with our principle of *no taxation without representation.* Since we are, in effect, taxing future generations by the exploitation of their resources, they should have their say in the process. Since they are too young to vote or not even born yet, offices should be instituted where pronouncements can be made on their behalf.

One possibility already has a precedent of sorts in the congressional office of the representative of the District of Columbia. Although without a legislative vote, Reverend Fauntroy is provided with the means to represent his constituency and bring their views and needs to the attention of Congress. Although, as Jim Wallis makes clear in this volume, the District of Columbia *should* have a vote, I suggest that this practice be used as a model, that we have a nonvoting representative for the people of the future, to promote their needs and bring a larger perspective on time into legislative debates. This representative could be selected at a special three-day convention in Washington, which would in itself be a salutary exercise in developing understandings commensurate with the effects of our present policies on coming generations.

A second possibility has even greater potential for changing our society's consciousness of time. Let me propose the establishment of a third house of Congress, a House of Spokespersons for the future. Although without the power to pass laws, it would speak for the needs and rights of coming generations. Its members, or "Spokes," would be high school seniors, two from each state, chosen at statewide conventions on congressional election years. The House of Spokes would convene in Washington for a week three times a year (say, in early January, spring, and summer), evaluate bills before Congress, and suggest new legislation. During the balance of the year its members would still be heard from, as they point to the priorities they see as appropriate for a healthy and decent future for this country and this world.

In postmodern politics, the spectrum of political identifications will be reconceptualized—from spatial to temporal terms. Rifkin suggests that political persuasions and loyalties formerly assigned to categories of "left" and "right" will sort themselves out more accurately and usefully in terms of their orientation to rhythms and duration of time.

He sees the emerging political spectrum as moving between "power rhythms," on the one side, calling for an accelerated expedient, simulated environment, and, at the other pole, "empathetic rhythms" calling for a resocialization of life and informed by an ecological stewardship vision. The latter, drawing on a Deep Ecology orientation, aims to reintegrate our social and economic tempos with the natural tempos of the environment, so that the ecosystem can "heal itself and become a vibrant, living organism once again."[10]

Because we as a species have no future apart from the health of that organism, this return to a more organic, ecological experience of time is a matter of survival. It will also ground and expand our personal lives. Bringing us into felt connections with past and future generations, it will allow us to claim the full measure of our days.

NOTES

1. Tyrone Cashman, unpublished manuscript, 1989.

2. Robert Jay Lifton, *The Broken Connection* (New York: Simon & Schuster, 1979), 338.

3. Cashman, unpublished.

4. Jeremy Rifkin, *Time Wars: The Primary Conflict in Human History* (New York: Holt, 1987).

5. Larry Dossey, *Space, Time and Medicine* (Boulder, Colo: Shambhala, 1982), 49.

6. Ariane Barth, "Im Reisswolf der Geschwindigkeit," *Der Spiegel* 20 (1989): 210; my translation.

7. Thomas Berry, *The Dream of the Earth* (San Francisco: Sierra Club, 1988), 123.

8. Ibid., 127.

9. My essay is in John Seed, Joanna Macy, Pat Fleming, and Arne Naess, *Thinking Like a Mountain: Towards a Council of All Beings* (Philadelphia: New Society, 1988), 57–65.

10. Ibid.

11 Jeremy Rifkin, *Time Wars*, 198–200.

3

2020 Hindsight: A Retired Kansas Farmer Looks Back on the Revolution in Agriculture Between 1990 and 2020

Wes Jackson

I. Introduction: The Jeffersonian Ideal

The year is 2020, and we are already 20 percent of the way into the twenty-first century. Two millennia have passed since the rise of Christianity, and the apocalypse has still not arrived. Twice now the apocalypse has failed to arrive at the millennium. There was a joke going around then that even an apocalypse won't save us! Even the secularists of the previous century, unaware of the extent to which they were secularized Christians, anticipated an apocalypse—almost welcomed it.

The nuclear arsenal was so huge then that we all felt suspended in a great arc of history headed downward to an inevitable heat death, a heat to be released from the early fires of the creation. It was a poetic tragedy we lived with then. Early humanity, insisting on being participants in the creation by the invention of agriculture, had gambled extravagantly, placing its bets on the presumption that human knowledge alone was adequate for managing the earth. But toward the end of that turbulent twentieth century, suspended on that great arc with our minds concentrated, sense arrived, and enough of us acknowledged that our ignorance would serve us better than the false promises small amounts of knowledge would inspire.

We who are assembled here today in the year 2020 call this period by various names: The Great Transition, The Age of True Discovery, the Age of Recognition of Limits. It is convenient to think of a thirty-year period—from 1990 to the present—because it is in these three decades that the most dramatic turn in history has happened. We were told that the globe was getting warmer and that an ozone hole was expanding. The population continued to explode, even while thousands died each day from starvation. The nuclear arsenal carried a firepower thousands of times greater than that dropped on Japan in 1945. Meanwhile, farmers were going out of business, chemical contamination of the countryside was rampant, and soil erosion continued at high levels. The accidents at Three Mile Island and Chernobyl had occurred. Reindeer had been shot and forests burned down to assist in the Chernobyl cleanup. Twenty-seven towns and villages still stand mute; one had been home to fifty thousand people.

We had become an empire in decline, as the national debt we are struggling to pay today began rapidly to mount.

Within weeks after *Time* magazine featured the Earth on the front cover of its last issue for 1988, a tanker hauling Alaskan oil had an accident that polluted hundreds of miles of Alaskan shore life, an accident from which that area still has not fully recovered.

But my specific topic is the revolution in agriculture over the last thirty years, a change from modern to postmodern agriculture. We regard agriculture no longer as a satellite out there in orbit around the rest of the society, in need of a fix, as it was regarded in 1990, but rather as an integrated part of society. Let's not forget that modern agriculture, which was dominant prior to 1990, had three major assumptions: (1) that nature was to be subdued or ignored in the interest of agricultural production; (2) that the goal of farming and agricultural research was to increase the productive capacity of our various crops and livestock; and (3) that agriculture was to serve as an instrument for the expansion of industry. Subdue nature, increase production, expand industry.

Unfortunately, with our emphasis on yield, we narrowed the germ plasm of our crops and livestock. The bovine growth hormone was popular then—the hormone that increased milk production by 30 percent and would have driven 30 percent of the dairy farmers out of business. It was phased out by 1995, partly because of the activism of the animal rights organizations and partly because cows were experiencing only two lactations before they had to be slaughtered. Calcium was being sucked from their bones faster than they could biologically replace it. Numerous calcium-deficiency diseases developed, which made the job for the animal rights activists easier.

In the mid-1980s, USDA scientists had spliced a human growth hormone gene into swine. Hogs did gain faster and were leaner, satisfying both the commercial grower and the yuppies. The attitude of the time seemed to be, "So what if these hogs are arthritic and cross-eyed? Isn't that just a matter of fine-tuning the hog?" It is an appalling thought today, but it was the consequence of the assumption that the goal of farming and agricultural research should be to increase the productive capacity of our various crops and livestock.

The third assumption, that agriculture was to serve as an instrument for the expansion of industry, was even more deeply ingrained in the American mind than we thought. The secretary of agriculture in those days was little more than the administrative assistant or deputy to the secretary of commerce. Food for export was the policy, and in the late 1970s America exported as much as $45 billion worth of food. This was seen as necessary to offset the cost of foreign oil.

In any case, these three assumptions were challenged, partly because they directly threatened Thomas Jefferson's vision of a nation of farmers and free citizens as the best bet for a healthy democracy. Those who promoted the abandonment of these three assumptions were accused of nostalgia. But the nation came to its senses. In forum after forum, in small groups of five, twenty-five, fifty, a hundred, and sometimes more, the basic question was debated: *Is the Jeffersonian ideal of the family farm and strong rural community mere nostalgia or a practical necessity in a world of declining energy and material resources?*

If our bottom line is an assured food supply into a distant future, how were we to protect the resource base necessary to make that possible? Soil erosion would have to be reduced to natural replacement levels. Dependency on petroleum would have to end. The water supplies for humans and livestock would have to receive a drastically reduced rate of alien chemicals with which vertebrate tissues have had no evolutionary experience. Biological nitrogen fixation would have to replace nitrogen fertilizer for which natural gas is the feed stock, which meant that crop rotations involving legumes would have to return. The essential crumb structure found in healthy soils is enhanced by having animals on the farm so that manure is returned. "We have to get animals back on the land," they said. Conserving our agricultural base for the long run, in other words, required that our farms meet certain ecological standards similar to those in natural ecosystems such as prairies. The key here is to feature diversity and a manageable scale: a high "eyes-to-acres" ratio. People must return to the land, therefore, if we are to place agriculture back on its biological feet. These were key elements in the shift to postmodern agriculture.

We learned that when a bottom line is so narrow that it can accommodate only profit, the bottom line breaks the system. The farm crisis had been brought on mostly by overproduction.

It became apparent that rural communities must be large enough that the family farm is as much a derivative of rural community as a contributor. Without community, the money that farm families received was returned to the city prematurely. Without small businesses, money could not roll over and over long enough to support the rural schools, rural churches, rural baseball. Large corporations owning farms were such willing participants in the extractive economy of agribusiness and so uninterested in the potentially renewable economy of agriculture that they were quickly made unlawful. Land under cultivation, especially land that slopes, needs to be watched. Lots of slow knowledge—the accumulated mistakes and successes—had to be handed down again from generation to generation. The purpose of land is not to serve as an instrument for yielding a simple cipher in a quarterly report. The land needs sympathy and love. A seamless web of people, land, and community is the only thing that would satisfy the ecological and cultural requirements for a sustainable agriculture.

The dramatic transition began when we as a people, in both cities and the country, decided that Jefferson's idea that the strength of the nation was dependent on the "free person" on the land was not some archaic two-hundred-year-old idea whose utility has vanished. It was already an old idea two hundred years ago, an idea in Western civilization almost from the beginning. It was there with the Hebrews at Mt. Sinai, with the desert and Egypt behind them, as they looked forward to the Promised Land of Canaan, where they each would sit under their own fig trees and trim their own vineyards. This democratic ideal, thankfully, was also an ecological ideal, for it accommodated the possibility and necessity of lots of people paying close attention to what Thoreau called "meeting the expectations of the land."

II. THE EMERGENCE OF THE BIG IDEA

A Big Idea gradually emerged in the American mind. As minds were concentrated, it became apparent that our problem with the earth was that we had assumed control of the earth with an inadequate understanding of nature's arrangements. We had been trying to understand agriculture by looking exclusively to agriculture and to what industry had to offer. Because nature had the most sustainable ecosystems, and because ultimately agriculture comes out of nature, a few began to suspect that our standard for a sustainable world should be the most sustainable ecosystems. "Nature as the measure," "nature as an analogy," "nature as the standard" became the phrases shortly after 1990. An expanding number of agriculturists and ecologists began seriously to explore the possibility of a marriage of ecology and agriculture, including agricultural science. This Big Idea was crucial in the transition from modern to postmodern agriculture.

This was not the first time humans have advocated that we return to nature as our primary teacher. Before 1990, Wendell Berry traced some of the literary history of this idea from Job to its re-emergence in the early part of the nineteenth century.[1] It really is an old idea, as Berry pointed out nearly thirty-five years ago:

Job, hundreds of years before Jesus of Nazareth, said:

Ask now the beasts, and they shall teach thee; and the fowls of the air, and they shall tell thee:
    Or speak to the earth, and it shall teach thee; and the fishes of the sea shall declare unto thee.

Virgil, at the beginning of *The Georgics* (36–29 B.C.), informs us that

    . . . before we plow an unfamiliar patch
    It is well to be informed about the winds,
    About the variations in the sky,
    The native traits and habits of the place,
    What each locale permits, and what each denies.

Continuing in the literary tradition, Milton, in *Comus*, has the lady say

> she, good cateress,
> Means her provision only to the good
> That live according to her sober laws
> And holy dictate of spare Temperance.

For the Great Plains, think of Virgil's admonition that "before we plow an unfamiliar patch it is well to be informed about the winds." What if the settlers and children of settlers who gave our continent the dust bowl nearly a hundred years ago had heeded this two-thousand-year-old advice? And Milton's insight about the good cateress who "means her provision only to the good that live according to her sober laws and holy dictate of spare Temperance"?

When this theme surfaces again, Berry tells us, it does so among the agricultural writers, first in 1905 in a book by Liberty Hyde Bailey entitled *The Outlook to Nature*. The grand old dean at Cornell thought nature was "the norm." "If nature is the norm, then the necessity for correcting and amending abuses of civilization becomes baldly apparent by very contrast." He continues: "The return to nature affords the very means of acquiring the incentive and energy for ambitious and constructive work of a high order."[2]

Work at the Land Institute in Salina, Kansas, began in 1976, nearly a half century ago, with the assumption that the best agriculture best mimics the natural ecosystems. A small group of researchers set out to build domestic prairies that would produce grain. That work, however, had its origin *ignorant* of a literary and scientific tradition, but, as Wendell Berry said about these poets and scientists, their understanding probably came "out of the familial and communal handing down in the agrarian common culture, rather than in any succession of teachers and students in the literary culture or in the schools." As far as the literary-scientific tradition is concerned, Berry pointed out that it is a series, not a succession. The succession is only in the agrarian common culture. Those who came off the farm and began work on nature as measure must have had a "memory" embedded in that agrarian common culture. Walt Whitman said that "perfect memory is perfect forgetfulness." To know something well is to not know where it came from.

In any case, the Big Idea of nature as the measure suddenly gave nature more respect, and the assumptions surrounding agriculture were quickly reversed.

Rather than subdue or ignore nature, we now ask, What was here? What will nature require of us here? And Berry's question, What will nature help us to do here?[3] Berry also pointed out that, as we have been cutting the forests and plowing the great prairies, "we have never known what we were doing because we have never known what we were undoing."[4]

And rather than thinking only of maximizing production, our primary goal, we now realize, is a livelihood in which the land is a place for people to live out their lives; a place to work, rest, contemplate, and establish their relationship with the universe; a place to develop a becoming existence.

Because of the courage exercised during the 1990s, it is easier now to "just say no" to the extractive economy. To use agriculture as an instrument for industrial expansion is now no longer acceptable. Instead, we ask what the earth requires of us.

Edgar Mitchell, one of the astronauts who had gone to the moon, provided us with the metaphor. Once asked what it was like to experience the moon, he replied that he was "too busy being operational to experience the moon." As we employed our knowledge and tinkered with the earth to accommodate our demands, we created acid rain, global warming, depletion of the ozone layer, and contaminated ground water. We became increasingly busy, more operational, with less and less time to experience the Earth.

III. New Laws Related to the Big Idea

A law that came to be recognized by the year 2000 was that high energy tends to destroy information of both the biological and the cultural varieties. This was hard to visualize in 1990 when people were still worrying where they were going to obtain the energy to support the kinds of lives they felt necessary without resorting to drudgery. But gradually we all learned. As the scale of an operation expands or decreases, the relationship between information and energy changes dramatically. Most farms in those years suffered from too much energy, too large a scale, and too little information, meaning too little diversity. An abundance of energy, especially of the fossil-fuel variety, has a way of homogenizing the farm ecosystem. With too much energy, there is a strong incentive to reduce diversity in order to simplify the farm structure and, in so doing, to break down the complementarities in the biotic and cultural diversity on the farm. Discovering the right balance of cultural and biological information and the right balance between information and energy, given the scale of an operation, is necessary for sustainability, a synonym for homeostasis.

There is another reality the culture came to understand pretty thoroughly about two decades ago, and that is how our values have the ability to penetrate the innermost recesses of nature. It is obvious that our values have led to the splitting of the atom, but our values have also become encoded in the chemistry of life, in the DNA. Our values have dictated the genotype of both major and minor crops: Corn, wheat, soybeans, and others now contain what we might call "Chicago Board of Trade genes." In other words, there were ensembles of genes in our major crops that would not have existed in their particular constellation were there not a Chicago Board of Trade, where a major share of the agricultural transactions took place thirty years ago.

Another principle related to the Big Idea had a radicalizing impact once it was recognized. The extractive economy was so pervasive that it dictated the terms of the renewable economy. We always believed that it was all right to mine coal and burn it, pump oil and use it, and hope for alternatives before the stock was gone. There were no illusions—it would one day be gone; people had the story straight on nonrenewables. But what was not comprehended was that the *economic* arrangements surrounding this extractive mentality would dictate the terms of the *renewable* or potentially renewable categories of our economy. Once it became clear that the renewable sector was being forced to obey the rules of the extractive economy, our citizenry became alarmed. A plant breeder at Oregon State University said it well some thirty-five years ago when he said that his main concern was *how to spend the rest of the genetic variation in his crop wisely.* This, of course, was the same concern about spending the fossil fuels.

Plant breeders became alarmed early, and the USDA built an expensive and highly inadequate facility for seed storage at Fort Collins, Colorado. But to preserve germ plasm through technology, rather than in nature and culture where it evolved and had been preserved, did not work. Genetic truncation of our major crops continued, and eventually we came to recognize that the first law of nature mentioned above was at work: *High energy destroys information.* We gradually caught on to the fact that the extractive economy, fueled by high energy that is dependent on burning the nonrenewable stock, requires the burning of the potentially renewable stock as well. It was like killing the goose that lays the egg.

IV. THE SHIFT TO AN ECOLOGICAL WORLDVIEW

In the 1950s a man named Feibleman wrote the twelve laws of integrative levels.[5] Beginning with atoms and molecules, followed by cells, tissues, organs, organ systems, and organisms, we see a hierarchy of structure. At each of these levels are emergent qualities that more or less define the field. Some biologists wondered what came next after organism: Species? Populations? What?

Stan Rowe, a Saskatchewan ecologist, thought about that question and concluded that, because the other categories in the hierarchy all had *volume*, the next category should have volume, too.[6] Neither species nor populations have contiguous volume, but an ecosystem does. Stan Rowe's volumetric criterion for thinghood catapulted *ecosystem* to a standing that ranks with the other categories in the hierarchy.

Granting to ecology a standing on a par with other disciplines—whether physics, chemistry, or organismic biology—was a great boost for agricultural science. In 1972, P. W. Anderson had explained in a *Science* article that there are laws at each level of the hierarchy as basic as the laws of physics. Ecologists no longer had to suffer from physics envy. With confidence in themselves and their field, they could turn to practical problems, not just do basic research. Agriculture gained.

With nature as the measure, ecology became the primary discipline. The challenge ecologists faced at the time the culture was ready to look to nature as the measure was immense. It was an exciting time, and a heartening one, too, for so many young scientists began to work on a new way to think about farming. The number of young ecologists in the field increased thirty-fold within only one decade—from 1990 to 2000.

The adoption of the Big Idea and the shift to ecology as the primary discipline helped bring about a shift to an ecological understanding of the world. We all began to understand more fully the silliness of placing priority on part over whole, recognizing that part affects whole and that whole affects part. The world of Bacon and Descartes was left behind.

V. The Practical Implementation
of the Big Idea

Neither the Gaia concept nor the photo from space was alone able to stop the destruction of the Earth. A necessary element in changing course in a major way came from an unexpected quarter. Simply stated, technological proliferation was threatening our democratic institutions. Biotechnology called this to our attention. In the early days of biotechnology, a few people were warning of genetic monsters to be derived from the new techniques. The public became aware, however, that the true monsters were the people who saw nothing wrong with arthritic, cross-eyed hogs. Citizens became more and more worried about the speed with which the new techniques could create potential problems. They worried that the billions of dollars being spent in the public and private sectors to bring biotechnology on fast and extensively made it impossible sufficiently to assess the implications. All new technologies require assessment time, and citizens have even less time now fully to assess a situation than at any time since the atom was split. Ordinary good citizenship in a democratic society requires that we be knowledgable about current events. Biotechnology robbed countless citizens of weeks of leisure and professional time in those years. The moral considerations, in other words, went far beyond whether it is right to produce miserable, arthritic, cross-eyed hogs. In short, there was a breed of scientific troublemakers operating faster than the scientific and citizen watchdogs could deal with them.

The Big Idea has changed our attitudes about farm animals and plants. Before, our domesticated livestock and crops were regarded primarily as our property. Now they are primarily regarded as relatives of wild things that had an evolution in a context not of our making. Acknowledging that the hog was a forest animal, the beef cow a grazer of grasslands, and the chicken a jungle fowl at the time of domestication changed our ideas about the dense confinement operations many of these animals had experienced.

Breeding and management of our animals and plants now reflect this acknowledgment. By streamlining for production in the previous century, we had begun to interfere with *re*production. Domestic beef animals were having calves so large that assistance was needed at calving time. Most turkeys had to be artificially inseminated. Looking to the original context has led to more humane treatment in the last decade or so, and the agenda for research has been drastically altered.

The transition to postmodern practices has not been easy. We all had to learn how difficult, if not impossible, it is positively to influence our philosophical enemies. Yet loving our enemy is essential for societal change.

A just and equitable world has not arrived, but we now at least realize the necessity of identity with poverty as a way of understanding the state of mind of the impoverished. It is striking that it is out of the writings of those who chose voluntary poverty in the last twenty years that we have learned the great insights for living in a world of increasing scarcity.

VI. RESULTING CHANGES

In the 1990s, political campaigns became more exciting than before, as sustainability became the number one issue. Aldo Leopold's "land ethic" was mentioned repeatedly on the campaign trail, and the consequences of an economy based on nature's plunder were repeated at every stop.

The candidates got down to issues. An opponent from Iowa asked a candidate from Nebraska why, if he was so opposed to the extractive economy, he had not taken measures to cease the mining of the Ogallala aquifer in his own state. It was a good question, because the Ogallala aquifer is the largest freshwater body in the world, and most of it lies under Nebraska. Irrigators had been withdrawing twenty million acre feet a year, two-fifths of the annual flow of the Missouri River at Kansas City. The candidate from Nebraska said that "indeed the mining of the Ogallala is serious, but in addition we should quit growing corn and soybeans on the sloping fields of Iowa where soil erosion averages eighteen tons per acre per year. The recharge rate of Iowa soils is far less than the recharge rate of the Ogallala." He continued: "Deplete the Ogallala, and we can pray for rain. Deplete the soils of the Midwest and we had better pray for mercy." He then proposed an export policy that would require that the energy cost for producing an equivalent amount of energy in alcohol would be added to the cost of the food itself. Not to be outdone, another candidate said we should include the energy cost to return an equivalent amount of nutrients to the fields that produced the crops for export.

By 1995, Latin American immigrants were the largest minority in the United States. It was a crucial time in the mid-1990s, for how we regarded and treated Mexico reflected how we would treat the third world in general. Much of the problem stemmed from the cheap food policy we had adopted long ago and from an unwillingness of Americans to do stoop labor at such low wages. Once the prices for food tripled, particularly those foods requiring stoop labor, household members began to question whether they might not be better off financially by producing a garden themselves. For many of those who had had a garden, it had been mostly a hobby, but when it became serious business requiring the involvement of the entire family, the immigration problem took on another dimension.

By reducing exports of grains in particular, the Conservation Reserve Program, started in the mid-1980s due to the 1985 Farm Bill, expanded from twenty-five million acres to one hundred million acres, one-fourth of our till agriculture land. Agriculture research in our land-grant institutions changed. At Kansas State University, biologists studying the nine-thousand-acre, never-plowed, native Konza Prairie, bought by the Nature Conservancy and managed by Kansas State, began a cooperative effort with the College of Agriculture at KSU. One radical Kansan had declared that the research going on at the

Konza was of more importance to the long-term agricultural effort than what was going on in the research plots at the experimentation station. Discussion and heated debate followed, but a small amount of clarification of the implications of "nature as measure" took place.

Policy changes came slowly but only to the extent that citizens made radical proposals for discussion. One disgruntled farmer called for a separation of science and state, declaring that if Jefferson were alive today setting up a new republic, he would insist on such. The farmer continued by saying that the science-state alliance had been many times more destructive than the church-state alliance ever was. He was not calling for a church-state alliance but declaring that Jefferson misidentified the most serious potential problem. "It's the aggregation of power I oppose," said the farmer. No presidential candidate picked up the proposal at the time, but by 2010 it was not a taboo subject.

Economists following the ideas of Herman Daly, the oldest living proponent of the steady-state society, are working closely with ecologists to explore how nature's economy has worked. The capitalistic model built on the accumulation of capital is no longer relevant in a world of declining resources. John Maynard Keynes, one of the architects of capitalism, had said that "foul was useful and fair is not" and "that we must have foul a little longer," foul being greed and envy, which he saw as necessary to open up the mines and wellheads and make more materials available for all. Once done, we were to suspend greed and envy. Unfortunately, these qualities, which the ancients regarded as sins, and on which the system was built, were not so easily dismissed when they were no longer deemed useful. But a new economic order that widens the range of considerations is being developed. The book published in 1989 by Herman Daly and John Cobb, *For the Common Good*, was a great stimulus.

Agricultural science is undergoing radical change, too. The way young scientists look at the world is radically different now from what it was in the twentieth century. Crops grown in polycultures using the natural integrities of nature have caused workers to have a different attitude about the pests. A species is introduced into the polyculture with varying degrees of susceptibility to insects or pathogens as a way of keeping that species sufficiently tamed down so that it does not overrun the plot. Here is an example of loving the historical enemies of humanity and putting them to our use. The ecological model for agriculture has introduced a wide range of such considerations.

Communities across the land are bidding to have seven to ten young Amish families locate next to their town each year instead of inviting new industry. In 1995, a poll showed that American agriculture could gain valuable information from the Amish. The Amish practiced a form of postmodern farming, sporting digital clocks in their buggies but using draft animals for traction. They used small engines on their haying and threshing equipment but steel wheels on their wagons. They assessed their technology against standards in which they sought to avoid the sin of pride. They acknowledged that as individuals acting alone, they could not control pride. This required help from the community.

Most of our legislative efforts over the last twenty years have been directed as much toward supporting rural community as toward saving the family farm. The exodus of capital from the countryside in the 1980s forced the human capital to go, too. Our legislation in the 1980s that was allegedly intended to save the family farm really made the family farmer only someone who would launder government subsidies to the suppliers of inputs. That has stopped.

One of the main destroyers of our national wealth was finally identified: the shopping centers that had sprung up all over the land. Some communities would get two within a decade, the newer malls driving the older one out just as *it* had made the original business district wither. Lots of good agricultural land was paved in the process, and now many of these centers, cheaply built and vacant, are falling down. Some towns have elected to keep them there as reminders of an excessive life in the past, in much the same way the Israelis keep tanks and crashed planes around as reminders of their wars. The shopping centers—promoters of consumerism, makers of the need for huge landfills, and destroyers of communities—now stand mostly idle across the landscape of an indebted nation. (By 1990 all of the federal taxes collected from west of the Mississippi were necessary simply to pay the interest on the national debt.) The automobile of the last century is almost gone, replaced by highly efficient small vehicles and a new mass transit system.

The Disney World Epcot Center in Florida, the land pavilion that attracted thousands of visitors each year, is now maintained as a source of amusement. This hydroponic gee-whiz world was described in the 1980s by Stephen Jay Gould, a popular professor at Harvard, as a technological *tour de force* but a conceptual desert. It was clearly the product of a centralist philosophy with little attention given to the land as organism. The energy and chemical demands were huge.

A large part of the problems we are only now overcoming were due to centralization. With that in mind, there is a final set of reminders our culture keeps around. Around Amarillo, Texas, the former Pantex plant, which once assembled all nuclear weapons produced in the United States, is closed now, and, perhaps as important, so is a nearby slaughtering plant once owned by Iowa Beef. Iowa Beef once had a total processing capacity of eight million animals a year for all of their plants combined. In the mid-1980s, at an antinuclear rally opposite the Pantex plant, an environmentalist declared that we had to be as opposed to Iowa Beef and the huge feedlots positioned nearby that supplied it as to the Pantex plant. Iowa and Kansas needed those animals on their farms, not on some commercial feedlot where their manure created a nuisance and their bodies required heavy doses of antibiotics. *The kind of economy that would make massive livestock confinement and processing possible would make Pantex necessary.* The speaker concluded "Shut down Pantex, shut down Iowa Beef!" to a bewildered audience. I am happy to report here in 2020 that, because both are shut down, the battle between those with a centralist philosophy and those with a peripheralist philosophy was won by the latter.

I don't mean to imply that the centralists never have their way. We still have lots of problems. For example, in spite of the thirty nuclear accidents of varying degrees of severity, mostly in the last fifteen years worldwide, nuclear power remains appealing to many who believe it will one day be possible to make it safe.

We are now firmly into the postmodern ecological age, and much of the ecologically destructive past is behind us. The public laboratories no longer have an assignment that is similar to the chemical industry. The era in which the public facilities tested the pesticides produced by the chemical companies for the purposes of promotion is over. The consciousness of the population is now sufficiently raised that, when questions arise about the possible harmful effects of pesticides, the people do not allow the scope of inquiry to be restricted to the immediate, direct, and measurable. We know that the ecosystem is strongly interconnected, highly variable, and vulnerable. We know that the things of the world are not isolated but richly interacting. We know that we cannot simply consider the *average* behavior of chemicals and organisms, because the world is very uneven. We no longer believe in magic bullets for solutions. We have developed ways to detect economic interests and theoretical biases when a particular approach is being promoted.

What has been accomplished in the last thirty years is truly revolutionary. Remember our long history. Four hundred years ago, Francis Bacon (1561–1626), the father of the modern science promoted in the twentieth century, advocated that we control nature for our benefit. He explicitly argued for an ethic that would sanction our exploitation of the natural world. The idea of progress was emerging out of an old order. Bacon's motives were high. He wanted the entire human race to benefit from science. It sounded right. He probably could not have seen it very clearly, but the loser would be Nature, which includes us. Rather than Nature as our teacher, his license called for making her our slave.

Bacon's *New Atlantis* was published in 1624, only two years before Bacon died. The scientist was the highest member in his utopia. Salomon's house in his New Atlantis community of Bensalem was the research institute. In this forerunner of the modern research institute, there was a total lack of political process. The scientists, those who held the secrets of nature, were simply to be trusted. This priesthood would decide what would be revealed and what held back from the state.

We are more democratic now, and our hope is that the strictly Baconian worldview and practice are behind us.

As a culture, we have moved from the notion of "smart resource management" to an acknowledgment of relationships and therefore of ecological context. Nearly all sustainable agricultural research and practice in the past were devoted to the human becoming only "smarter." Finally, we began to draw on the "intelligence" embedded in the ecological context, an intelligence that goes far beyond whatever "smart" capabilities the human can muster.

We had our own evolution at the Land Institute. In the early days, we said we were working on "perennial polycultures for grain production." We were never quite comfortable with the expression and usually laced the phrase with humor when saying it aloud. We did it almost unconsciously, because the expression carried a certain brittleness, a certain "smartness," and emphasized *our* clever agronomic arrangement, which forced us to feel more informed than we deserved to feel. It never captured the spirit of what we were about. Gradually we began to say that we were out to build a "domestic prairie featuring grain production." This shifted the focus from us to nature as the reservoir of intelligence. Attention was then drawn away from us as major agents of manipulation to an acknowledgment that we were students of nature bent on discovery, students who wanted to build arrangements that imitate or mimic, as much as possible, the current local results of the long evolutionary process.

The two questions mentioned earlier—"What was here? What will nature require of us?"—still dictate the terms of the Land Institute's research agenda. As we received answers to these two questions, we gained insight into the third implied question articulated by Wendell Berry—"What will nature help us do here?" Few agricultural researchers or even farmers, maybe all the way back to Plato and Job, asked such questions. But as long as all agricultural species, from corn plants to Holstein cows, were regarded as the property of humans, rather than as relatives of wild things which had most of their evolution in a context not of our making, then the best we could hope for was to become "smart resource managers." That was too limiting to prevent soil erosion or, for that matter, any other desecration of the agricultural landscape or, ultimately, of us humans.

So in 1990, even as we cheered the progress being made by farmers who were adopting practices that are less harmful to the soil and water, we knew that, for agriculture to be *sustainable*, we had to make a mental shift in how we see the world. Nearly a century earlier, Sir Albert Howard of England had said we should farm like the forest. He could have said we should farm like the prairie. Our work to develop several domestic mimics of the prairie mosaic signaled our willingness to step out of the "smart resource management" paradigm into a world in which we set out to discover the best fit with nature, both agriculturally and economically.

A major surprise is that a different economic order emerged from these values. Agroecology has made us better community accountants and, for that matter, better global accountants. With this shift, accounting becomes a most important and interesting discipline, because an accountant is really a student of boundaries, a person who thinks about both the nature of boundaries and the classification of boundaries. From Maine to California, ecological accountants now think about what we should allow through the boundaries of various communities and at what rate. An input-and-output analysis now forces us to examine the dynamics within those boundaries if we are to prevent squandering and pollution and efficiently to use the materials and energy in a conserving spirit.

NOTES

1. Wendell Berry, "A Practical Harmony," in *What Are People For?* (San Francisco: North Point Press, 1990).

2. Liberty H. Bailey, *The Outlook to Nature* (New York: Macmillan, 1905).

3. Wendell Berry, "Wildness," in *Home Economics* (San Francisco: North Point Press, 1987), 146.

4. Wendell Berry, personal conversation.

5. J. K. Feibleman, "Theory of Integration Levels," *British Journal of the Philosophy of Science* 5 (1954): 59–66.

6. J. S. Rowe, "The Level of Integration Concept and Ecology," *Ecology* 42 (1961):420–27.

4

THE "VISION THING," THE PRESIDENCY, AND THE ECOLOGICAL CRISIS, OR THE GREENHOUSE EFFECT AND THE "WHITE HOUSE EFFECT"

David Ray Griffin

In this essay I will argue the following theses:

I. The human race is in an unprecedented situation: Its own activities threaten to bring about its own demise and that of much of the life of the planet millions or even billions of years prematurely.

II. An examination of major dimensions of the ecological crisis shows that a wait-and-see approach will probably be suicidal and that we need instead an immediate and massive response.

III. This ecological crisis has been brought on by the modern world and can be surmounted only if we quickly make the transition to a postmodern world.

IV. The United States of America is the nation with the greatest responsibility for making this transition, both because it is more responsible than any other nation for causing the ecological crisis and because it, in spite of recent declines in economic and political power, still has the greatest capacity for exercising the needed leadership.

V. The president of the United States has far more power to bring about the needed changes in our way of life, through both direct action and the exercise of moral and symbolic leadership, than any other individual or institution. Therefore, although we need political vision and leadership at every level of our national life, including the grassroots level, there is little hope for success unless we have wise and courageous leadership exercised by the holders of the office of the presidency in the coming decades, beginning immediately.

VI. Our presidents need to lead the United States in recognizing the ecological crisis for what it is—the greatest challenge ever faced by the human race, which probably must be met, if it is to be met, during the coming two or three decades—and in responding with the biggest crash program of all time.

The title of this essay is based upon two statements made by the person who occupied the office of the presidency while this essay was written, George Bush. In one of these statements, he, upon being asked by a reporter about his vision of the presidency, made fun of the "vision thing." But according to biblical wisdom, vision is nothing to ridicule. As Jim Wallis reminds us in his essay in this volume, Proverbs 29:18 says that "where there is no vision, the people perish." This wisdom in our times means that, because of the theses summarized above, without vision in our political leaders, especially our presidents, the people and most of the millions of other forms of life brought forth by the Creative Source of all life will perish. Unfortunately, Bush's promise to be devoid of vision is one campaign promise he kept.

The other statement alluded to by the title was made by Bush while he was campaigning for the presidency on August 31, 1988, which was a time in which the environment had become a hot political issue. Candidate Bush said: "Those who think we're powerless to do anything about the 'greenhouse effect' are forgetting about the 'White House effect.' As President, I intend to do something about it."[1] Unfortunately, what Bush as president has done about the greenhouse effect is primarily to belittle it. He has used the "White House effect" not to lead the modern, industrialized nations in a crash program to save the planet, but to dilute and retard the quite modest proposals favored by most of these other nations.

Insofar as George Bush *has* exercised presidential leadership, it has been based upon an outdated, modernist vision—the kind of vision that created the ecological crisis in the first place—according to which the good life depends upon the domination of nature for human benefit, according to which politics has primarily to do with controlling as much of nature as possible (such as its oil) for one's own nation's benefit, and according to which economics does not have to take ecology into account. Bush has continued to say that we need to seek a "balance" between economic and ecological concerns, showing that he has not caught the part of the postmodern vision that recognizes that even the human economy is not sustainable if it is not harmoniously integrated into the one truly global economy—the economy of nature. Far less has he caught the larger postmodern vision that sees the human species not as the only form of life worthy of moral concern, but as one of millions of species, all of which should be allowed to flourish, for their own sakes and their Creator's as well as ours. In short, the Bush administration, like the Reagan administration before it, has exercised just the kind of leadership that we do not need, the kind that has probably already doomed us to unprecedented suffering in the coming century, and the kind that, unless it is reversed quickly, will doom us to the same fate that we are already inflicting upon other species at an unprecedented rate—extinction.

Given this introductory overview of my argument, I will support it in terms of the above six theses.

I. OUR UNPRECEDENTED SITUATION

At the end of every year, the news media ask what the "biggest story" of the year was. They do this on a somewhat larger scale at the end of every decade. So we can imagine that, as the century draws to a close, we will be inundated by opinions as to what the biggest story of the century was. Many pundits will single out the battle against fascism in World War II. Many more, probably, will point to the rise of Communist governments, the cold war, and the failure of Communism. But these and similar answers would be far off the mark or, at best, only portions of the truly big story.

The judgment as to the really big story can be made with some objectivity. We, after all, are facing not only the end of a century, but the end of a millennium. If one of the stories of the past one hundred years coincided with the biggest story of the past one thousand years, then it would clearly be the biggest story of our century as well. And this would be all the more the case if this same story were the biggest story of all human history. And—to drive the point home with an only apparently extreme claim—there would be no doubt whatsoever if this same story could be seen to be the biggest story since the rise of life itself. And yet this is indeed the case.

What is this biggest of all stories? It is that *one of the millions of species of life on our planet has now, in our century, developed the power to threaten not only its own existence but also that of most of the other species of life on our planet.* This has never happened before. From a cosmic standpoint, it has to be the biggest story not only of our time, but of the adventure of life on planet Earth itself. (For all we know, it may be the first time this has happened in the entire universe; but to have simply the biggest story in the history of our planet occur in our time is probably grandiose enough, even for twentieth-century Americans.)

An increasing number of thinkers are pointing out the momentous nature of the transition through which we are living. For example, Bill McKibben means by the title of his recent book, *The End of Nature*, that "we have ended the thing that has . . . defined nature—for us—its separation from human society." His point is that, whereas in the past, human efforts were tiny compared with the size of the planet, the way of life in one part of the world is now altering every inch of the globe. He describes the implications of this change of our situation in theological terms: "In [ending nature], we exhibit a kind of power thought in the past to be divine . . . . We as a race turn out to be stronger than we suspected—much stronger. In a sense we turn out to be God's equal—or, at least, his rival—able to destroy creation."[2] Less dramatically, Herman Daly and John Cobb begin their recent book on sustainable economics by citing a number of "wild facts" that, they say, point to "one central underlying fact: the scale of human activity relative to the biosphere has grown too large."[3] Barry Commoner, whose recent book *Making Peace with the Planet* is oriented around the notion of a war between the ecosphere and the "technosphere," introduces this notion in terms of "a basic fact: that in the short span of its history, human society has exerted an effect on its planetary habitat that matches the size and impact of the natural processes that until now solely governed the global condition."[4] Or, if Daly, Cobb, and Commoner are discounted because they hold heretical economic views, we can look at statements made by Lester Brown's Worldwatch Institute, whose *State of the World* series is supported by foundations associated with names such as Rockefeller, Hewlett, Mellon, and others whose support of modern capitalism cannot be doubted. In *State of the World 1989* one finds the following statements:

> The deterioration of the earth's physical condition that we documented in past volumes of this report is now accelerating. . . . We are now in a race to stop environmental deterioration before it becomes unmanageable. . . . Many societies have been severely tested over the several thousand years since civilization began. . . . But the world as a whole has never been so challenged as it is today.[5]

The same point has been made increasingly in countless other publications. An unprecedented change in relationships has occurred, and this confronts us with an unprecedented challenge, one that requires an unprecedented response. The authors of the same volume of *State of the World* say: "One of these years we would like to be able to write an upbeat *State of the World*, one in which we can report that the trends undermining the human prospect have been reversed. It now seems that if we cannot write such a report in the nineties, we may not be able to write it at all." Accordingly, they say, "the nineties needs to be a 'turnaround decade.' "[6]

But, if this is the big story of our time, and in fact the biggest challenge ever faced by the human race, you would never know it from the statements and actions of most of our political leaders. Although the environmental crisis evoked a few statements of concern in the 1988 presidential campaign, such as the one from candidate Bush cited earlier, the candidates campaigned as if this issue were of secondary importance at best. Since being elected, our president and most of our other leaders have acted as if the environmental crisis were no crisis at all. One of the best-known symbols of visionless leadership is that of Nero fiddling while Rome was burning. And yet, in a time when the problems of acid rain, toxic wastes, global warming, and a growing ozone hole are well known, a majority of the American politicians seem to get more exercised by the burning of our flag than by the burning of our planet. We desperately need political leaders with a larger vision. (The selection of Albert Gore as the Democratic vice-presidential candidate, made just before this book went to press, provided hope that the 1992 campaign would be better in this respect.)

II. MAJOR DIMENSIONS OF THE ECOLOGICAL CRISIS AND THE NEED FOR AN IMMEDIATE RESPONSE

Although there are many interconnected dimensions of the overall ecological crisis, I will focus here primarily on two of the most global and most potentially catastrophic dimensions: the hole in the ozone layer and global warming.

The Ozone Hole

Ozone, a noxious gas at ground level, is crucial in the upper atmosphere for life on earth, being the only gas that prevents deadly ultraviolet radiation, UV-B, from reaching the earth's surface. Most of this ozone is found from twelve to twenty-five kilometers above the earth, but even there the so-called ozone layer is very thin, with ozone molecules constituting only a few parts per million. This layer is so thin that at sea-level pressure it would be only one fourth of a millimeter thick.

Significant destruction of this fragile layer of protection will be devastating for life on earth. Much attention has been given to the fact that ozone depletion will increase skin cancer in humans. Donald Hodel, secretary of the interior in the Reagan administration, perhaps never explicitly made the remark that was widely attributed to him— that no regulations on substances destructive of the ozone layer were necessary because people could simply wear hats, sun-glasses, and skin lotions; but he evidently did suggest that a policy of "personal protection" and "lifestyle change" be presented to the president in lieu of working for a meaningful accord.[7] As serious as an increase in human skin cancers will be, however, it may be the least of the problems created. Evidently something like two-thirds of the forms of plant life are adversely affected to a significant extent by UV-B. One of the most ominous facts may be that the phytoplankton and zooplankton at the base of the food chain are damaged by UV-B, which can penetrate the ocean to a depth of sixty feet. The krill in the ocean depend so completely on the phytoplankton that, as one expert has said, "if anything happens to the krill, the whole ecosystem [of the ocean] will absolutely collapse."[8]

The discovery that the ozone shield has indeed been depleted has been dramatic. A scientific study published in 1974 by Mario Molina and Sherwood Rowland[9] said that chlorofluorocarbons (CFCs), which are used in aerosol spray cans as well as in coolants and polyurethane, will destroy ozone molecules. When released into the atmosphere, they waft their way up to the upper layer of the atmosphere, where they are broken apart by ultraviolet rays, so that free chlorine atoms result. These chlorine atoms can last for a hundred years, and each atom is capable of destroying tens of thousands of ozone molecules. (Later it was learned that CFCs were not the only culprits. Halons, widely used for firefighting, release bromine, which is also long-lived and even more destructive of ozone than chlorine.)

The scientific community was somewhat divided about this prediction in the 1970s (as it is now on the predictions about global warming), but some limited action was taken. The United States, Canada, and Sweden banned CFCs from aerosol cans; but then most people forgot about the problem, or even ridiculed it.[10] (Lawyers for the Du Pont Corporation, the world's largest manufacturer of CFCs, successfully argued in congressional hearings that it would be folly to outlaw their product on the basis of such remote dangers.)[11] Reports in 1985 and 1988, however, revealed not only that the ozone hole over the South Pole was much bigger than the scientific models had predicted (being larger than the USA and higher than Mr. Everest), but also that considerable thinning was occurring over other parts of the planet as well.[12]

After the discovery in 1985, the United States under the Reagan administration actually led the way in getting an international agreement—the Montreal Protocol—on substances that deplete the ozone layer. This was due, however, less to courageous presidential leadership than to the fact that Du Pont let it be known that, with the right incentives, it could produce a benign refrigerant within five years.[13] (Had the Reagan administration not reduced pressure in the first six years of its reign, these substitutes could have been on the market many years earlier, which would have prevented billions of deadly chlorine atoms from reaching the upper atmosphere [about eight thousand thousand tons of CFCs were produced in 1985].)[14] And even then the 1987 Montreal Protocol was far too weak. Rather than calling for greatly reduced emissions of CFCs immediately and an outright ban within five years, it called merely for a freeze (at 1986 levels) by 1989, a 20 percent reduction by 1993, and another 30 percent cut by 1998. Halon production was not reduced at all, but was simply to be frozen at 1986 levels (six thousand tons) by 1992. The agreement would not arrest depletion of the ozone layer, but merely slow its acceleration.[15]

The Montreal agreement was strengthened in 1990, after the scientific finding that ozone destruction, while greatest over the South

Pole, was not limited to that region, that there was already significant loss in the Northern Hemisphere—for example, over the United States and Great Britain. But the United States, rather than leading the way in strengthening the agreement as much as possible, effectively argued for a weaker plan than most of the other nations involved wanted. Whereas others wanted to have all CFCs banned within five years, the Bush administration argued successfully for seven years.

The threat from the ozone hole is so serious that such a difference could be crucial. In fact, the threat is so great that political leaders with vision and courage would have pressed for an immediate ban on all the destructive substances, even if no substitutes were in the offing. After all, the world got along without CFCs before 1928, when they were synthesized, and it could get along without them or substitutes now. This might cause some discomfort, but what is that when the very survival of most forms of life is possibly at stake?

An immediate ban was the only reasonable course of action, because of a combination of several factors. Some of these have already been mentioned: the destructiveness of UV-B to so many forms of life, and the fact that the ozone destroyers last for about a hundred years. Another factor is the lag effect: It takes these substances six to eight years to waft their way up to the upper atmosphere—which means that most of the destructive atoms that were released during the Reagan administration had by 1990 not yet begun to do their work. It is possible—the amount of the destruction has consistently outstripped scientific predictions quite considerably—that the ozone-destroying substances released had by 1990 already doomed us; we do not know. But in light of the possibility that this was not so, but that we were then very close to the edge, it was absolute folly to continue pouring twenty-seven hundred tons of these substances into the atmosphere per day for even another week, let alone for several more years.

Finally, in 1992, after further scientific studies showed that the hole over the United States was—again—even larger than predicted, President Bush declared that the use of CFCs would be phased out. But his announcement came only after Du Pont and other chemical corporations had said that CFCs would have to be discontinued. As was the case with Reagan, presidential "leadership" came only after the business sector had spoken. And again, there was no issuance of an order for an immediate ban. Those who had been profiting from destroying our planet's viability would need to be given time to adjust so that their profits would not be interrupted. Gangsters, presumably, should be allowed to continue robbing and killing people for a few years while they become retrained for another line of work.

Although presidential leadership has not been close to adequate with regard to the depletion of the ozone layer, I turn now to an issue on which it has been even worse.

Global Warming

There is a growing consensus among climatic scientists that global warming has *already* begun; there is an *overwhelming* consensus that, if it has not already begun, it *will* occur, and quite dramatically, in the coming decades, especially if the human activities responsible for it continue largely unchanged.

Global warming is caused by certain gases in the atmosphere that act somewhat like a greenhouse, letting heat from the sun in but then not letting it escape.

Carbon dioxide (CO_2) is the most plentiful of these greenhouse gases. It is now 25 percent more plentiful in the atmosphere than in preindustrial times. This increase is due primarily to the burning of fossil fuels. It has been said that the Industrial Revolution should really be called the Industrial Eruption: "Human beings are injecting at least one hundred times more carbon dioxide gas each year than all the volcanoes of the world."[16] But the metaphor of an eruption is somewhat misleading, because the amount of matter spewed into the atmosphere keeps increasing each decade. Whereas we put eighty billion tons of carbon into the atmosphere in the one hundred years between 1860 and 1960 (and each ton of carbon leads to 3.7 tons of CO_2), we added that same amount in the thirty years between 1960 and 1990. We are now putting in about six billion tons of carbon into the air every year —one ton per human being. Of course, we do not all account for the same amount: The United States, with about 5 percent of the world's human population, is responsible for almost 20 percent of its carbon output from fossil fuels.

But CO_2 is only one of over twenty greenhouse gases. Nitrous oxide is 19 percent more plentiful now than in preindustrial times, and methane, which is twenty-five times more effective than CO_2 in trapping heat, is 100 percent more plentiful now. The CFCs, mentioned in connection with the ozone hole, are also greenhouse gases. CFC-12, for example, is twenty thousand times more effective than CO_2 in trapping heat.

The threats from global warming are manifold and ominous. One threat is that some areas of the world will simply become more uncomfortable in the summer. The summer of 1988, which many Americans found close to unbearable, was only 1.5 degrees (Fahrenheit) hotter than normal. And yet predictions call for the global temperature to rise by 5 to 10 degrees in the next century. And that is only the global *average*—the predictions call for even higher rises in the Northern Hemisphere. Higher temperatures will, furthermore, create even greater demand for air conditioning, which will, if we are still using fossil fuels for electricity, lead in turn to even greater global warming.

A greater threat is to food supply. Because the United States, which is one of the world's major producers of food, is in the zone that will suffer the greatest increase in temperature, global food production will be greatly reduced. We should not imagine, incidentally, that Canada and Russia, which will then have a climate more suitable for agriculture, will be able to take up the slack, because their soil is thin, due to the fact that their topsoil was scraped away during the last Ice Age.

Perhaps the greatest threat is that of a dramatic rise in the level of the oceans, due both to the heating of the water, which will cause it to expand, and to the melting of polar ice caps (which are not now *in* the ocean). A rise of two to three feet seems already in the works in the coming decades, and, unless dramatic changes are instituted, the rise may be as much as eight feet by the middle of the next century. This would cause massive dislocation in coastal cities around the world and virtually inundate several low-lying countries. But there is an even worse possibility: If the western portion of the Antarctic ice sheet, which is unstable, melts enough to fall into the sea, the oceans could rise fifteen to twenty feet. Scientists believe that this will not happen, if at all, for several centuries; but they do not know for sure. And in any case, it should be cause for concern. How would we feel about our ancestors in the eighteenth century if they did nothing about a problem because its effects would not be felt until late in the twentieth century?

The Reagan and Bush administrations have, unfortunately, taken an attitude of "let's wait and see" toward the threat of global warming, just as they had with regard to the ozone hole, claiming that the evidence is not conclusive enough to warrant drastic changes. There are reasons, however, that make this policy probably suicidal.

First, as with the depletion of the ozone layer, there is the lag-time factor. As Michael Oppenheimer and Robert Boyle point out: "The full extent of the warming that will accompany any particular level of greenhouse gases will be realized about forty years after their release into the atmosphere."[17] The main reason for this lag is that the ocean is slow to warm, so it will keep the planet relatively cool in the meantime. But once it warms up, the average temperature of the planet will rise dramatically—just as a stuffed turkey finishes cooking quite quickly after the stuffing finally gets hot. Another factor contributing to lag time is that much of the CO_2 released into the atmosphere in the industrial period has probably been absorbed by the world's forests and oceans. (The reason for this assumption is that, given the amount of CO_2 that has been released into the air in the modern period, there should otherwise be about twice as much of it in the air as there in fact is.)[18] Once the forests and oceans reach their saturation points, the level of CO_2 in the atmosphere will climb dramatically if we have continued to spew it forth in great quantities.

The other major reason why the wait-and-see attitude is probably suicidal is that the process of global warming is irreversible for all practical purposes. Once the greenhouse gases are in the air, they will remain there for hundreds or even thousands of years.[19] As Oppenheimer and Boyle conclude:

> Lag time and irreversibility cut the legs out from under the politicians' responses of 'Let's see how bad things get before we spend any money' or 'We need more research.' . . . The shroud of uncertainty will not be lifted until after the fact, and by then the situation will be effectively irreversible.[20]

The wait-and-see approach is based, furthermore, on the assumption that global warming, when it occurs, will be gradual, and this assumption is probably false. As one scientist says:

> Earth's climate does not respond in a smooth and gradual way; rather it responds in sharp jumps. These jumps appear to involve large-scale reorganizations of the Earth system. If this reading of the natural record is correct, then we must consider the possibility that the major responses of the system to our greenhouse provocation will come in jumps whose timing and magnitude are unpredictable. Coping with this type of change is clearly a far more serious matter than coping with gradual warming.[21]

The wait-and-see attitude taken by most of our politicians understandably makes scientists frustrated. As Sherwood Rowland, one of the discoverers of the ozone hole, put it: "What's the use of having developed a science well enough to make predictions, if in the end all we're willing to do is stand around and wait for them to come true?"[22] Our politicians did this for far too long with regard to the hole in the ozone layer; they are continuing to do the same thing with regard to global warming.

It is true that we do not have absolute certainty on these matters, and even that scientists differ somewhat in their predictions. But this is almost always the case when dealing with threats. Political wisdom lies in assuming that the worst predictions, or at least something close to them, may be correct and acting accordingly. During the cold war with the Soviet Union we had no certainty about Soviet capabilities and even less about intentions, but our military preparations were generally based upon "worst-case scenarios." With the prospect of global climate change we face a far more likely and serious threat. We should assume that the worst-case analyses may be correct. As Secretary of State James Baker said in January 1989 at the opening of the Intergovern-mental Panel on Climate Change: "We can probably not afford to wait until all the uncertainties have been resolved before we do act."[23] We can only hope that his view will soon prevail.

Furthermore, the element of uncertainty works both ways: Just as the ozone hole and the greenhouse effect may turn out to be less seri-ous than scientists predicted, they may turn out to be even *more* serious (as has repeatedly been the case with the ozone hole already). For example, certain types of positive feedback may accelerate the deterio-ration of the ecosphere more rapidly than scientists have predicted. One example is already known: The air above the South Pole in Octo-ber and November is now eighteen degrees colder than it was in the 1970s, due to the loss of ozone (which is a greenhouse gas). Because of the colder temperature, more ice crystals form, and ice crystals pick up chlorine atoms and make them thousands of times more destructive of ozone molecules. Because of this positive feedback, the destruction of the ozone shield *accelerates* each year.

Positive feedback will occur also in relation to global warming. For example, water vapor, which contributes to global warming, will itself be *increased* by global warming. Another example: Continued global warming will eventually cause the Arctic ice-cap to begin disap-pearing (sooner than the Antarctic ice sheet, perhaps within the next fifty years). When it does begin to disappear, it will begin exposing the dark polar waters and the dark tundra, which will soak up much more heat than did the ice. The North Pole will therefore heat up even more, thereby accelerating the melting of the ice cap, which will expose more dark waters and tundra, and so on.[24]

Besides this kind of positive feedback within the processes of global warming and ozone-layer destruction, respectively, there are also positive feedback relationships between the two processes. For example, some of the phytoplankton, which suck up carbon dioxide and put the carbon on the ocean floor, will be killed by the ultraviolet radiation coming through the ozone hole. The ozone hole will thereby accelerate the greenhouse effect.

Besides the various positive feedback relationships scientists already know about, there are likely several more about which they now have no inkling. Accordingly, the fact that we have no certainty about exactly what will happen provides no basis for ecological brinkmanship; it should instead provide an additional basis for a drastic crash program.

Other Dimensions

The fact that I have focused here only upon the ozone hole and global warming is not to say that these two problems are the only truly serious ones. For example, even though the tension between East and West has reduced, the threat of instant annihilation through nuclear weapons is not abolished: Tensions between North and South will probably continue to increase, and all the old problems—such as nuclear terrorism and accidental nuclear war—remain. And little has been done to reduce the multiple threats posed by nuclear power plants, including the extremely long-term problem (addressed by Joanna Macy's essay in this volume) created by nuclear wastes.

Also—to lift up yet a fourth problem of gargantuan proportions—we are now living through the biggest holocaust in the planet's history. The best estimates say that the various species of plants and animals are now being destroyed at something like ten thousand times their natural extinction rate. According to some estimates, we will, if we continue at our current rate of habitat destruction, destroy by the year 2000 between five hundred thousand and one million species of living things. Each of these species took millions, even billions, of years to evolve; each is unique and, once it is gone, it will never return. Besides the fact, often mentioned, that many of these species surely contain elements that would be of great benefit to human beings, perhaps medically, many of them probably also play an essential role in the ecological cycle of life. Beyond all this, each one can be considered, as Thomas Berry says, a unique mode of divine presence.[25] And yet we continue to exterminate them at the rate of dozens, perhaps hundreds—only God knows—per day.

Furthermore, beyond the threat of nuclear holocaust and the already occurring biological holocaust, the problems of deadly air, acid rain, topsoil loss and degradation, groundwater shortage and pollution, and the pollution of our oceans, rivers, and lakes also require immediate and extensive action. We have an interconnected set of crises that will challenge us as never before to live up to our self-given name: *Homo sapiens sapiens*—the doubly wise humans.

III. MODERNITY AS THE SOURCE OF THE ECOLOGICAL CRISIS

To develop a vision of the way out of the ecological crisis, it is necessary to understand its root cause. Otherwise we will likely not understand the depth of the challenge that it poses to our present way of life, nor envisage a response proportionate to the challenge.

Although to some extent we can look back to the rise of agriculture and of city-based civilizations as the beginning of the problem, the human threat to the survival of the ecosphere did not begin in earnest until the modern industrial revolution of the eighteenth and nineteenth centuries, which had *its* roots, of course, in the "modern scientific revolution" of the seventeenth century.

This so-called scientific revolution was really a change in worldview. The distinctively modern worldview has regarded nature not as an organism, not even as a created order in which the divine creator is immanent, but as a machine. This new worldview is radically dualistic and anthropocentric. Human beings are regarded as wholly different from, and as outside of, "nature," which is seen to be devoid of intrinsic value. Nature's only positive value is as a resource for human welfare; negatively, nature is seen as a threat. Nature is there to be dominated and exploited by human beings; in fact, the domination of nature is regarded as the human calling.

This modern worldview by itself would not, of course, have led to a global crisis; it did this only as it became expressed through modern economics and the accompanying industrial revolution, which together have increasingly come to dominate modern life in general. Even modern industrial life in its earlier stages, although it created many local problems (such as the notorious air pollution in London), did not pose a danger to the global ecosystem. But, as the human population dramatically increased in the twentieth century, and as, simultaneously, the industrial system and its products became increasingly modern as well as widespread, especially since World War II, the threat implicit in modernity from the outset became manifest quite suddenly on many fronts.

Modernity has brought about these changes primarily through three explosions (a useful metaphor in spite of its aforementioned inadequacy): (1) the modern industrial system, which, being based on fossil fuels both for energy and as raw material for its products, has resulted in an explosion of pollutants into the air, land, and water; (2) modern medicine and agriculture, which together with a lack of policy have led to a population explosion; (3) modern economics, which has resulted in an unprecedented explosion of wealth in a significant portion of the human population and a corresponding explosion of consumer products. Any one of these explosions by itself would have put a severe strain on the planet's carrying capacity; combined, they are now overloading it.

The most distinctive feature of modern industry is its reliance upon fossil fuels. Whereas people in premodern eras derived energy from permanent or renewable sources, such as the sun, rivers, wind, wood, dung, and muscles, the modern world has relied primarily on indirect solar energy that it took nature millions or even billions of years to form, mainly coal, oil, natural gas, and uranium (with wood remaining a constant).

Michael Oppenheimer and Robert Boyle suggest a helpful way of looking at our present situation. The industrial age has thus far gone through four waves. In the first wave, from roughly the 1780s through the 1820s, water was the major source of energy; in the second wave, from the 1830s to the 1890s, steam power was dominant; from the 1890s through the 1930s the dominant form of power was electricity based upon wood and coal; and from the 1940s until now, the fourth wave, oil has been dominant. But this wave is now coming to an end, and we are making a transition to the fifth wave, which will be oriented around direct solar power. We must eventually make this transition in any case. But "the challenge is to speed the transformation and channel the economy toward the quickest and most complete substitution for fossil fuels before the world is overwhelmed by climatic change."[26]

Another way to put the issue is in economic terms: We have been on an irresponsible binge as a society, living off of our capital (nonrenewable resources) rather than our income (renewable resources). Any financial planner would tell a family that this path leads to self-destruction; and yet this is what our economists have been encouraging us as a society to do. And then, as Daly and Cobb point out, they lead us in self-congratulatory cheers every year that we manage to deplete more of our capital than we did in the preceding year—because that depletion is what the GNP now primarily measures. So another way to describe the next "wave" is that it will involve a return to living primarily off of income.

In this book we are speaking of a transition from the modern to the postmodern world. This transition will not be easy, because modernity is essentially a religious vision, as Thomas Berry has suggested in *The Dream of the Earth*. The modern mind is entranced by the modern dream, which is perhaps "the most powerful dream that has ever taken possession of human imagination."[27] This dream involves visions of nature as "a vast realm of natural resources for exploitation and consumption" and of "industrially driven consumer society" as a process that will lead to a millennium of freedom and abundance.[28] Although the dream is now turning into a nightmare, we are like drug addicts who cannot overcome their addiction to a way of life that they rationally know is killing them.

What we need is a generation of political leaders who have broken free from this self-destructive modern vision, having replaced it with a postmodern vision of humanity living in a harmonious and sustainable way with the rest of nature. This harmonious and sustainable relationship with nature, reflected in our economic system, will be a necessary condition, as John Cobb points out in this volume, for harmonious relationships among nations; otherwise, resource wars will be even more prevalent than in the past.

Essential to this harmonious relationship will be a curbing of human population growth and probably even a shrinkage of the population. Whether we date the origin of our species with the rise of the human race four million years ago, with the rise of *Homo sapiens* some three hundred thousand years ago, or with the rise of *Homo sapiens sapiens* some fifty thousand years ago, it took us a long time to reach our first billion members, which occurred in 1800. The second billion, now that the modern industrial age had arrived, took only a century. We then added two more billion in seventy-five years. Now we have over five billion and are adding a billion each decade. Most of this growth is occurring in the third world. And yet growth in the heavily industrialized world, although it is much slower, is equally serious. As Paul and Anne Ehrlich point out, "a baby born in the United States represents twice the destructive impact on Earth's ecosystems and the services they provide as one born in Sweden, three times one born in Italy, 13 times one born in Brazil, 35 times one in India, 140 times one in Bangladesh or Kenya, and 280 times one in Chad, Rwanda, Haiti, or Nepal. . . . [Therefore] population shrinkage is essential among the rich."[29] And yet, between 1970 and 1988 the population of the USA rose 21 percent.

So, a sustainable world will necessarily include not only a postmodern energy system and a postmodern economic system, but also a new attitude about human population and a heretofore lacking willingness to curb its growth. There is no issue on which vigorous leadership is more urgent; there is no issue on which wise and courageous leadership will be more needed.

IV. AMERICAN RESPONSIBILITY

The United States of America has a special responsibility to lead the way in overcoming the global ecological crisis for two reasons. First, America is directly more responsible for the crisis than any other nation. For example, with something like 5 percent of the global population, America is responsible for about 25 percent of the greenhouse gases.

Second, America serves as a symbol and model for much of the rest of the world. Other nations want the things Americans have. There will be hope that third-world countries will not "modernize," but will "postmodernize"—that is, develop in environmentally sustainable ways—only if they see that we are moving in this direction, thereby signaling that modernization is more a thing of the past than the wave of the future. America, the most modern of all nations, must now lead the world in becoming postmodern.

Furthermore, America can exert moral leadership in this area around the world only if it puts its own house in order, because the rest of the world knows full well our role in creating the problem.

So, if the United States would institute a crash program to change its own ways, this would do more than any other nation can do to alleviate the global crisis directly. And this change will have two indirect effects: Our symbolic power will begin to influence other nations in an environmentally positive, rather than in a negative, manner; and we can begin to exert credible moral leadership in this area.

V. THE NEED FOR PRESIDENTIAL LEADERSHIP

The idea that we will need presidential leadership to solve the ecological crisis often evokes strong objections. For some people, the idea conjures up a vision of a father figure who is expected to do everything for us. Rather than a vision like this, which will simply reinforce the passivity of the citizenry, it is said, we must emphasize the idea that the problem will be solved only by massive grassroots activism. For some people, the call for vigorous presidential leadership is a call for top-down solutions, whereas the only solutions that ever work are bottom-up solutions. The call for a solution from the president and other political leaders is, furthermore, said to rest on the naive view that politicians are leaders, whereas the truth is that they are followers. They will exercise leadership with regard to the ecological crisis only when they see that the citizenry is ahead of them—that is, when they see that that is where the votes are.

There is much truth in the points of view expressed in such objections. But just as it would be naive to believe that effective solutions could come from the presidential level *alone*, or even from this combined with that of the governors and the national and state congresses, it would be equally naive to assume that effective solutions could be found, especially in time, *apart from* political leadership at these levels, especially that of the presidency. The argument here is not for presidential leadership *instead of* leadership at other levels, including grassroots activism and individual and corporate responsibility, but for presidential leadership that will *supplement*, *inspire*, and *encourage* leadership, activism, and responsibility at all the other levels.

The reason no simple solution—whether focused on the president, state and local politicians, corporations, or grassroots activism, whether stressing top-down or bottom-up solutions—can be adequate is that the problem is extremely complex, with many dimensions and levels. Some of the problems can be addressed effectively at one level, whereas other problems must be addressed at other levels. The focus of the present essay is on what can and must be done at the presidential level—without denying the importance of the other levels—if there is to be hope. For example, grassroots organizations can do little directly to stop the worldwide use of greenhouse gases and ozone-depleting substances, to change the national agricultural and energy policies, to develop a new national transportation policy, to change industry-wide pollution standards, to change the national economic and military policies, to name only a few things. At the same time, it is also true that the *ideas* for solutions arise best from outside the government—ideas for new agricultural, economic, and transportation policies, for substitutes for environmentally destructive chemicals, and so on. (The present book, indeed, is seeking to suggest and spread some such ideas.) This is part of the truth of the bottom-up emphasis. But these ideas will do little good unless political leaders implement them, or at least pass legislation that encourages their implementation. Aroused citizens can bring much pressure to bear to have a nuclear power plant shut down. But they can do little to guarantee that the alternative will not be a nuclear power plant in a neighboring state. They can do little to see that the nation advances to solar power rather than retreats to coal.

The example of citizens pressuring a governor to shut down a nuclear power plant raises another element of truth in the objections mentioned above—namely, that most politicians are guided less by their vision of the long-term good of the planet than by their concern to be reelected. They are, in this sense, leaders less than followers, following what they believe the majority of their constituents want. Accordingly, one could say, rather than calling for new leaders, we need to develop a more concerned and informed electorate, out of which more ecologically responsible politicians will emerge.

On the one hand, it is certainly right to emphasize the need for a more concerned and informed electorate, because only in this way will we get better politicians. This side of the truth is stressed by several of the authors in this volume and is in no tension with the point that we need better political leaders.

On the other hand, it is also the case that politicians sometimes do act courageously, voting for something because they believe it is right even though they suspect it may threaten their reelection. We should encourage politicians to do this with respect to the environment. Furthermore, although in general politicians follow public opinion polls, they also help *shape* public opinion. This point is true especially of presidents, who have vast resources at their disposal for forming public opinion (see *Manufacturing Consent*, by Noam Chomsky and Edward S. Herman); I discuss this point below in the section on symbolic-moral leadership.

One of the reasons the importance of political leadership with regard to the ecological crisis is sometimes minimized is the idea—comforting to politicians and giant corporations alike—that the ecological crisis is due primarily to the habits of consumers, so that the solution must also lie with them. But as Barry Commoner has said, "Pogo's analysis of the environmental crisis—'We have met the enemy and he is us'—is appealing but untrue."[30] Of course, there are certain things that we as individuals can do within the present system, such as drive less and recycle more. But most of the decisions that make a big difference are made by corporations and at the city, state, and especially federal levels. If the kind of massive change needed is to come about, especially fast enough, the support of individuals and institutions of various kinds—political, educational, communications—and at every level will be required. And this is likely to occur only through presidential leadership.

There are at least two reasons why presidential leadership is required. First, the executive branch of the federal government can directly do, and get Congress to do, many of the things that need doing.

Second, through the symbolic power of the presidency and the moral leadership its occupant can exert, the cooperation of other segments of society can be enlisted. In the following sections I will refer to some to the things that the executive branch can do in terms of direct action and promoting legislation, and then address the issue of symbolic-moral leadership.

IV. A CRASH PROGRAM

Because we have not responded adequately to the environmental crisis since becoming aware of it as a society in the late 1960s, and especially because many of the gains made during the 1970s, minimal as they were, were undone in the 1980s, "a crash program is now essential," as Worldwatch Institute says.[31] I will describe some of the elements of such a program and some illustrations of what presidential leadership can do to promote this program. The major areas to address are energy efficiency, energy supply, transportation, forests, militarization, economics, agriculture, toxic chemicals, and population.

Energy Efficiency

One of the most shameful aspects of the American economy is how much of the energy from fossil fuels, for which we are willing to go to war, would be unneeded if only we would engage in a massive program to make our buildings, our transportation system, and our production system more energy efficient. An indication of how wasteful we are is provided by the fact that the Swiss, who do not have a noticeably lower standard of living than we do (and who have a much colder climate to boot), put only one-fourth as much carbon per person into the atmosphere as do Americans.[32]

Partly because we have been so wasteful, energy efficiency is by far the greatest potential source of new energy for America. Already in the 1980s, with rather modest changes, we got, as Amory and Hunter Lovins point out, seven times as much energy from savings as we did from the expansion of supplies.[33] And, far greater savings are possible in the future. Yet, our political and business leaders have not gotten the message: "The supply options got about six times as much investment and at least 20 times as much government subsidy as the more cost-effective efficiency improvements."[34]

As the Lovinses emphasize, not only will this efficiency be good for the planet; it will also be economical, even in the short run. If the efficiency measures that are now available were fully implemented, *three-fourths* of all the electricity now used in the United States could be saved, and at a price of less than the *operating* cost of coal or nuclear plants (even if their construction cost were zero). To put this in other terms: We can save four times as much electricity as we now get from nuclear power plants, and at less than the cost of simply operating those plants (ignoring the tremendous costs involved in building and then dismantling them).[35] Likewise, if presently existing oil- and gas-saving technologies (such as "superwindows" in buildings, refrigerators and light bulbs that take four times less electricity than standard ones, and automobiles that get over a hundred miles per gallon) were fully implemented, four-fifths of all the oil used in the United States could be saved.[36] Again, this could be done economically: Only *"one year's* worth of the roughly $50 billion per year that we are spending on forces whose mission is to protect or seize Mideast oilfields, if spent to make American buildings more heat-tight, would *eliminate* imports of Mideast oil."[37] Driving home the amount the American economy could save, while also saving the planet from American waste and wars, the Lovinses state that "the energy still wasted today in the United States costs more than $300 billion per year—*more than the entire military budget*, or about twice the federal budget deficit."[38] The moral for wise leadership is clear.

Energy Supply

The dependence of the modern economy upon fossil fuels is doubly tragic—and foolish. Besides the fact that these fuels are killing the planet, being the chief source of air pollution, water pollution, acid rain, global warming, and the ozone hole, an economy based on fossil fuels is inherently unsustainable, because these fuels are finite. We will, in fact, begin running out of oil early in the next century. The implication would seem to be obvious: *Because the fossil-fuel economy is killing the planet, and because we must soon shift from it to a sustainable economy anyway, we should begin doing so immediately, while there still may be time to prevent catastrophic global changes.*

One way to attempt to avoid this obvious conclusion is to argue thus: "Because we are running out of fossil fuels anyway, we need not take any special governmental action. The finitude of the fossil fuels can be accepted as a godsend that will save us from global warming and other catastrophes, and, as these fuels become increasingly scarce, market forces will lead future generations to make the transition to renewable forms of energy." Unfortunately for this scenario, there is enough coal and oil left to raise the level of carbon dioxide ten times higher than the doubling that is expected in the next century.[39] Although the easily extractable oil will indeed be depleted soon, coal reserves will last, even if used at currently projected rates, well into the twenty-third century. Also, although shortages of oil will soon make renewable forms of energy increasingly attractive from an economic standpoint, we cannot leave the solution to the market. As Oppenheimer and Boyle say, "left to its own devices, the global economy would not make the transition nearly fast enough to avoid environmental catastrophe. . . . The only tool at hand for speeding a global transition to the fifth wave [solar energy] is government."[40] This does not mean that the government should be directly involved in producing the new technologies, only that it needs to provide the appropriate types of incentives. These incentives should be aimed at moving us as rapidly as possible away from the present system, in which about 90 percent of our energy is produced from fossil fuels, to a system in which most of our energy comes from renewable, nonpolluting energy—a combination of solar thermal, solar photovoltaic, wind, tidal, geothermal, and biomass energy. Government can make this transition likely or unlikely.

Solar energy provides a demonstration of the ability of the president to effect change for good or ill. When the Reagan administration slashed support for renewable energy, orders for solar hot-water systems dropped 80 percent. Those incentives, in strengthened form, need to be reinstated. But perhaps the most important form of renewable energy will be electricity from photovoltaic cells. The development of more efficient and less expensive photovoltaics can be promoted simply through the purchasing power of the government. Unfortunately, Jimmy Carter while president, although he was much more enlightened in this area than his successors, vetoed a bill that could have mandated the purchase of nearly a half billion dollars' worth of photovoltaic cells for federal installations. This move, estimates had it, would have brought the price of electricity per watt down from $20 to 50¢ in five years, which would have made them competitive and greatly expanded the market;[41] this plan should be revived immediately.

American energy experts and politicians have long belittled renewable forms of energy, thinking—or at least publically *saying*— that they could never supply more than a tiny fraction of American needs. But that idea was based in large part on the assumption that we need far more energy than we do. With the kinds of energy efficiency discussed above, renewable energy could, the Lovinses say, "cost-effectively supply up to thirty-five percent of total national needs in the year 2000—and approximately one hundred percent within a few decades thereafter. Sustainable resources, not exhaustion, would then underpin long-term prosperity and security."[42] Besides benefiting the planet and our economy, this development, the Lovinses stress, would greatly enhance the nation's security. Another point stressed by the Lovinses is that renewable forms of energy do not need government subsidies; they need only to have the subsidies removed from nuclear and fossil-fuel energy: If they had a level playing field, they would be able to compete.

An important element in dealing with energy will be, as Oppenheimer and Boyle have stressed, free transfers of solar technologies to third-world nations.[43] A central part of the postmodern sensibility is the recognition—driven home by global warming and the ozone hole—that all of our fates are interconnected, so that we help ourselves by helping others.

Transportation

The problem of transportation is second to none. It is responsible for something like a third of the world's use of energy and therefore close to a fourth of the world's greenhouse gases. Driving motor vehicles causes more air pollution than any other single human activity. Motor vehicles in the United States produce more CO_2 than *all* of the activities of any other country except China and the former Soviet Union.

Modern transportation illustrates especially well the interconnection of the various modern sources of the environmental crisis. It is energized by fossil fuels. It is terribly inefficient, being based primarily around the private automobile (especially in the United States which, with 4 percent of the world's population, has over one-third of its five hundred million automobiles). It is not only inherently much less efficient than other forms of transportation, such as trains; it is far less efficient than it need be: Automobile prototypes *four times* more efficient than current models already exist. There is much more transportation going on than would be necessary if cities were designed so that people lived near their work, or at least so that mass transit were practical for most people, and if the economy stressed local self-sufficiency rather than trade between remote areas (see Cobb's essay in this volume). And the problem of transporting people and goods multiplies every time the population multiplies. Transportation takes two-thirds of the oil used by Americans, and automobiles alone take one-half of this amount.

The United States should have begun a complete overhaul of its transportation system in the early 1970s, when the environmental and energy crises became well known. (Had our nation implemented the existing possibilities in the past two decades, the terribly immoral Gulf War[44] would not have seemed necessary.) Such an overhaul is even more urgent now. The aim of this overhaul should be, on the one hand, to make the automobile as planet-friendly as possible and, on the other, to institute new incentives and disincentives that will discourage the use of automobiles and trucks and encourage the development of more energy-efficient options.

Various proposals have been offered for making the automobile less polluting. Most immediately, through a combination of removing government subsidies for gasoline and passing efficiency legislation, we should get the gas-guzzlers off the road and get the prototypes that get from 80 to 120 miles per gallon into mass production. (The recent proposal, in the light of the Gulf crisis, that legislation be passed to require that automobiles get 40 miles per gallon by the end of the decade, shows how timid and/or uninformed most of our national political leaders are.) At the same time, the number of electric cars (with batteries charged by solar power) should be greatly expanded. This can be done immediately for vehicles for which the hundred-mile limit between rechargings poses no difficulty; and further research and development on ways to overcome this problem (such as quick-change batteries) should be promoted. One of the best candidates for extensive research and development is the solar hydrogen engine (the hydrogen is derived from electrolysis of water using electricity derived from photovoltaic cells; a photovoltaic-hydrogen plant is now being built in Germany), which would provide a high-performance, long-range vehicle that would be virtually nonpolluting. (Prototypes have been produced by BMW and the Perris Smogless Automobile Association of California, among others.)[45] Another good possibility is solar methane. This possibility is one of the reasons why, among alternative fuels presently discussed to be used temporarily, natural gas would be preferable to ethanol and methanol. Besides the facts that ethanol increases hydrocarbon emissions, uses grain that is needed for food, and uses up more energy in production than it provides, and that methanol (which the EPA has pushed) increases emissions of nitrogen oxides and emits (carcinogenic) formaldehyde, the pipelines used for natural gas could later be used for solar methane.[46] Surely the most important prototypes for the long-range future, finally, are those that are powered by photovoltaic cells on the automobile.

Although it is important to make the automobile as planet-friendly as possible, it is at least equally important to move away from an automobile-centered transportation system for a host of reasons, including these: Whatever forms of fuel replace gasoline, it will be important to make our transportation system as energy-efficient as possible; our cities and freeways are already too clogged with traffic; our arable land is already too covered with asphalt and cement; and the automobile is by far the most lethal form of transportation (it has killed more Americans—between two and three million—than all the wars of the twentieth century combined).

Because public forms of transportation have been neglected for so long in this country (due not simply to the alleged "love affair" between Americans and their automobiles, but to collusion, leaving Americans little choice—80 percent of the driving in Los Angeles is work-related), rectifying the situation will be expensive, but it must be done. The national railway system needs to be reinvigorated, with old lines repaired and new ones built for "bullet trains." Subsidies heretofore given to the highway and airline systems should now be given to the railway system instead. All cities now without them need interlocking light-rail, monorail, subway, and bus systems.

Besides public transportation, the use of bicycles should be vigorously promoted, as it is successfully in China, Japan, the Netherlands, Denmark, and, within the United States, in Davis and Palo Alto, California. This means building bike lanes and bike paths throughout all towns and cities; requiring businesses and mass transit stops to provide showers, lockers, and safe parking spaces; providing financial incentives for biking to work; and using the media to make biking to work a source of prestige.[47]

The other major factor in the transportation package is urban redesign. Among the aims of this redesign would be to get people living closer to their work (so that they can walk, bike, take public transportation, or drive a low-polluting vehicle only a short distance) and to make it possible for some form of public transit to reach every part of the city.

The assumption, incidentally, that none of these things will get people out of their automobiles is false. People will change their habits, if the incentives to do so are sufficient, especially if economic incentives are combined with appeals to support the health of one's nation and the planet.

Presidential leadership would be crucial to, and effective in, all these dimensions of the transportation overhaul. The rebuilding and improvement of the national rail system would take the kind of presidential backing given to the space program. Urban redesign and the related development of biking and various forms of public transportation would require legislative incentives based on an overall vision that could probably come only from the executive branch. The research and development needed for such things as more practical solar-powered automobiles would need governmental support. And the government could spur the development of many of the promising technologies, and the lowering of their price, by using the purchasing power of the federal government (which, for example, buys over $7 billion worth of autos and trucks annually). One of the most immediate things presidential leadership could do would be to get legislation passed requiring energy-efficient automobiles, then making sure that the deadlines are not postponed and that the standards are enforced. To illustrate the importance of such action: If even the modest regulations for automobile efficiency that were instituted in the 1970s had been left in place, instead of terminated, by the Reagan administration, the amount of gasoline saved in a decade or so would have equaled all the oil estimated to lie under the Arctic National Wildlife Refuge (for which, of course, the Reagan and Bush administrations have wanted to drill).

Forests

Deforestation is responsible for a significant amount of the greenhouse gases. One fifth or more of the carbon poured into the atmosphere results from the burning of forests; and the loss of forests lessens the planet's capacity to absorb CO_2. Most of the discussion in the United States about deforestation has been about the tropical forests; and yet "the temperate rainforests of the Pacific Northwest produce four times more organic matter than tropical rainforests, making them the single most important carbon-storing mechanism on the surface of the Earth."[48] Particularly serious is the loss of the virgin or old-growth forests, 97 percent of which have been cut down in the last two hundred years. Their loss destroys habitat for various species, contributes to soil erosion, and makes forests, because of loss of diversity, much more vulnerable. And yet present policies of the U.S. Congress will lead to the virtual elimination of our native forests—especially if, as evidently desired by the Bush administration and much of the Congress, a way around the Endangered Species Act can be found.

This issue provides a good example of the point made earlier, that we cannot exert credible moral leadership until we change our own ways. The United States has been putting pressure on Brazil to change those of its policies that are responsible for the destruction of the Brazilian rain forests. In 1989, Brazil's President Sarney called U.S. pronouncements about deforestation in Brazil "an insidious, cruel and untruthful campaign" to distract attention from its own environmental degradation.[49] The fact is that what the United States has said about Brazilian deforestation is, tragically, true; but what Sarney said is also true, even with regard to deforestation in particular. Among other things, we have been, thanks to congressional legislation, selling old-growth trees from the Tongass National Forest in Alaska to a Japanese pulp mill (and, to boot, we are selling these trees, which would bring about $300 each on the open market, for about $2 each).[50] We cannot expect Brazil or any other nation to listen to our concerns about global warming when we are doing such things.

Modern Militarization

Militarization has been responsible for global degradation in almost countless ways. Military exercises and battles account for a significant portion of the world's fossil-fuel use. Nuclear weapons and power plants exist thanks to military-driven research and design (R&D). Military battles are destructive of land and forests—as a visit to Vietnam makes clear. And military spending takes such an enormous amount of the national and global budget that far too little is left for social and environmental programs. The U.S. budget for 1990 contained about $45 *billion* for military R&D and only $190 *million* for environmental R&D. We will have a chance of surviving the ecological crisis only if most of the resources previously devoted to the military are now turned to the environment. (One sensible proposal for how to reduce military spending drastically, while not reducing "defensive" capability, is to merge the four branches of the U.S. armed forces into a single military, thereby eliminating "outrageously wasteful duplication, triplication and sometimes even quadruplication of effort.")[51]

We come now to the final four problems mentioned earlier—economics, agriculture, toxic chemicals, and population. The issues of economics and agriculture, however, are passed over here, because they are the subjects of entire essays in this volume by John Cobb[52] and Wes Jackson.[53] One of their points that bears repeating here is, however, is that the issues of economics and agriculture are closely intertwined with the issue of militarism. The main precondition for reducing global militarism is altering the global economic-agricultural system.

Toxic Chemicals

The question of toxic chemicals is well addressed in *Fighting Toxics*, edited by Gary Cohen and John O'Connor, and by Barry Commoner in *Making Peace with the Planet*.[54] Their all-important point is that none of the various kinds of pollution can be successfully addressed through efforts at pollution *control*. Government and industry have thus far spent billions on pollution control to very little avail. The only effective means is pollution *prevention*: prohibiting the production of the polluting substance in the first place. One can only hope that federal, state, and local officials will listen.

Population

The issue of human *population* has been readdressed recently by Paul and Anne Ehrlich in *The Population Explosion.* (Commoner, unfortunately, regards the technology of production as the only real problem, foolishly belittling the issue of population; the Ehrlichs, by contrast, regard population as the most important issue, while dealing with technology in a more balanced way than Commoner deals with population.) To stress the crucial nature of this issue, the Ehrlichs cite the saying, "Whatever your cause, it's a lost cause without population control."[55] They are absolutely right. A crash program to deal with the human population, in rich and poor nations alike, must be a central part of the overall crash program needed if there is to be much hope of averting deaths in the billions due to wars and ecocatastrophes in the twenty-first century. Several workable plans to control and even reduce population have been proposed. Lacking are not ideas but political leaders with the vision, will, and courage.

To summarize the argument thus far: Whereas the bad news is that the global environmental crisis is extremely serious, the good news is that the ideas and the technological means for responding to the crisis in an adequate way are already at hand. What we need now is the political vision and the will to implement them. Which brings us to the other dimension of presidential leadership, the symbolic-moral dimension.

VII. PRESIDENTIAL SYMBOLIC-MORAL LEADERSHIP

If and when we get a president who is ready to be the "environmental president" in fact, not simply in campaign rhetoric, his or her symbolic and moral authority will be as important as the things the executive branch can do directly. There is only so much that can be accomplished by legislation (even if effectively enforced) and government spending. Beyond this, we need a president who will inspire the nation—everyone from hard-nosed, bottom-line corporate executives to potential cyclers and recyclers—to join the crusade to save the planet (and, at the same time, the American economy, not to mention its soul). Although an adequate American response to the environmental crisis will require strong presidential leadership, it will also require appropriate action at every level of American society.

Although some environmentalists stress top-down solutions, while others seek bottom-up solutions, there is, as argued earlier, no antithesis between the two. There are some issues that can be addressed only by the federal government, others that are best addressed by state governments, and still others that are best addressed by city governments; there are yet other issues that are best addressed by the private sector, and still others by volunteer organizations. More accurately, most issues require cooperation between different bodies. What presidential leadership can best do is establish a framework and atmosphere, through a combination of legislation, revenue sharing, example, symbolism, and rhetoric, in which the various things that are needed—such as research and development, adoption of appropriate technologies, state and local legislation, and recycling incentives—happen.

This kind of presidential leadership is needed if a sufficient proportion of the individuals and corporations in the nation are to get serious about this most serious issue of all time. There is a certain percent of the population—perhaps 5 to 10 percent—that is already firmly committed to environmental protection and restoration and is already doing all it can (within the confines of the present system). There is a much bigger percent—perhaps 40 to 50 percent of the population—that is intellectually and morally persuaded but not yet doing much. Many of these people believe that their efforts will count for little, given the fact that most of the country is carrying on with business as usual. This group is, we could say, waiting to be led. There is yet another portion of the population—perhaps 40 to 50 percent— that, for the most part, simply believes what the president and therefore (for the most part) the mainline mass media say. This group will take the environmental crisis seriously if and only if the president of the United States says that they should, and shows by his or her own actions that it is serious and yet that we can take effective action to overcome it.

What we need first of all, accordingly, is for a president to state the situation clearly and unequivocally, perhaps beginning with a "state of the world" address. The president needs to explain how serious are the various dimensions of the global crisis, America's responsibility in this matter, and then what America needs to do to respond to the challenge. The president needs to explain that this is the most serious challenge ever faced by the human race and that we need to respond accordingly. Because the threat to our national security is far greater than it was in World War II and the ensuing cold war with the Soviet

Union, the national effort will need to be far greater than it was even in those efforts. And then, not to make a mockery of all this, the president needs to announce a set of programs with a level of funding that backs up the statement that this cause is indeed even *more than* "the moral equivalent of war" (to cite the essay by William James that inspired, among other things, President Kennedy's Peace Corps).

Thereafter, the president should regularly, perhaps in monthly "non-fireside chats," report to the American people on recent developments in the national and global battle to save the planet, then encourage them to do all that they can do in their station in life—encouraging automakers even to exceed the new regulations for gasoline mileage, suggesting the various reasons why Americans should eat less meat, and encouraging us to plant as many trees as possible, to plant again the backyard gardens that were so important during World War II, to ride our bicycles and take public transportation as much as possible, to recycle as much as possible, and so on. In this way, the president could keep before us the fact that we are facing the greatest crisis of all time and could continue to draw more and more citizens and institutions into the effort.

An extremely important role would need to be played by the mass media, of course. The problem is that they are owned by corporate giants, in many cases precisely the corporations that are profiting most from the present arrangements (NBC, for example, is owned by General Electric). A most important feature of presidential leadership would be to convince these corporations that their true interests and those of the planet do in fact coincide. The work of the Lovinses can be especially helpful in this respect. *World Watch* magazine says: "The political challenge is to break free of the industrial interests that paralyze the U.S. government."[56] That statement reflects a realistic analysis of what has been going on (and therefore not going on) in the past (the fact is mentioned that of the top twenty-five companies in the Fortune 500, thirteen are automobile or energy companies). But the real challenge for political leadership now is to *convert* the industrial interests, to enlist them in the effort to save the nation and the planet, partly by moral persuasion, partly by showing them, in terms of hard figures, that their economic interests and the interests of nature's economy need not be in conflict. This would be leadership.

Far from excercising this kind of leadership, however, our presidents have, for the most part, done just the opposite. With regard to George Bush in particular, it had been known to environmentalists from the outset that Bush has been the greatest obstacle to agreement on meaningful accords among the industrialized nations. This fact became general knowledge in June 1992, due to the publicity given to U.S. recalcitrance at the "Earth Summit" in Brazil. The "balance" between the environment and the economy in terms of which Bush has justified his position generally means that (short-term) economic interests take precedence over ecological sustainability (and therefore long-term economic interests).

The degree to which the Bush administration has systematically sought to undermine environmental regulations in the name of economic interests has become even more fully understood through the attention recently given to the Council on Competitiveness, chaired at Bush's bequest by Vice President Dan Quayle. Assigned the task of reducing regulations perceived by industries as stifling economic growth, this council has been given virtual veto power over regulations written by most departments of the federal government. Members of the Environmental Protection Agency have said that this power has had a "chilling effect" within the EPA (*ABC World News Report*, 4-5 August, 1992).

The point here is not to attack Bush personally. Although he has surely been worse with regard to the environment than other possible occupants of the office might have been, the main problem is due not to his personal beliefs and insensitivities, but to the modern mind-set, of which he is simply a somewhat extreme embodiment, and the late modern world order, of which, as president of the United States, he is pressured from almost every side to be the chief defender. Until we elect people with postmodern sensibilities to that office, and make clear that we will support their efforts to move beyond the modern world order, the United States, both directly through its actions and indirectly by its example, will continue to lead the world to self-destruction.

VIII. Conclusion

This essay, indeed this book as a whole, argues that if there is to be hope for human life and even much of the rest of the life of the planet, we must have, among other things, wise and courageous political leadership, especially from presidents during the next twenty years. The record of the past, of course, provides ample basis for scepticism that we will get such leadership. For example, the Ehrlichs give this analysis:

> It is our guess . . . that any resolution of the human dilemma that might lead to [population] *stability* over even the medium term

(say, a few centuries) would have to be based on democratic decisions acceptable to most of the world's people—a mutually agreed-upon system, the major features of which were somehow mutually enforced by social pressures or other sanctions. To establish civilization on such a path will require inspired leadership, something that has been absent in the United States for some time.[57]

Such statements show up in virtually every publication one reads about the environmental crisis. For example, Oppenheimer and Boyle say that "there has been little leadership on the environment from U.S. politicians. Numbed by years of propaganda against federal intrusions, they often lack the wit and courage to proffer solutions."[58] Perhaps the most pessimistic statement I have encountered comes from Bill McKibben. After saying that "somehow, political leaders and government processes and budget makers must accustom themselves to a new way of thinking," he then reflects upon his own statement, adding: "Of all the quixotic ideas discussed here, that may top the list."[59]

We must hope, however, that this is *not* quixotic, that some presidents will arise from among us who do have "the vision thing" and are willing and able to use the "White House effect" to realize this vision—a postmodern vision of humanity living in harmony, for God's sake, with the rest of nature.

Notes

1. *New York Times*, 24 Sept. 1988; cited by Jonathan Weiner, *The Next One Hundred Years: Shaping the Fate of Our Living Earth* (New York: Bantam Books, 1990), 94.

2. Bill McKibben, *The End of Nature* (New York: Random House, 1989), 64, 78.

3. Herman E. Daly and John B. Cobb, Jr., *For the Common Good: Redirecting the Economy toward Community, the Environment, and a Sustainable Future* (Boston: Beacon Press, 1989), 2.

4. Barry Commoner, *Making Peace with the Planet* (New York: Pantheon Books, 1990), 6.

5. Lester R. Brown, Christofer Flavin, and Sandra Postel, "Foreword" (xv–xvi) and chap. 10, "Outlining a Global Action Plan" (174–94), in *State of the World 1989: A Worldwatch Institute Report on Progress Toward a Sustainable Society*, by Lester R. Brown et al. (New York: Norton, 1989), xv, 174.

6. Ibid., xiv, xvi. Nothing in the 1990, 1991, and 1992 issues of *State of the World* retracts this dire assessment.

7. Michael Oppenheimer and Robert H. Boyle, *Dead Heat: The Race against the Greenhouse Effect* (New York: Basic Books, 1990), 47, 226.

8. Sayed El-Sayed, quoted by Weiner, *Next One Hundred Years*, 159.

9. Mario J. Molina and F.S. Rowland, "Stratospheric Sink for Chlorofluoromethanes: Chlorine Atom-Catalysed Destruction of Ozone," *Nature* 249 (1974):810–12.

10. Cynthia Polluck Shea, "Protecting the Ozone Layer" in Brown et al., *State of the World 1989*: 77–96, esp. 87.

11. Weiner, *Next One Hundred Years*, 141–42.

12. Ibid., 77; Oppenheimer and Boyle, *Dead Heat*, 46–48.

13. Oppenheimer and Boyle, *Dead Heat*, 159.

14. Brown, Flavin, and Postel, "Outlining a Global Action Plan," in Brown et al., *State of the World 1989:* 188.

15. Shea, "Protecting the Ozone Layer," 94.

16. Weiner, *Next One Hundred Years*, 41.

17. Oppenheimer and Boyle, *Dead Heat*, 82.

18. Weiner, *Next One Hundred Years*, 43.

19. Weiner, *Next One Hundred Years*, 109; Oppenheimer and Boyle, *Dead Heat*, 80.

20. Oppenheimer and Boyle, *Dead Heat*, 83.

21. Wallace S. Broecker in *The Challenge of Global Warming,* D. E. Abrahamson (Washington, D.C., and Covelo, Calif.: Island Press, 1989); quoted in Oppenheimer and Boyle, *Dead Heat*, 17.

22. Sherwood Rowland, one of the predictors of the ozone hole (see n. 9, above), as quoted in Weiner, *Next One Hundred Years*, 162.

23. Baker's comment is quoted by P. Shabecoff in "Joint Effort Urged to Guard Climate," *New York Times*, 31 January 1989: A9; I owe the quotation to Oppenheimer and Boyle, *Dead Heat*, 185.

24. Weiner, *Next One Hundred Years*, 116.

25. Thomas Berry, *The Dream of the Earth* (San Francisco: Sierra Club Books, 1988), 11.

26. Oppenheimer and Boyle, *Dead Heat*, 168–72, 3.

27. Berry, *Dream of the Earth*, 205.

28. Ibid., 40, 38, 41.

29. Paul R. Ehrlich and Anne H. Ehrlich, *The Population Explosion* (New York: Simon & Schuster, 1990), 134.

30. Commoner, *Making Peace*, 229.

31. Shea, "Protecting the Ozone Layer," 96.

32. Weiner, *Next One Hundred Years*, 42.

33. L. Hunter Lovins and Amory B. Lovins, "How Not to Parachute More Cats: The Hidden Links Between Energy and Security," 2. (This paper was presented at the conference from which the present volume arose, but could not, unfortunately, be included here.)

34. Ibid.

35. Ibid., 7.

36. Ibid., 6.

37. Ibid., 8.

38. Ibid., 11.

39. Weiner, *Next Hundred Years*, 103.

40. Oppenheimer and Boyle, *Dead Heat*, 4, 5.

41. Commoner, *Making Peace*, 206–07.

42. Amory B. Lovins and L. Hunter Lovins, *Brittle Power: Energy Strategy for National Security* (Andover, Mass.: Brick House, 1982), 263.

43. Oppenheimer and Boyle, *Dead Heat*, 5.

44. On the Gulf War, see Thomas C. Fox, *Iraq: Military Victory and Moral Defeat* (Kansas City: Sheed & Ward, 1991); Kenneth L. Vaux, *Ethics and the Gulf War: Religion, Rhetoric, and Righteousness* (Boulder and Oxford: Westview Press, 1992); and the series of articles in the *Los Angeles Times* the week of 24–28 February, 1992.

45. Oppenheimer and Boyle, *Dead Heat*, 122–23.

46. Commoner, *Making Peace*, 197–98.

47. Marcia D. Lowe, "Cycling into the Future," in *State of the World 1990*, by Lester Brown et al. (New York: Norton, 1990), 119–34.

48. Kate Crockett, "The Deforestation of America," *Earth Island Journal*, Spring 1990:14.

49. Quoted in Oppenheimer and Boyle, *Dead Heat*, 150.

50. Ibid.

51. Leslie H. Gelb (of *The New York Times*), "Putting a Plug in the Vast Military Rat Hole," *Santa Barbara News-Press*, 28 July 1992:A9.

52. See note 3, above, and Herman E. Daly, "The Steady-State Economy: Postmodern Alternative to Growthmania," in *Spirituality and Society: Postmodern Visions*, ed. David Ray Griffin (Albany: State University of New York Press, 1988), 107–22.

53. On postmodern economics, see also also Dean Freudenberger, "Agriculture in a Postmodern World," in Griffin, *Spirituality and Society*, 123–32.

54. See note 4, above, and Gary Cohen and John O'Connor, eds., *Fighting Toxics: A Manual for Protecting Your Family, Community, and Workplace* (Washington, D.C., and Covelo, Calif.: Island Press., 1990).

55. Ehrlich and Ehrlich, *Population Explosion*, 26.

56. *World Watch* 3/3 (May-June 1990), 25.

57. Ehrlich and Ehrlich, *Population Explosion*, 182.

58. Oppenheimer and Boyle, *Dead Heat*, 186.

59. McKibben, *End of Nature*, 146.

5

WITHOUT A VISION THE PEOPLE PERISH: WASHINGTON, D.C., AS PARABLE

Jim Wallis

Where there is no vision,
the people perish.
　　　—Proverbs 29:18

I. A TALE OF TWO CITIES

It was only a few weeks before the 1988 presidential election. I was driving home from work through the streets of Washington, D.C., listening to a National Public Radio discussion on the lackluster campaign. The panel of experts, of both Democratic and Republican persuasions, were trying to determine why no real issues of substance had emerged in the electoral contest between the two major parties' nominees.

In the end, they all more or less agreed that the lack of sharp political debate in 1988 was due to the fact that there were no really pressing issues to discuss. These commentators (all white, male, national-level journalists) concurred that the nation was experiencing "good times" and that, in such a positive climate of peace and prosperity, substantial political differences always tend to be muted.

I arrived home at my neighborhood of Columbia Heights, in the inner city of the nation's capital. As I turned off the radio and got out of the car, the words of the experts flooded my mind: "We are living in good times—there are no real issues to discuss." Standing there in the street for a few moments, I looked around at the obvious signs of a community fighting for its very survival—and losing.

Then it dawned on me: We just don't exist here. Neighborhoods like this one, and their counterparts in every American city, simply do not count in the minds of the political analysts and decision makers. The people who live here don't matter to the discussion and are not factored into the debate. It's as if the poor are just not there.

But they are there, and their numbers are growing. On a global scale, they are now the majority.

What we have yet to understand is that our destinies are all tied together. It is that failure to comprehend our common bond with one another, and with the earth, that is at the heart of our present crisis. Without that vision, we will surely perish.

Columbia Heights runs along Fourteenth Street, a scene of the much-publicized, so-called riots in Washington, D.C., following the assassination of Martin Luther King, Jr., in the bitter spring of 1968. The now-infamous "riot corridor," as the area is still called, even today bears the scars of the frustrated and angry violence that erupted when people's hopes were suddenly and brutally cut down. Burned-out buildings and vacant lots remain after more than twenty years. The once-bustling commercial center in the black community has never been restored. Neither has the expectant sense of promise that filled these streets during the peak years of the civil rights movement.

Several years ago, my sister Barbara was walking up one of those streets with her five-year-old son, Michael. They were on their way to the neighborhood day-care center that had been opened by Sojourners Community. Michael surveyed the scene on the block and, looking up at his mother with puzzlement, asked, "Mommy, was there a war here?"

Indeed, the empty shells of buildings, piles of rubble, and general devastation all around could easily give that impression. Perhaps the eyes of a child can see what jaded adult vision quickly passes over or too easily accepts: There was and is a war here. It goes on every day, and the casualties are everywhere.

The people who inhabit this and similar neighborhoods are not only neglected and ignored by political decision makers; they are war victims. They are the dead and wounded of a system that has ravaged their lives and their communities. It is no wonder that those who make it through refer to themselves as "survivors." But many are not surviving. The forces that have declared war on them are global and impersonal, but the consequences for the people here are very personal indeed.

For most of the fourteen years Sojourners Community has lived in Washington, D.C., the inner-city neighborhoods of the capital have been invisible to the nation. Everyone knows "official Washington," with its marble, monuments, and malls. But "the other Washington" has been off-limits to the blue-and-white tour buses and to the consciousness of the rest of the country.

Here are substandard tenements instead of stately government offices. Here children play in back alleys strewn with glass, trash, and syringes, instead of running in beautiful parks. Here the only monuments are to neglect, indifference, and the stranglehold of entrenched racism on the city that proclaims itself a beacon of freedom to the world. Here the homeless huddle literally in the shadows of the great houses of state power, trying to keep warm by sleeping on the heating grates that expel hot air from the heating systems of the State Department, the Pentagon, and the halls of Congress.

Even the name, *Washington, D.C.*, tells the tale of two cities. The white residents and professionals who run the federal capital live in "Washington." The black residents who are the city's vast majority (70 percent) are from "D.C."—the District of Columbia. This capital of the "free world" is still virtually a segregated city, especially in housing, schools, and social interchange.

A word heard often in D.C. is *colony*. The District of Columbia didn't obtain even partial home rule until 1974. But still, District residents (seven hundred thousand people) have no voting representation in the Congress, and all actions taken by the elected city government are subject to outside Congressional veto.

The forces of housing gentrification and real estate speculation are slowly pushing black residents into more overcrowded neighborhoods or out of the city altogether. Once-poor ghetto neighborhoods are being transformed into upscale yuppie enclaves with prices too high for any of their former inhabitants.

Many D.C. blacks are convinced all this is part of a deliberate scheme on the part of the white power structures of the city: Through what is often referred to as "The Plan," whites will eventually become the majority and retake the city from its present black political leadership. Then, it is believed, full home rule or even statehood will finally be granted—once the city has passed from black to white power.

Most white residents, the white-controlled media, and other blacks scoff at talk of "The Plan," but many black residents are convinced of it. And whether or not a deliberate conspiracy exists, "The Plan" does describe what indeed is happening in Washington, D.C., these days.

But, neither its extremes of wealth and poverty, nor its racial polarization have been well known beyond the Beltway. For most Americans, at least most white Americans, the nation's capital has been best known as the site for great high school trips, or for the Cherry Blossom Festival, or as the home of the Redskins. Mostly, Washington, D.C., is known as the most powerful city in the world, and it is no wonder that its powerless underside has been so easily and so long overlooked.

But suddenly, Washington, D.C., began making national and international headlines, not as the center of power but as the murder capital of the nation. Quickly the media cameras, so used to turning away from "the other Washington," focused their attention on neighborhoods overrun with drugs and guns. D.C. got famous. *Newsweek* did cover stories that spoke of the "two Washingtons," while nervous local officials rushed to assure anxious tourists that the killing was limited to only "certain parts of the city."

As it turns out, Columbia Heights has become the murder capital of the murder capital, according to the Metropolitan Police Department. The killings continue unabated on the streets where we of the Sojourners Community live, and in recent months they have come very close to home. At a recent meeting in the Sojourners Neighborhood Center, one local resident asked, "What does it mean to live in the most murderous neighborhood in the most murderous city in the most murderous nation in the world?"

In 1983, I traveled to the war zones of Nicaragua on the first team of a project known as Witness for Peace. In a refugee resettlement camp I met a thirteen-year-old boy named Agenor, who made a great impression on me. His baseball cap, tattered shirt, and beat-up tennis shoes reminded me of the kids who run up and down the streets of my own neighborhood. But this skinny Nicaraguan boy carried a heavy automatic weapon on his back. He was a member of the citizens' militia, defending against Contra attacks and a feared U.S. invasion. As I returned home, Agenor's face, with its searching brown eyes and shy smile, was etched in my memory.

I met Eddie on the street the day I got back. He also was thirteen. While telling Eddie about my trip, I had a terrible thought. If the U.S. government continued to escalate its war in Nicaragua and eventually sent troops, Eddie—a young black man from a poor family with few other options—would be among the first to go. That had been the pattern in Vietnam.

In that moment, I imagined the awful possibility of Eddie and Agenor meeting on some Nicaraguan battlefield, raising their guns to aim at each other, and one or both being killed. The great ideological confrontation between East and West would come down to Eddie and Agenor shooting each other—two young men, one black and one brown, dying in the name of a global conflict between two white superpowers. Instead of that horrible picture, I tried to imagine Eddie and Agenor playing baseball together.

Eddie never died on a Nicaraguan battlefield, as I had feared he would. But Eddie did die, in March 1989 on the streets of his own neighborhood. He became the latest victim, and the newest statistic, in the city's epidemic of violence.

One month later, we at Sojourners were all gathered in church on Sunday morning. During the intercessions, the news was announced that another young man, Anthony, had been killed a few nights earlier. I watched faces around the room grimace in pain and the tears begin to flow. Anthony had been a student in our community's day-care center many years earlier. We know the whole family. After the service, Martha, who had been Anthony's teacher, flashed with anger, "He was such a sweet and sensitive boy. It has to be the system!"

After church that day, I found myself in a funeral home, viewing the body of a handsome, vital young man, now cold and dead. His grieving mother and brothers and sisters were all there. There wasn't much to say.

We are losing a whole generation of young people in our cities to poverty, drugs, and violence. Washington, D.C., is a city out of control, reeling from the brutal consequences and tremendous suffering of a global economic, social, and spiritual crisis that has yet to be named, understood, or addressed. It is a crisis of the highest magnitude, and it points to a global reality that we must recognize and squarely face.

II. WASHINGTON, D.C., AS A PARABLE

Through these painful and soul-searching events, something has become quite clear to me: Washington, D.C., stands now as *a parable unto the world.* The crisis in the capital of the wealthiest and most powerful nation tells the story of the crisis the whole world now faces. In Washington, D.C., today, we see a mirror of what the modern global system has become. The brutal paradoxes of the most famous city on earth have become a parable that can teach us what we must learn if we are to survive.

Washington, D.C. is *the* symbol of power. People stream to the official city to exercise power, to influence power, or just to be around power. The power holders and the power groupies alike are intoxicated with the smell of it. The key word here is *access*—access to power. That's what everyone is always fighting for in this town. Power, like money, becomes its own justification. How you get it and what it is used for are beside the point. Having power is what's important.

As power defines official Washington, powerlessness defines "the other Washington." Here are the people who clean the hotel rooms, cook the food, and drive the cabs—if they have work at all. The lack of industry and of a strong union and a strong labor movement have reduced the work force to an underemployed labor pool supplying the bottom rungs of the service economy.

The federal government, which provides some middle-level jobs for many D.C. residents, is, of course, almost entirely in white hands. Even the city government, which has become a safe haven for black political leadership, must still have its legislation and budget approved by the congressional overlords. If Washington is the most powerful city in the nation, D.C. is the most powerless, without control even over its own affairs and destiny. As the "last colony," D.C. symbolizes the relationship many other parts of the world have with official Washington.

The revealing paradoxes exist on almost every level of life in Washington, D.C. Housing costs are among the highest in the country, as are the rates of homelessness. Infant mortality is at third-world levels in the city that has more lawyers and real estate developers than any other. Black youth unemployment is upward of 60 percent, while white professional couples with two incomes search for investments. SAT test scores for D.C. public school students are one hundred points below the national norm, while the city's private school students score one hundred points above it.

Nineteen million tourists spend $1.5 billion in Washington each year, while the D.C. jail runs out of money for toilet paper. Some 30.5 percent of the total square feet of office and retail space in Washington, D.C., is owned by foreign investors, while the number of loans to black-owned businesses continues to decline. The downtown hotel business is booming, while more and more women and children move into the city's shelters or onto the streets.

Washington's affluent suburbs are rated among the most desirable places to live in the nation, while the black death rate in D.C. increases due to a lack of good health care. Young white men pay some of the highest college tuition rates in the country at local universities, while their black counterparts are nine times more likely to be the victims of a homicide.

Washington, D.C., is a microcosm of the dynamics that now govern the world order. The current drug war brings all these contradictions into sharp relief.

No one knows the exact numbers, but an extraordinary percentage of D.C. youth are involved in the drug traffic. As in source countries such as Colombia, drug trafficking has become a livelihood for the poor. In the high-stakes atmosphere of drugs and money, life becomes cheap indeed. In Colombia, now, it costs only $40 to have someone murdered. In both Colombia and Washington, D.C., poverty sets the stage for tragedy, and the drama of drugs simply carries out the executions.

In the current economic and cultural environment, it becomes very difficult to tell young people to "just say no to drugs." What we are telling them, in effect, is to be content working part-time at McDonald's (the eighth-largest employer in D.C.) and to pursue the American dream as best they can. In a changing economy, the better jobs and brighter future we want to promise inner-city children are just not there.

Meanwhile, the images that assault them daily—through TV, movies, and popular music—all tell young people that their very worth as human beings comes from how much they can possess and consume. Fancy clothes, new cars, a nice house, and lots of gold around their necks become the aspirations of inner-city youth. In that, they are no different from most Americans. In fact, interviews with drug dealers reveal that they have the same materialistic values and goals as those of the surrounding society.

The crucial difference is that these inner-city youth are virtually denied access to the alluring attractions of American consumer culture. They are blocked out by an economy that has no room for them.

Washington, D.C., like the rest of the global system, is now run by a two-tiered economy. At the top is a highly lucrative and booming sector of managerial and professional elites, while at the bottom are increasingly impoverished masses who service the high-tech economy but whose labor and even consumption are less and less needed. Whole sectors of the global population are now simply defined outside of the economic mainstream. And to be shut out of the global economy means to be consigned to death.

There are more and more children in poverty in America. One out of every five children and half of all black children are born poor. The gap between rich and poor has steadily grown as a changing economy leaves more and more people behind. The swelling ranks of the hungry and homeless, now including many families, are a highly visible moral contradiction in a nation that prides itself on its standard of living.

The earth itself suffers along with the poor. A politically neglected and continually poisoned environment poses real threats from global warming trends, ozone depletion, acid rain, contaminated water, unhealthful food, polluted air, toxic and nuclear wastes, and ravaged wildlife. We will not escape the consequences of our behavior. As Chief Seattle said, "This we know. The earth does not belong to people. People belong to the earth. This we know. All things are connected. Whatever befalls the earth befalls the people of the earth. We did not weave the web of life. We are but a mere strand in it. Whatever we do to the web, we do to ourselves!"

Public school education, health care, low-cost housing, the family farm, and the industrial workplace are all in a state of crisis in the United States. Drugs and crime are out of control, while the proposed solutions fail to deal with either underlying causes or individual responsibility, neglecting both perpetrators and victims.

The fight against racism has been halted at the highest levels of government, and its ugly resurgence is upon us. Hard-fought progress made by women for equal rights is now under attack from many quarters. The nation's foreign policy continues to violate its expressed values and causes untold human suffering principally to poor people of color. Our collective conscience has been numbed, and the sanctity of life is diminished with each passing year of moral accommodation to nuclear weapons.

These realities are especially hard on the young black and brown minorities that inhabit our inner cities. They are the ones being left behind. They are the ones whose dreams and hopes for the future have been denied. They are the ones who are offered no real normal or legal path to a decent and abundant life. There is no room for them in this society, and they know it. With no place, no stake, and no future available to them, they are finding their own road to "success." And it is a very dangerous road, indeed, with many casualties strewn along the way.

III. A QUESTION OF VALUES

In our neighborhood, children eight, nine, and ten years old wear beepers on their belts. It is not because they are little lawyers and doctors, but because drug dealers call the children at play when a drug run has to be made. It is safer for the dealers to use children for their drug runs, because it makes their detection and punishment less likely.

By running drugs, young people can make more money in a day or a week than they ever dreamed possible. Thousands of dollars are available to them in an economy that has never offered them more than uncertain, part-time employment at minimum wage. And many are taking the option. My sister Barbara tells me that virtually all the kids her two sons grew up with are now on the streets involved in the lucrative but lethal drug traffic.

In April 1989 the *Washington Post* ran a front-page series of articles called "At the Roots of the Violence." The second installment described the unwritten "code of conduct" of the drug dealers in these words: "Never back down. . . . Be willing to kill or die to defend your honor. . . . Protect your reputation and manhood at all costs." The drug dealers who live by this code are known as "soldiers." A reporter asked one of them why they are always so ready to shoot. He answered: "I guess it's greed for that money."

The *Post* then said of the code of the streets: "It is a way of behaving that flies in the face of traditional American values."

Really? What values are reflected in American foreign policy? What code of ethics governs the wars of Wall Street? Does not the enshrinement of greed and the glorification of violence every day on TV sets and movie screens reinforce cultural values? What message does their society give young people every day about what is most important in life? Have they not been convinced, like most other Americans, that status and success come by way of material acquisition? Does the way people get rich even matter in America?

Perhaps our cultural values now reflect the emptiness of our situation most of all. Television now rules the popular culture. Consumption has become our highest cultural value and social purpose. In fact, material consumption is the only universal form of social participation that Americans have left. Everything else has been either marginalized or completely co-opted by the frenzied desire for things. Consumption is the thing that both the rich and the poor, and everyone in between, seem to care most about. Not only does consumption define the culture; materialism has *become* the culture in America. There is no longer any doubt that things are more valued than people and that people have, themselves, become commodities. We are faced with an almost totally economic definition of life. The result is a culture that has lost its very soul.

With great danger to themselves and others, are not these children pursuing the same glittering materialistic dream of others, in the quickest and perhaps only way they see open to them? Entertainers and sport stars line up to tell kids to say no to drugs. Hardly anyone comments on the irony of role models negotiating million-dollar contracts while encouraging young black children to settle for fast-food minimum wages and to resist the constant temptation to make thousands of dollars a week selling drugs.

The violent underside of American society is not a social aberration that we can safely and morally distance from "traditional American values." Rather, the frightening carnage is a frustrated mirror image of the twisted values that now govern the wider society.

The crisis of our inner cities will not change until we change. Social transformation will not occur without a transformation of values.

Why is real estate development that evicts the poor from neighborhoods like ours regarded as shrewd capitalism instead of criminal offense? Why are housing, education, and health care treated as commodities available to the highest bidder instead of as human rights? Why does the unrestricted mobility of corporate capital take precedence over people's access to good, safe, and meaningful work? Why do prevailing assumptions of national security go unchallenged when resources spent for instruments of destruction leave nothing for child nutrition? Why is our professed commitment to democracy so flagrantly violated by our own foreign policy? And why do the poor of our own country still wait for that democratic process to be fulfilled?

IV. VALUES AND THE PRESIDENCY

The presidential election of 1988 was decided without ever coming to grips with the two things the nation most needs: an honest facing-up to pressing social and ecological realities, and a courageous offering of moral vision. Social and ecological reality and moral vision were the most avoided topics in that most dismal campaign. The 1992 campaign at this writing promises to be little better.

It is not only the country's "infrastructure" (highways, bridges, factories, and so on) that is deteriorating; the moral structures and foundations of the nation are also unraveling. This is the state of the union that was not addressed in the 1988 presidential election. Instead, the campaign was dominated by images, symbols, and illusions. The triumph of technique over substance now governs American politics, with television as the controlling medium of political discourse.

The modern presidency is utterly bereft of political and spiritual vision. In fact, the White House exhibits no long-term social vision of any kind. Presidential goals are both short-term and shortsighted. The goals of the modern presidency have to do with maintaining power rather than with offering leadership; with managing crises rather than with getting to their causes; and with controlling media images rather than with charting new directions.

A system has emerged in the modern world whose primary reality is economic. The modern presidency serves merely to protect and maintain that system. The trouble is that the system is leading us to death.

A postmodern presidency would fundamentally challenge that system at its roots and offer genuine alternatives to it based on the critical moral values that we must hope we still possess. Because such a challenge and such an alternative are unlikely to come from the top of American society, where the modern presidency is firmly controlled, the vision necessary will have to originate from the bottom, the margins, and those middle sectors of society where dislocation and/or more independent social values offer the possibilities of new imagination.

Two promising constituencies for such a task are the poor who are organizing themselves and places within the religious community where fresh thinking and renewal are now taking place. The postmodern presidency will not be constructed from the mere shuffling of elite personnel at the top, but rather will be a response to a transformation of values and action at the grassroots.

During the election year of 1988, another campaign was fought that did try to face many of these realities, while also articulating some new visions for America's future. Jesse Jackson made a moral appeal, and the response to it began to show the possibilities of a new coalition for change, which crossed boundaries of race, class, and issues.

V. A SOURCE OF MORAL VISION

Despite the lack of recognition of it in the 1988 presidential campaign, we are indeed in a social crisis. It is a crisis that confronts us with choices—critical choices of national values and direction. Honest truthtelling and bold moral vision for the future are urgently needed. The combination of the two is in fact the essence of what political leadership must be in the days ahead.

A discernible hunger exists in the nation for just such leadership. Whether it is strong enough to produce a winning electoral possibility in the near future is a question we can't answer yet. But the American people deserve to be offered such a choice. And, even more importantly, those of us who claim the biblical heritage have a religious responsibility to offer it. That has always been the prophetic vocation.

The prophets challenged the way things were, while at the same time helping people to imagine new possibilities. They were not afraid to confront the king, to defend the poor, or to say that what God had in mind was far different from what most people had settled for. Rankled by injustice, sickened by violence, and outraged by oppression, the prophets defined true religion as "doing justice, loving mercy, and walking humbly with your God" (Micah 6:8).

The political convictions of those of us whose religious convictions are rooted in the biblical tradition should grow out of that kind of faith—a faith that does justice. We should be less interested in the ideologies of left and right than whether justice is really being done—especially to the marginalized and the downtrodden for whom the God of the Bible seems to have such a special concern. That same biblical perspective sees the accumulation of wealth and weapons as the wrong road to national security and instead offers the possibility of an economy that has room for everyone, an environment treated as a sacred trust, and a commitment to resolving our conflicts in ways that do not threaten the very survival of the planet. That political vision directly confronts the barriers of race, class, and sex, which so violate God's creative purpose and still wreak such violence among us.

To enjoy a culture in which human values and creativity can truly flourish will mean being set free from our captivity to consumption and its totally economic definition of life. What is most human, rather than what is most profitable, must become the critical question. Our primary concern is for the values of the culture rather than for the economic value of the culture.

The prophetic religious tradition invokes the values, ideals, and even the faith that stands above the behavior of the people and the practices of the nation. On the basis of transcendent faith and moral values, it calls the people and the nation to accountability.

Martin Luther King, Jr., stood firmly in that tradition as he spoke to the nation about living up to the challenge of both biblical faith and the best ideals and aspirations of America. Dorothy Day, by stubbornly espousing and living out true biblical values, exposed the hypocrisy of a nation that regarded itself as biblically rooted while it exploited the poor and found its identity in possessions and its security in weapons.

Even a president, Abraham Lincoln, called for national penitence for slavery and civil war. He reminded a divided nation that both sides in the war read the same Bible and prayed to the same God, whom each side believed to be on its side. The prophetic stream of American religion has been faithfully persistent but never dominant. The function of prophetic religion is to bring the nation under judgment and call the people to repentance. The fact that America has become increasingly pluralistic in religious orientation does not relieve us who stand in one of the biblically based religions from the responsibility of living politically in terms of the highest values of our tradition.

One final story graphically depicts the crisis we face and suggests from where the vision needed may come.

On a flight home recently, I found myself on an airport shuttle bus with other travelers. Two handsome young white couples were having a loud conversation about their favorite restaurants around the world. Many of the rest of us would have preferred not to listen, but the close quarters left us no choice. Finally, one of them exclaimed in praise of their very favorite place, "It's just a wonderful restaurant—you can spend $300 for dinner in your shorts!"

The next day was Saturday, and the food line formed early outside the Sojourners Neighborhood Center, only three miles from the White House. Three hundred families each receive a bag of groceries which is critical to them for getting through the week. Just before the doors are opened, all those who helped prepare and sort the food join hands to pray. The prayer is normally offered by Mrs. Mary Glover, a sixty-year-old black woman who knows what it is to be poor and who knows how to pray. She thanks God for the gift of another day. Then she prays, "Lord, we know that you'll be coming through this line today, so help us to treat you well." Mrs. Glover's prayer is a better commentary on a well-known gospel passage than any we will ever read from an elite seminary. She knows very well who it is that waits in line with the hungry and huddles with the homeless to keep warm on the heating grates of Washington, D.C.

6

A POSTMODERN VISION OF EDUCATION FOR A LIVING PLANET

Douglas Sloan

Our instructions in preparing our addresses for this conference were for us to go about it as if we had "the undivided attention for thirty or forty minutes of an intelligent, concerned president of the United States," and to set forth the vision we would like that president to have. So, Ms. President, I am very grateful to have this opportunity to talk to you about "a postmodern vision of education for a living planet."

And, Ms. President, so there will be no misunderstanding from the outset, I want to begin by saying something about the word *vision* itself. I take vision here to mean not a fantasy, not a figment of wishful thinking, not even primarily that activity familiar to many of us, the imaging of desirable futures—although this last meaning will certainly be involved. I take vision to mean something much stronger: *a perception, an actual grasp of realities, and a being grasped by realities*, in this case by realities that can sustain and guide us in protecting a living planet and creating a just and caring society. In seeking such a vision for education, we are asking: How do we nourish the forces both within and without that will enable us and our children to make such a world and community living realities?

To be concerned about the future of our dear planet and kindred creatures faces us immediately with educational tasks. There is not a major problem facing humankind today—whether environmental, economic, political, medical, social, personal, or spiritual—that does not directly involve education. And education is repeatedly called upon to be our main source for solving these problems.

Of course, the faith that education can actually provide solutions has been increasingly called into question. It has become more and more apparent that education is itself involved in all these problems—sometimes weakened as a victim of them, sometimes implicated as a contributor to them. Our challenge, then, is twofold: We educators have to think and act in such ways that we are engaged in self-healing at the same time that we strive to release healing and strengthening forces in the world around us.

In any case, in our concern for a living planet, education is at the heart of the matter. In the first place, education has fundamentally to do with the future of our children. If we permit the planet to be destroyed, or kill it, the children have no future.

In the second place, education has to do with how we know the world, and how we equip our children to know the world. Knowledge and our ways of knowing are at the center of education. It is through knowing that we come, in a very real sense, to have a world, because *our* world is the world as we perceive it and relate to it. If our ways of knowing are themselves overly narrow, if knowledge itself is of only one kind, then the world that we create for ourselves to live in through our knowledge will itself be impoverished.

The kind of knowledge that has become dominant in all modern education—from colleges and universities on down to the elementary and, alas, preschool levels—is more and more of one narrow kind. It can increasingly deal only with the quantitative, technical, and instrumental. Instrumental and quantitative ways of knowing are powerful and important. But if they are our only ways of knowing everything, then a lot gets left out—a lot of what is most important.

The main things that are eliminated are the *qualitative realities* that bind the world together and that are the essence of life, beauty, and meaning. Our predominantly quantitative way of knowing must reduce all such qualities to data to be manipulated for instrumental purposes. In our dominant forms of modern knowing, therefore, the intrinsic importance of life, beauty, and meaning disappears. And because our world is given to us by our ways of knowing, life, beauty, and meaning disappear from our world. Moreover, if the conception of knowledge is unrelievedly one of taking things apart—we call it the "reductive/analytic method"—then the world of our reality, with its nature, human communities, and human selves, also fragments, falls apart, and begins to die.[1]

The splittings of the two nuclei—the nucleus of the atom and the nucleus of the living cell—have been heralded as the greatest achievements of modern science. They are the quintessential, characteristic achievements of modern knowledge and, therefore, of modern education. Were they to have occurred within a larger, qualitative context that could have supplied meaning and direction, we might be able to view them with more hope for their human promise. But to the extent that they epitomize a way of knowing and a view of reality that dominate the modern world at the expense of all other ways of knowing and other views of reality, they are more ominous than hopeful.

A few years ago, in *The Fate of the Earth*, Jonathan Schell described the ecological damage of the planet that a nuclear war would unleash. Not only would human society be destroyed, the ecological life-systems of the planet would be imperiled. This would involve the extinction of birds and beasts and many ocean species all over the world, the pollution of the earth's waters, the alteration of the earth's atmosphere and climate, the destruction of plants and forests around the world, the increase of ultraviolet light, the possible poisoning of all living creatures, and so on.[2] This ecological damage described by Schell, this spoliation of our planet earth, is already well under way. It is taking place without a nuclear war.

Is it possible that there is some deep connection between our attitudes toward the earth, and treatment of her, and the kind of thinking and ways of knowing that have also produced things like nuclear bombs? If so, then our situation is even more serious than we may have suspected. It means that in our efforts to ensure the future of the earth we will require more than renewed moral commitment and political action. We will require also, and more fundamentally, *a transformation of the ways we think about the world and come to know her.* And, because our dominant modern forms of education are tied to the modern, narrow conception of knowledge and its correspondingly inadequate understanding of the human being, our efforts for the future of the earth will also require a new, *postmodern vision of education* in which *the fullness of knowing and the fullness of the human being are joined throughout.* What the substance of this postmodern vision of education will involve is what we must now turn to.

And so, Ms. President, I want to introduce a cliché that you will hear from almost everyone who talks about educational reform—the cliché that we "need to educate the whole child." Everyone who has some kind of new educational idea, or is pushing an old educational idea, nearly always says, "We're going to educate the whole child." Clichés are often clichés because they have a truth to them. The truth here is that, indeed, the whole child or person has to be educated. What makes it a cliché, however, is that it is often uttered as a generality that no one can really disagree with, but that no one quite knows what to do with, either.

If we look carefully at it, however, this idea of educating the whole person can give us an anchor for thinking about an adequate vision of education. For what can education be in its fullest sense other than the development of the whole human being? Such an education would require, first, the development of individual *self-confidence* and self-esteem. From this self-confidence can come the autonomy and the strength necessary for the development of a second central dimension of the human being: the capacity for *caring*, a capacity for compassion and love and openness to others and to the earth. And from these two, self-confidence and caring, can come a third essential human dimension: the capacity for *meaning*, the desire and the ability to find what is significant and true in life, and to develop that to its fullest. All three dimensions, it must be stressed, have to be held together.

It is impossible, for example, really to care for someone else if we are constantly worrying about whether we are worth anything. It takes someone who has a deep sense of self-confidence really to care. And caring is in turn related to consciousness and the quest for meaning. We find meaning in that which we really care about—for example, the earth, other people, and ideas. It is the person who does not care who is often the most unconscious and the most devoid of a sense of meaning.

And the development of confidence, caring, and the capacity for meaning implies the education of the whole person. By the whole person I mean the thinking, willing, feeling, imaging, valuing person. Thinking, willing, feeling, imaging, valuing—each is involved with the others, and all are involved in knowing in its most powerful and insightful sense. It is an error of the modern world to assume that feeling, willing, and valuing have little to do with thinking and almost nothing to do with knowing. All are also involved in the development of confidence, caring, and the capacity for meaning, but each in its own way. Another way to make the point is to say that education must involve the education of the human imagination, one definition of which is that imagination is the whole person involved in knowing—the thinking, willing, feeling, imaging, valuing person.[3]

What is required for an education of the imagination, of the whole person, the thinking, willing, feeling, imaging, valuing person? Can this idea give us a necessary and crucial starting point for whatever else we might also think is essential to an adequate vision of education?

Although I do not here give primary attention to the actual content of the curriculum, it should not be thought that I consider the content of a postmodern education of little importance. On the contrary! A new awareness must enter into all our education of the momentous issues we now confront and must learn to deal with if we are to gain a future for our children and our planet Earth: issues of war and peace, of ecological realities, of a just world social order, of respect for all persons, and of the meaning and possibilities of human life. Such issues must become integral to the whole content and substance of the curriculum.

Even more important than content, however, is the education of the human capacities necessary for dealing creatively and responsibly with that content. If, as so often happens in modern education, new content is taught in habitual, old ways that stifle the development of the human capacities for insight, understanding, and commitment, then the emphasis on new content will miscarry badly. It will also go awry if we assume that what may be educationally sound for adults is equally appropriate for the young and school-age child. In curriculum and teaching, in content and method, therefore, an understanding of the human capacities for knowing and living in their fullness, and of what is necessary for the wholesome development of these capacities, is essential.

This is what I now want to explore with you, Ms. President. Just so that credit is given where credit is due, I want to make clear that my suggestions are indebted to the work of Rudolf Steiner and to Waldorf Education, which is based on Rudolf Steiner's insights. In Waldorf Education we have a vision of education for a living planet that has already been tested by nearly half a century of experience and practice.[4] What I want to do here is to try to develop some central aspects of the vision in a way that I hope will be suggestive for all education, not least for public education.

What is involved in the education of the whole person, the thinking, willing, feeling, imaging, valuing person? As we begin to address this question, it is important to realize that none of these activities exist in closed compartments isolated from the others. Thinking, feeling, and willing, for example, all interpenetrate, and even in those moments of experience and stages of human development when one of them may predominate, the others are not entirely absent. There is no thinking in which aspects of feeling and willing are not at work; no willing in which some elements of thinking and feeling are utterly lacking; no feeling that has not gained some connection with thinking and willing. At the same time, each has its own distinct and all-important part to play in human development, experience, knowing, and education. And if we consider valuing as that multifarious activity in and by which we seek to apprehend, work to understand, and strive to live in the light of the truly valuable, then we can come to see that thinking, feeling, and willing are all deeply and intimately involved with valuing in the work of knowing and in the tasks of education. In what follows, I will look separately at thinking, feeling, willing, and imaging and, in doing so, will also attempt at least to indicate the crucial connection of each with valuing.

I. THINKING

Thinking is terribly important. As I said earlier, in many ways thinking creates the world we experience, and the quality of our thinking greatly determines the kind of world we live in. Stanislaw Ulam, a mathematician who worked on the development of the first atomic bomb, expressed vividly the importance of thinking for our experience. "It is still an unending source of surprise for me," said Ulam, "to see how a few scribbles on a blackboard or on a sheet of paper could change the course of human affairs."[5] Thinking not only largely creates our world; it can also destroy the world. The quality and level of our thinking is, therefore, all-important.

Modern thinking is unique as a part of knowing, because it is that aspect of knowing that tends toward abstraction, detachment, and separation from what we would want to know. We stand back in detachment, observe the world, form concepts—and these concepts then give us a certain power over the world. With them we can begin to manipulate the world, to take it apart and move it around, to understand many of its inner relationships. We need this kind of abstract, conceptual knowing, and we need it to be powerful. Many of the most important achievements of the modern world have been made possible by this kind of analytical, conceptual thinking.

An adequate vision of education, then, will not seek to get rid of instrumental and quantitative thinking, despite my earlier criticisms of making it the essence of all knowing and knowledge. Instrumentalism and quantification are of crucial importance. An adequate vision of education, however, will see that they are placed firmly within the larger context of the wholeness of thinking.

What, then, is necessary for the full development of thinking? Let us, in other words, from this standpoint think carefully about thinking. In doing so, it is important to observe that analytical, conceptual thinking really first begins to come into its own in the adolescent years. As we shall see, this has important educational consequences.

Thinking has many components. One component is the conceptual abstraction I have already mentioned. Another component is the ability to follow a chain of argument, to recognize its premises and follow through the logic involved. Yet another component is the actual content, the information that we are thinking about. And a fourth component being stressed by many people today is critical awareness, the ability to ask whose interests particular ideas may be serving.

These are all part of thinking. However, there are two further components that must also be present throughout, if everything else is not to go wrong. These are (1) a sense for truth and (2) what I call "insight-imagination."[6]

Here is where the observation that thinking in its fullest sense first begins to emerge in adolescence becomes important. Young people passing through puberty aware of their new powers and have a deep thirst to know the truth about things—about the world, about themselves. "Who am I really?" they are asking, and "What is my real relation to the world and to other human beings?"

The first requirement for finding satisfactory answers is that they have teachers and adults who are also fellow seekers after truth and who support them in their quest. They need adults who are able to take their hard questions, for they want to know what kind of persons we are also. And, they need adults capable of recognizing, in the midst of what is often a lot of turmoil, chaos, and upheaval, the real person, the individual human spirit that is struggling to emerge within them.

There are powerful voices in education today calling for the abandonment of the concept of truth. This is fully in keeping with the dominance of purely quantitative and instrumentalist conceptions of knowing, which are themselves uninterested in any notion of truth—other than instrumental truths—and incapable of dealing with truth. Rather than the quest for truth, we are asked to settle instead for instrumental results, on the one hand, and for communal consensus, on the other. Often proposed as a safeguard against dogmatism and the self-righteousness of any who claim to possess truth—something a genuinely true statement or true person would never claim—the denial of a sense for truth and the quest for truth promises to have the most fateful consequences.[7]

For one thing, a purely instrumental and reductionist way of knowing that is not governed and guided by a sense of truth will take the world apart without ever knowing or caring what it is doing. And we see that happening all around us. For another thing, to make an appeal to the consensus of the group the final determiner of what counts as truths seems, as Leszek Kolakowski has put it, ultimately a form of collective, group solipsism.[8] Finally, where there is no burning quest for truth in one's own inner core, then a vacuum appears that is filled either with cynicism or just as likely with all the unexamined, unconscious, conventional truisms and assumptions of the times.[9] Then the possibility of fundamental transformation is simply foreclosed.

Here we can see clearly that all education is moral education, that personal being, the fullness of thinking, and a sense for truth all go hand in hand. Is it not possible that the cynicism, the rage, and the heart-rending despair and apathy that many young people display to the world reflects a disappointed idealism—a deep wound inflicted by a society that is not present to them as persons, that does not share their concern for truth, and that underestimates their desire to face the real problems of life?

All this has political-social implications, for if a society's leaders relentlessly try to avoid dealing with its real problems, do not even want to recognize that there are real problems, or in the face of them look out only for "number one," they signal the youth that they are not really serious about either the truth or them and their future.

The other element necessary to healthy thinking is insight. By *insight* I mean that by which newness and life enter into our thinking. Without insight, thinking is dead. Simply learning abstract concepts without insight results in what Alfred North Whitehead called "the acquirement of inert knowledge."[10] Critical thinking without the life and interest of insight tends to become destructive and cynical. Logic without insight can still be powerful, but all the more locked into habitual ruts and outworn assumptions. Logic without insight becomes dead, and often deadly. We live in a world in which there is a highly developed, powerful, logical rationality that is extremely dangerous because it is locked into certain narrow ruts and driven by certain unexamined assumptions that run over everything else.[11]

Where does insight come from?

II. WILLING

We have examined thinking in the narrow, analytic, conceptual sense. Let us leave it on one end of the spectrum and move all the way over to examine the other end, willing. Willing is also involved in knowing. Here we can begin to get a sense of the deep sources of insight.

We can get a sense of the nature of willing by comparing it with the kind of experience we have seen in conceptual, analytic thinking. Analytic thinking is highly conscious; it is also separative and detached. It stands back and abstracts out of the given immediacy. When we look at the realm of will we find by contrast a very different experience arising out of a different relationship to the world. Volition, willing, brings us into an immediate involvement and identification with the world. We have difficulty even in conceiving of volition apart from some activity that involves moving, touching, or shaping something, an activity that always includes some kind of immediate engagement with the world.

Within and through this realm of will, the very young child first comes to experience and to know the world. The stupendous will of the young child is legendary. What is important is that, as A. C. Harwood has put it, when the child begins to perceive the world, it is the activity of the world that captures the child's attention, and the child responds with an activity of its own. "It is the moving object which catches his eye," writes Harwood, "and his looking is always closely associated with the movement of the limbs. It is not enough for a child to see—he wants to handle and touch."[12] And often we can add, "to taste and eat." Through its willing activity, the child first comes to know the world by identifying with it. The young child begins its development, and its engagement with the activity of the world, with an almost unlimited desire and capacity to imitate and play in that world, and through this play and imitation to make the world its own.

The will works in realms that for the most part are inaccessible to thinking consciousness, even for adults. I may decide to get up and close the window, and then do so. In the process I am aware of my conscious intention and of the results in the movements of my arms and legs. However, what happens within my body to effectuate the intention and actually to move my limbs remains utterly in the realm of my unconscious. Our immediate conscious intention, which we sometimes mistakenly identify with the whole of our willing, is continuous with a deeper realm, in which the forces of our being, orientation, and action in the world have their source. Within this unconscious realm of willing activity in the young child, however, a tremendous wisdom is at work. We can almost say that the intelligence of the young child awakens first of all in the willing activity of the physical body.

Rudolf Steiner often pointed to three complex and wonderful things that the child achieves during the first years of its life. For all of us, in fact, these may in many ways be the most remarkable accomplishments of our entire lives. During her or his first two years or so, the child learns to stand and walk, to speak, and to think. And, the little child does them all without the help of any school or professional educator. Standing and walking are clearly activities of the will, as is the child's imitative work in learning to speak. And, from these come the first intimations of thinking. As the developmental psychologist Kurt Fischer has written, "All cognition starts with action. . . . [T]he higher-level cognition of childhood and adulthood derive from these sensor motor actions."[13] In the willing activity of play and imitation, children begin to discover the wider intelligence at work in the world and within themselves.

Perhaps we can get some further sense of the nature and importance of this active, participative knowing of the child by considering what Michael Polanyi has called "tacit knowing."[14] Polanyi has spoken of a deep knowing at the level of the unconscious that, even for us as adults, informs and provides the basis for all of our other knowing. While there is not an exact correspondence between tacit knowing, as Polanyi describes it, and the participative knowing of the young child, there are important similarities and connections between them. Indeed, the way and extent to which children in their early years are able to play, imitate, and explore the world through their own willing activity may very well determine the quality of the tacit knowing that Polanyi argues is so essential to all our knowing in later years.

Polanyi talks about this deep, tacit knowledge as knowledge that is always more than we can say. An example is bicycle riding. You may have had the experience of not having ridden a bicycle for twenty years, and then a friend says, "Let's go biking." You get on the bike, you wobble for a moment, and then you are pedaling away. You knew how to ride the bicycle all along. It was tacit knowledge, in your bones, your muscles, your body fluids even. You were not especially conscious of knowing how; you probably even had doubts that you did. In fact, if you were to think much about how you were riding the bicycle, you would probably find yourself in the ditch. It is essential that tacit knowledge be developed and that it flow into our conceptual, conscious thinking.

Rudolf Steiner pointed out that the child's early experience of mathematics is of this kind. The child really first experiences mathematics on the playground, on the teeter-totters and swings, in running and playing. In these, the child has an immediate, lived experience of vectors and forces and angles, and so forth, that later on can be abstracted out in a formal, powerful, conceptual way. Steiner even uses the nice expression *body geometry* to describe this early lived knowledge.[15] The power of the later concept will often depend on the child's having had that strong, lived experience in its early years.

If we do not have that lived experience, or if we intrude upon it too quickly, making it abstract and conscious too soon, we damage the power of thinking that will come later in life. It is extremely important, therefore, to realize that the child comes into the world with a deep, deep wisdom that has to be respected and nourished, if the foundation for insight and imagination is to develop.

What kind of education, then, is needed for the young child who comes into the world with this living wisdom? It must be an education that recognizes that the most important way in which the young child comes to know the world and to make the world his or her own is through play and other activities, and through imitation of others. What is primarily required, therefore, is an environment that is worthy of the young child and that can support that child's own efforts to gain the lived experience that can later form the foundation for really insightful, new dynamic thinking. And it is precisely in having that experience of security in knowing the world in an immediate way that the foundation is laid for a self-confidence and a security that will be with the child throughout the rest of her or his life. This early sense of security can then be the source from which the child later on can be truly adventurous. It is a commonplace among therapists that the person who has a sense of inner security is also the person most able to be adventurous and to take the risks that life often demands.

At this point we can also see how critically important the moral dimension, what we have called the "valuing" dimension, is for the participative experience and knowing of young children. In this connection, however, the moral, valuing task lies in the first instance primarily with us as parents and teachers, and as a society. Young children come into the world not only with a nearly insatiable capacity for imitation, but also with a deep, unconscious confidence that the world is good and worthy of being imitated. That children not be fundamentally disappointed in this faith is crucial. Children's experience of goodness is essential both for their own self-confidence and trust in being and for their capacity in the later years of life to recognize and stand by the true and the good.

This means that in considering the kind of environment worthy of the growing child, we must pay careful heed to the kind of persons who are also part of that environment and into whose care the child has been entrusted. The child takes in not only the physical, but also the psychological-intellectual attitudes and intentions of those around it. Rudolf Steiner once described the young child as "but one great sense organ," imitating and absorbing its whole environment, including the attitudes and emotions of those around.[16] Jean Piaget has similarly written: "At this most imitative stage, the child mimics with his whole being, identifying himself with his model."[17] From this perspective, the presence to the child of warm, caring, trustworthy, and clear-thinking persons is essential.

This vision is the very opposite of the proposal now popular in some quarters—a proposal already being put into practice in places—to introduce training in conceptual, analytical skills at the earliest age possible. This proposal is actually sometimes referred to by its proponents as "hot-housing" very young children in reading. writing, and problem-solving skills at an ever earlier age.[18] This is an intrusion that threatens the development of the tacit knowing necessary for truly powerful, creative cognition later on.

And, the increasing tendency in modern education to rely on tapes, films, television, and movies as surrogates for real human beings at an earlier and earlier age betrays a lack of understanding of the most important needs of children.

Similarly with the back-to-the-basics movement that would have us teaching reading, writing, and arithmetic almost as soon, it seems, as the baby drops from the womb. One of the problems with the back-to-the-basics movement, especially when it is imposed on the preschool child, is that it has forgotten that the basics of education are *not* reading, writing, and arithmetic. *The real basics are wonder, interest, confidence, compassion, and courage.* Where these are, reading, writing, and arithmetic will be hard to keep back.

Of course, to provide our children with a trustworthy environment and the nourishment of caring adults is no easy task in our day. This very first requirement of a fully human education is lacking for millions and millions of children. Poverty, racism, unemployed single and teenage mothers, the lack of prenatal care and nutrition, the submission of the child to violence and abuse, even the damaging effects on the growing child of unceasing exposure to television—all these things and more mean that countless numbers of children today are condemned, from birth on, to desolate environments and to lives of fear and insecurity. Providing them with even the fundamentals of a trustworthy environment in which to grow confronts us immediately with exceedingly difficult political-social issues and challenges.

And in this, of course, Ms. President, we will need all the wisdom and courageous leadership you have to offer, because an adequate vision of education has political-social implications from the outset. What I want to stress, however, is that these political-social issues must be wrestled with in continual mindfulness of what the education of the whole person requires. Otherwise, the well-being of the developing child will quickly be sacrificed to other, noneducational purposes.

A prime example of this sacrifice, Ms. President, is the still widely cited 1983 report of the Presidential Commission on Excellence in Education, published under the title *A Nation at Risk.*[19] This report was concerned with high school education. It accurately pointed to many of the shortcomings and failures of American education. But the main concern that drove the commission was not educational in any true sense of that term; it was the fear that the American nation-state is losing out in its ability to compete with others, militarily and economically. The report saw the primary task of the schools to be that of restoring America's competitive edge, and to do so by increasing the emphasis on courses devoted to calculative, technological, utilitarian skills. A narrow conception of national interest thus became the driving force for a narrow conception of education. What we need from you, Ms. President, is courageous leadership based on a vision of what is required for the genuine education of human beings.

III. FEELING

We have analytic thinking on one end of the spectrum and willing on the other. One is separative and abstractive; the other is immediate, participatory, and concrete. Let us put feeling in the middle: It is feeling that joins the two. Feeling moves back and forth between them in a rhythmic way. Feeling is itself very important in knowing. One of the things that is left out in almost all modern education is the importance of the feelings in knowing, and the importance, therefore, of providing an education *of* the feelings. Is not our whole society awash in all kinds of unformed, uneducated feelings—from the maudlin and banal to the chaotic and violent?

This lack of attention to the education of feelings is doubly unfortunate, because elementary school-age children experience the world primarily through their feelings. And children of this age have an irrepressible desire to explore and express the many feelings that they find welling up within their own souls: sympathy and antipathy, joy and sorrow, love and anger, courage and fear, laughter and tears, beauty and ugliness—the whole rich gamut. They want to find out what these have to tell them about the world and themselves. During these years the intelligence of the child awakens primarily in the child's life of feeling. The analytic thinking, which will come into its own during adolescence, also begins to make an appearance, but in the school-age child even the first traces of this thinking lie essentially within the realm of the feelings.

Particularly characteristic of the intelligence of the child during these years is that it is pictorial. The feelings express themselves primarily in pictures and images. The essential qualities of the intelligence or, we can say, the pictorial thinking of the school-age child are those of the concreteness and wholeness characteristic of the image. It is especially important during these years to nourish these capacities and qualities, not least because the power and health of the later emerging conceptual thinking depends upon them.

The feelings are important in knowing in a number of ways.

In the first place, feelings are the very power sources for our knowing. They drive us. We say of a girl, for example, "She's really interested in her studies." What that expression says is that deep feelings power the girl in her thinking. In other words, feelings are important in knowing because it is in them that we care—or hate, or are indifferent. Moral education, for instance, that is unconcerned with the education of the feelings does not deserve the name.

There is another major way in which feelings are important in knowing. Feelings are themselves often one of our most important sources of knowledge. What is it that feelings enable us to know? They open up for us the qualitative dimensions of life and reality.

What is meant by "the qualitative"? It includes such ordinary things as color, sound, pattern, and rhythm. But it also includes all those constellations of qualities that we lump under the headings of meaning, significance, life, consciousness, truth, goodness, beauty, personhood, and spirit. These qualities constitute the essence of what makes human experience human.

If these qualities are left out of education because they do not fit a narrow view of knowledge, the possibility of a life-affirming and life-bestowing education is choked off. And, because these essentially human concerns are also what is most exciting and interesting about our lives, an overly narrow, technical, utilitarian education is itself dehumanized, impoverished, ultimately boring and dead, and most likely even deadly. One wants very badly to drop out of it.

The primary way we come to perceive and to know the qualitative dimensions of reality—in ourselves, in others, in the world—is through an educated, discriminating feeling life. Our valuing activity, our capacity for ascertaining what is truly of worth, is intimately bound up, therefore, with the education of the feelings. To speak of bringing the warmth of heart into our thinking need not be mere sentiment; it can be a very concrete expression of the possibility of making accessible to our thinking the full range of the qualitative realities given to an educated feeling life.

There is yet a third critical role that feelings play in knowing. The feelings move between the realms of unconscious will and conscious awareness, and it is through the feelings that the two are brought into connection and harmony—or not. Because it participates in the qualities of both, the feeling life can connect the separating, distancing, antipathetic nature of conceptual thinking with the open, participative, sympathetic nature of the will impulses. And if there is attained in the soul the rhythmic harmony to which the feeling life naturally aspires, provided it has the proper nourishment and support, then the feelings themselves become the pivot for a balanced working-together of feeling, thinking, and willing. Where the feeling life is chaotic or undeveloped, thinking often is cold, detached from the realities of life, and vulnerable to being driven by arbitrary and blind impulses of will. A harmonious, rhythmic feeling life can enable us to bring the deeper steadiness and power of the will increasingly into our conscious intentions, and at the same time to illuminate our deeds and actions with the clarity of conscious thought.

Especially important during the elementary years, therefore, when the child's feeling life is abloom, is an education that is socially and artistically rich and nourishing. Again, the critical influence of the teacher in such an education can hardly be overestimated. Children during these years need trusted teachers to whom they can rightly look with love and respect and whose sound judgment they can rely on and identify with. In their respect and love for such teachers, children can discover and bring to expression their own deepest feeling-sense for the reality of the other. And the care and knowledge of such teachers will bring stability into the tumultuous and often polar extremes of the children's burgeoning feeling life, providing a framework of trust within which their own autonomous feeling-based judgments of good and bad, of what is of value and what is not, can mature and grow in strength.

In the arts, the feelings especially come into play. An artistic education is not simply a matter of having art classes in the curriculum. Rather, it is one that is rhythmical, balanced, and filled through and through with the qualitative dimensions and experiences that the arts consist of and convey. An artistic education, or education as an art, is an education that, in the teaching of mathematics, science, history, geography, and so forth, is pervaded by storytelling, drama, color, painting, singing, the playing of instruments, handwork, modeling, movement, and rhythmic relationships of all kinds.

A couple of brief examples, from many possible ones, might help illustrate the nature of such an education.[20] A classroom pervaded with storytelling—and the acting out and illustrating of stories—is a powerful influence in the teaching of reading and, more than that, in creating in the student a genuine interest in learning and a deep love of words, of their sounds and meaning. It is the importance and power of the feeling quality of words in story, poem, and drama that is often forgotten in many modern educational discussions of the teaching of reading as mainly the functional decoding of signs for utilitarian purposes—an approach that does not seem to have been particularly successful even on its own terms. Creative storytelling by the teacher, in which an emphasis is not placed on the reciting of facts to be memorized but on eliciting feelings of sympathy and antipathy, will engage the interest of the student and, at the same time, contribute indirectly and all the more powerfully to the development of memory. And the telling and reliving of stories will strengthen the students' capacities for their own powers of expression and understanding.

The teaching of mathematics can offer another example. An artistic teaching of arithmetic can lay the basis for a delight in mathematics and a power and mobility of thought. The introduction of numbers with rhythmic games, poems, and songs, the walking out of number relationships, a sense for the qualities of numbers—the unity of one, the duality of two, and so on, perhaps illustrated and made pictorially vivid in the telling and acting out of archetypal fairy tales—can make the study of arithmetic a living experience from the beginning. As students become more concrete and outgoing in their interests, the active exploration by them of the applications of mathematics in everyday life will provide a sense of its usefulness and power. And as abstract capacities begin to grow stronger in the later elementary years, the activity of geometrical design and form drawing can make palpable the inherent beauty of logical relationships and abstract forms. Although we have only touched here upon the possibilities, a similar artistic approach in the teaching of all the sciences, with the awareness never lost of the relation of the sciences to the human being and to living nature, is of utmost importance in a postmodern education for a living planet.

An artistic education will be a rhythmic education. This includes not only the rhythms of song, movement, stories, games, and so forth, but also a careful attending to the rhythms of the day, of sleeping and waking, of the season and year, and of the course curriculum. The full development of thinking, feeling, and willing depends upon the rhythmic and harmonious interplay of all together.

In the arts, the qualities that nourish the feelings and with which the feelings work are directly present. The arts, moreover, engage the will forces in connection with the feelings. This is also why, for instance, the handcrafts will find a firm place in an artistic education. The handcrafts provide opportunities for the development of fine motor skills, the training of the will in repetitive and disciplined activity (which, if it is rhythmic, children love), and the creation of useful and beautiful objects, all as a unified activity.

And, finally, in the arts, thinking, logical relationships, ratio, and order are present as lived experience. This is also why—ironically so, in light of the low order of priority enjoyed by the arts in most of modern education—an artistic education in the school-age years is also the best preparation for the development of sharp, penetrating, mobile, analytical intelligence later on. John Dewey was one who began to see this years ago. Dewey said: "To think effectively in terms of relations of qualities is as severe a demand upon thought as to think in terms of symbols, verbal and mathematical." And then he added: "The production of a work of genuine art probably demands more intelligence than does most of the so-called thinking that goes on among those who pride themselves on being intellectual."[21] In the 1930s and 1940s, he called for a totally new awareness among educators of the fundamental importance of an artistic approach in all education, from the teaching of literature to the teaching of mathematics.[22] This, he maintained, was essential for an education of the imagination. "Imagination," Dewey said, "is the chief instrument of the good."[23] But on this subject American education has ignored John Dewey almost altogether. It was not Dewey's emphasis on the imagination, but his emphasis on instrumental problem-solving, that captured the attention of American educators.

The healthy development of the feelings, and ultimately of the will and of thinking, requires an artistic education. And such an education is essential to the healthy unfolding of our valuing capacities. The education of the feeling life is the foundation of our caring, for caring rests in a feeling-sense of the reality and worth of the other, in a sense of beauty, a sense of harmony, a reverence for life.

IV. IMAGING

The role of the image in all our knowing deserves much more attention than we customarily give it. It is in the image that we can grasp perhaps most vividly the concrete coming together of thinking, willing, feeling, and valuing in our knowing. Of course, the image has a particular relationship with feeling. We have observed in the school-age child the pictorial quality of our feeling life, and it is chiefly our feelings that bring the image to life within us. The feelings supply the qualitative substance of the image and present this to us as an integrated whole. But as with the feelings in general, imagery also bridges the realms of thinking and willing, and we can see this in that the right image can infuse and endow our knowing with life, power, and meaning.

On one side, the image plays a decisive role in mobilizing the forces of will and, unless we find or produce the empowering image, our actions may never really take wing. Kenneth Boulding vividly brought this out in a little classic entitled *The Image*. He said, for example: "All the horsecollars in the world did not suffice to abolish slavery until the image of a free society became dominant."[24] And whenever that image has faded, so too have our freedoms. On the other side, imagery also plays an indispensable role in guiding our thinking, including our most conceptual, analytical thinking. In fact, whenever we want to understand, explain, and integrate the world, we bring the images within us to bear on what we are seeking to know. Even those scientists who deal most with a kind of imageless mathematical thinking must, nevertheless, draw immediately upon images whenever they turn to devising instruments and experiments to test their formal calculations.

It is in the image also that we can see clearly the importance of our valuing in the work of knowing. The quality of our images largely determines the kind of world we experience and create for ourselves and for others. We therefore have a responsibility for the kind of images that shape our world and for the ways in which we use them. We can only exercise that responsibility, however, by bringing our images to consciousness. But that alone is not enough. We must also be able, if necessary, to transform our images, to bring to birth new images and to apply them effectively and appropriately. Both of these are acts of self-transformation that require trained will, clarity of consciousness, and a vital image-making capacity.

If we are to exercise our responsibility in knowing, to be conscious in our valuing, it becomes very important for us to ask ourselves, "What are the images that dominate the modern world? that dominate our own mind? What are our images of nature, of the other person, of human being in general, of the future?"

If we begin to ask these questions, we soon realize that we carry with us a lot of unconscious imagery. Often this unconscious imagery is of the lowest level and of the narrowest kind. If we ask, "What is the dominant image of nature today?" one answer would be this: nature as a machine. And the power of the image is such that if we continue to think of the earth as a machine, we will find more and more that we have, indeed, a machinelike world. And then increasingly we will have little machine selves to go with it. And this is largely what we have, because this image of nature as machine has been becoming increasingly dominant over the past three centuries.

What is our image of the other? Often it is that of the stranger or the enemy, and then we react accordingly out of that very powerful image. What are some of the main images today of the human being? An advertisement for a health club reads, "Be an animal." But that image of the human being is not limited to the health clubs of our time. The image of the human being as nothing but an animal is dominant in modern higher education today.

And what about our images of the future? Two exceedingly powerful images at first had a beneficial effect because they jolted us awake. One is Rachel Carson's "silent spring," and the other is Jonathan Schell's "fate of the earth." While these images of a stricken future earth initially shocked us out of our complacency, they are so powerful and so negative that now they may work to paralyze us. We desperately need to bring to birth within us even more powerful, positive images of the future that will open us up to the larger realities on which we can draw for insight, energy, and courage.

This need points to an all-important task of education, that of developing the image-making capacity of the individual. Increasingly in our culture, and in our education, we are leaving it up to others to supply us and our children with images. Without a lively image-making capacity of our own, we and our children are forever at the mercy of the conventional, given images of the larger society. In movies, on television, in the street, often in the uncritical exposure of young children to computer education—the images come to us and into our children from all sides.

These images, especially in the case of movies and television, are often banal, tasteless, and violent. But even more serious educationally is the fact that they are *somebody else's* images. Children are given less and less opportunity to develop that all-important image-making capacity of their own. Children are being robbed of their own imagination — and with the imagination go not only moral capacities but also other crucial abilities and opportunities.

We must begin to think more and more earnestly about the kind of pictures we want for ourselves and our children and about the capacities we nurture for bringing those pictures to life within ourselves. Increasingly we seem to be a culture that has a kind of Walt Disney or some other Hollywood world in our heads. In an age of atomic bombs, genetic engineering, and environmental catastrophe, could anything be more dangerous than a Mickey Mouse imagination? Of course there could—a Rambo imagination.

But suppose that the images on television were just terrific, the best, most uplifting we and our children could possibly look at. They would still be somebody else's pictures, somebody else's pictures creating a world for us and them. Where the children are deprived of the chance to develop their own image-making, imaginative power, they are also deprived of their chance to have a world of their own. Developing a powerful, self-directed, image-making capacity is absolutely essential to an education that equips for the real challenges and uncertainties of life.

V. Conclusion

The concept of the education of the whole person has momentous implications for the rest of society. We cannot seriously conceive of educating for meaning, caring, and self-confidence and, at the same time, tolerate the meaninglessness, the ugliness, and the fearfulness presented by soul- and body-destroying neighborhoods, the disintegration of cities and farms, and the spoliation of our planet. But the two tasks, the educational and the social-cultural, go hand in hand. It is the education of the whole person that will equip us and our children to bring insight and staying power into the political, social, and spiritual challenges that now confront us as a nation and as a world.

Providing the kind of postmodern education being described here, Ms. President, is of utmost urgency. And it will require the utmost in intelligence, care, and commitment from all of us. First of all, we are fast sacrificing an entire generation of children. This is patently clear for the hundreds of thousands of poverty-stricken and neglected children in our society who have not the basic conditions for security and self-confidence, to say nothing of the chance to develop the emotional, social, and intellectual abilities that life will demand of them. But the so-called privileged are also at risk. An education, however well-intentioned, that stresses only a narrow intellectualism at an ever-earlier age deprives children of the foundations of truly powerful and mobile thinking capacities. An education in which beauty, social feeling, and wonder are not central—in which they are not recognized as the foundations of imaginative knowing, caring responsibility, and meaning-filled experience—may produce little virtuosos of calculation and competition. But it also results in a disaster for the society in which these children will be the leaders, and it leaves their own inner lives a desert.

The urgency of providing an education of the whole person is, therefore, to be seen also in the glaring need, wherever we turn, for imaginative political and social leadership. The common inclination of our leaders, and of us all, to rely increasingly on purely technical solutions for all our problems treats only symptoms and bespeaks a deep deficiency in our political, moral, and intellectual imagination. We see this, for example, in the growing tendency of our leaders to abandon the patience and understanding necessary for creative diplomacy, and to have immediate recourse instead to the military solution and its often exquisite technical rationality (as in "smart bombs"). Without imagination and insight we become less and less capable of penetrating to the heart of the mounting chaos and totalitarian forces vying for control of our world. Growing social unrest, wrenching human needs, and rampant fear and desire, all in a world permeated by unrestrained exploitation of nature and by weapons of unfathomable destructiveness, demand as never before an education in which self-confidence, caring, and meaningful insight are truly developed as our most needed and important human capacities.

Finally, the continuing and unrelieved destruction of our beautiful planet confronts us with the urgency of an education in which a sense of life and beauty are central. A sense of life and a sense of beauty—in short, a capacity to recognize and nurture the qualities of existence—are not luxuries for those few who like and can afford that sort of thing. They are the indispensable basis for truly powerful and imaginative conceptual thinking. And they are the foundations for a caring that is also powerful and effective. A purely utilitarian and instrumental education by itself, without the context and direction of the qualitative, despite good intentions and dazzling technologies, can only hasten the destruction of our planet. We need as never before an education of our capacities to recognize and respond to the qualities of existence—an education for the development of a sense of beauty, of a reverence for life, of a grasp of the complex and fragile relationships among beings, and not least of all a conceptuality suffused and informed by all these qualities: a living thinking. At the current rate of environmental destruction, do we have much more than a decade to make such an education a reality?

An education of the whole person presents us with the difficult task of having to be concerned about both the short term and the long term at the same time. We face the short-term task of marshaling all available resources to turn the present situation around. We face the long-term task of forming the capacities of consciousness and the structures of society that alone can make possible a meaningful and enduring society. If we focus only on the long term, we are in danger of losing the sense for the urgency of our time. But if we are preoccupied only with the short term, we are in danger of neglecting the careful thought necessary for an education that does not simply revert to the convenient truisms and conventional practices inherited in the moment. The long-term task is essential, for the tasks of maintaining a just and meaningful human society and a living nature are now with us, humanly speaking, forever. The short term and the long term are both necessary and must be carried out simultaneously: the first making breathing room for the second, and the second more and more informing and strengthening the first. The difficulties in such a tension-filled undertaking are manifold; the necessity and urgency of it are inescapable.

When caring, grounded in self-confidence, is poured into our thinking, thinking itself not only will be powerful, but also will be full of insight, life, and meaning. To be grasped by this postmodern vision of education can itself begin to call forth in us the strengthened impulses of the will, the enlivened feelings, and the moral sensitivity and steadfastness that a living thinking requires. Such a living thinking will alone secure for us a living planet.

That, Ms. President, is mainly what I wanted to say to you, and I am grateful for the opportunity.

NOTES

1. David Bohm describes clearly the fragmenting nature of our dominant modern ways of knowing, and the consequences for nature and society, in *Wholeness and the Implicate Order* (London: Routledge & Kegan Paul, 1980), 1–26; also see Bohm's "Postmodern Science and a Postmodern World," in *The*

Reenchantment of Science: Postmodern Proposals, ed. David Ray Griffin (Albany: State University of New York Press, 1988), 57–68.

2. Jonathan Schell, *The Fate of the Earth* (New York: Knopf, 1982); see esp. 1–96.

3. For a brilliant, rich exploration of the full nature of imagination as essential to the future of the human being and a living earth, see Owen Barfield, *Saving the Appearances: A Study in Idolatry* (New York: Harcourt, Brace & World, n.d.; reissued by Wesleyan University Press, 1988).

4. Waldorf Education, based on the work of Rudolf Steiner, encompasses a holistic understanding of the human person and a detailed view of child development. It has a curriculum and teaching methods that are at once intellectual, aesthetic, and social. My remarks in this article only touch on the richness of Waldorf Education and Steiner's pedagogical insights. For introductions to Waldorf Education, see especially A. C. Harwood, *The Recovery of Man in Childhood: A Study in the Educational Work of Rudolf Steiner* (London: Hodder & Stoughton, 1958); Mary Caroline Richards, *Toward Wholeness: Rudolf Steiner Education in America* (Middletown, Conn.: Wesleyan University Press, 1980); and Henry Barnes, Alan Howard, John Davy, and Hope Leichter, "An Introduction to Waldorf Education," *Teachers College Record* 81 (Spring 1980): 322–70. Among Rudolf Steiner's many lecture cycles on education, the following provide introductions to Waldorf Education: *The Education of the Child in the Light of Anthroposophy* (London: Rudolf Steiner Press, 1965); *The Essentials of Education* (London: Rudolf Steiner Press, 1982); *Kingdom of Childhood* (Hudson, N.Y.: Anthroposophic Press, 1982); *The Child's Changing Consciousness and Waldorf Education* (Hudson, N.Y.: Anthroposophic Press, 1988).

5. Quoted in Richard Rhodes, *The Making of the Atomic Bomb* (New York: Simon & Schuster, 1986), 11.

6. See Douglas Sloan, *Insight-Imagination: The Emancipation of Thought and the Modern World* (Westport, Conn.: Greenwood Press, 1983).

7. For example, see Richard Rorty, "Education, Socialization, and Individuation," *Liberal Education* 75/4 (Sept./Oct. 1989): 2–9; also see my response to Rorty in this same issue of *Liberal Education*, 24–25. There are some sticky epistemological issues involved here, having to do with "the social construction of reality," which space does not permit exploring. Suffice it to say that much of Rorty's discussion in this article is admirable, because, like his model, John Dewey, Rorty is committed to liberal, Western, humane, democratic values. And his rejection of certain notions of truth seems unobjectionable. But also, as with Dewey, the tacit importation of these values into, and their standing within, an exclusively instrumentalist, consensual notion of truth begs crucial questions.

8. Leszek Kolakowski, *Metaphysical Horror* (Oxford and New York: Basil Blackwell, 1988), 25.

9. For example, in the article cited above, Richard Rorty himself seems unconsciously, again like Dewey, to accept in fact several things as unquestionably true—for example, the propositions of received Darwinism, the bedrock conventionalism of the modern mind-set.

10. Alfred North Whitehead, *The Aims of Education* (New York: Free Press, 1967), 32.

11. Nikolai Berdyaev has commented: "Preparation for war is in the highest degree rational, and it presupposes the deliberately reasoned arming of states. This is a self-contradiction of war. The human masses are inoculated to produce a most irrational condition of the soul. War presupposes the arousing of erotic conditions, its nature is erotic, not ethical. In this particular case, I include in *eros, anti-eros* also, which has the same nature. Hate is an erotic phenomenon. And the mass of mankind is brought to a most irrational state of mind, to the madness of rational caring, it is upheld by rational discipline, it works on a technical basis. It is a demoniacal combination of extreme irrationalism, with extreme rationalism" (*Slavery and Freedom* [New York: Charles Scribner's Sons, 1944], 163). Berdyaev's observation here about war can be extended to many of the major activities of modern civilization.

12. Harwood, *Recovery of Man*, 34.

13. Kurt Fischer, "Theory of Cognitive Development," *Psychological Review* 87 (1980): 481, quoted in Arthur Zajonc, "Computer Technology: Questions Concerning the New Educational Technology," *Teachers College Record* 85 (Summer 1984): 521.

14. Michael Polanyi, *The Tacit Dimension* (Garden City, N.Y.: Doubleday, 1966).

15. Steiner, *Child's Changing Consciousness*, 17–20.

16. Ibid., 44.

17. Howard E. Gruber and J. Jacques Voneche, *The Essential Piaget* (New York: Basic Books, 1977), 71.

18. For journalists' reports on some instances, see, for example, Leslie Maitland Werner, "Parent Pressure Cited as Harmful; 2 Experts see Stress on Very Young Children, Asserting Education is No 'Race,' " *New York Times*, 16 Nov. 198:, 39; Glenn Collins, "Superbabies Aren't Happy Babies: One Crusade," *New York Times*, 17 Dec. 1987: C1; Glen Putka, "Tense Tots, Some Schools Press So Hard Kids Become Stressed and Fearful; Flashcards, Computers, Tests All Day Long Take a Toll On Fast-Track Students, Burning Out by the Age of 10," *Wall Street Journal*, 6 July 1988: 1. On the damaging effects of intruding too early into the child's life and play with essentially adult agen-

das, see especially David Elkind, *The Hurried Child* (Reading, Mass.: Addison-Wesley, 1981).

19. *A Nation at Risk: The Imperative for Educational Reform*, Report of the National Commission on Excellence in Education (Bell Commission) (Washington, D.C.: U.S. Department of Education, 1983).

20. I have here also drawn my examples from the actual practice of Waldorf Education. However, my drastically abbreviated descriptions do not begin to do justice to the richness of the teaching methods or to the range and depth of the curriculum in Waldorf Education. A. C. Harwood provides an excellent guide to Waldorf theory and practice in *The Recovery of Man in Childhood*. A fine, succinct description of Waldorf pedagogy and curriculum is Roberto Trostli, "Education as an Art: The Waldorf Approach," *Holistic Education Review* / (Spring 1988): 44–51.

21. John Dewey, *Art as Experience* (1934; New York: Capricorn Books, 1958), 46.

22. See Dewey, *Art as Experience* and "Experience, Nature and Art," in John Dewey et al., *Art and Education*, 2d. ed. (Merion, Penn.: Barnes Foundation Press, 1947). Nearly twenty years before Dewey's call for an artistic emphasis in education, Waldorf Schools had more than anticipated Dewey by actually putting into practice a full-fledged concept of education as an art. For Dewey later, the concept was only a beginning idea, which he never developed in any of its actual curricular and pedagogical details.

23. Dewey, *Art as Experience*, 348.

24. Kenneth Boulding, *The Image: Knowledge in Life and Society* (Ann Arbor: University of Michigan Press, 1956).

PART II

THE POLITICAL PROCESS AND THE PRESIDENCY

7

POLITICAL CULTURE AND THE PRESIDENCY: MEMORY AND THE SHIFT FROM MOSTMODERN TO POSTMODERN

Roger Wilkins

In my view, the postmodern world began when J. Robert Oppenheimer saw the explosion at Trinity and was reminded of the line from the *Bhagavad-Gita*:

Now I am become death, the destroyer of worlds.

That is the first record of an acknowledgment by a human mind that humans had created the capacity to destroy the world. This capacity is both the symbol of, and the crucial element in, the postmodern world.

In the first part of this essay, I look at the presidents from John F. Kennedy onward as examples of modern men dealing with postmodern problems, men whose behavior in office may give us some hints about pathways to a better future. Because these were presidents in postmodern times, they might be called "postmodern presidents." But they were not. Instead of adopting postmodern values, goals, and means to deal with this radically new global situation, they carried the values, goals, and means of the modern presidency to their extreme limits. I will accordingly—adopting David Griffin's term—refer to them as "mostmodern" presidents.

In the second part of this essay, I suggest some of the things we need to do if we want a genuinely postmodern politics, including a postmodern presidency. In all of this I will be suggesting that memory—including its recovery— is a necessary condition for the emergence of a postmodern political culture.

I. The Mostmodern Presidency

I watched from the vantage point of the State Department as John F. Kennedy sketched out the contours of what can be considered the first mostmodern presidency. My memory tells me that the office was shaped then by a compound of the American male's John Wayne-ness, American constitutional idealism, the magic and mystery of the national security state, hardball Massachusetts politics, and television.

Of those elements, our John Wayne acculturation and the seductions of the national security state have been most constant over the ensuing decades, with television being omnipresent as it oscillated, from administration to administration, between the roles of powerful presidential tool and relentlessly destructive Greek chorus.

The most remarkable thing about the office of the presidency is how profoundly American it is. The presidency was the most human of the governmental inventions that resulted from the American revolution. We thrust our aspirations into the office. The men who come to it are brimful of the cultural memory of this country and of fundamental American yearnings and attitudes. From the very first president, who cut his eyeteeth on forays into the western wilderness, the frontier spirit has been in us, in our presidents, and in the lore and spirit of the office they occupy. The forces, the politics, and the technology of the postmodern era have pumped those elements up to almost mythic proportions.

The threat of annihilation has dominated our consciousness over the last three decades and has, more than any other recent force, reshaped the presidential office. Moreover, the president's power to wreak annihilatory damage has puffed up our sense of the office and has worked on the consciousness of the man in it. We call him "the leader of the free world" and "the most powerful man on earth." We talk about his awesome burdens and about the button—the doomsday button—just there, under his hand. All of that has to weigh heavily on the psyches of the human beings who hold the office, and that weight has, in my judgment, led to defects in vision that have decreased our capacity to understand our world and to identify our problems. All of those developments have come about in very American ways.

Fundamentally, it seems to me that American presidents have met the threat of annihilation with the attempt to master and to dominate it. Americans and their presidents have responded to the nuclear peril, which (thus far in human experience) appears to be the ultimate in human-created uncertainty, by attempting to create certainty at the core of nuclear instability. In our responses, ranging from the creation of thermonuclear weapons to the covert magic of the CIA, our presidents have sought to shape our power in ways that could destroy, control, and contain the threats posed by an unstable and unpredictable world.

But being Americans, how could we have reacted differently? For a century and a half after the creation of the nation, our oceans seemed to provide us with more certainty than almost any other people ever had in the dangerous, roiling, and tumultuous evolution of nations through the recorded history of humankind. And within our borders we had most favorable conditions as we were left largely unimpeded by the earth's great powers as we bludgeoned out our fate on this lush, wide land of ours.

Americans are a self-confident people. We learn from our history that, when we have problems, we face up to them and solve them with whatever means are necessary. If we are oppressed by a dim-witted British monarch, we rebel, persevere, and establish our own country. If we find the country isn't working quite right, the wise men convene in Philadelphia and devise a plan to fix it. We are also self-confident because there was always more—west of the Hudson, west of the Allegheny, west of the Cascades—there was always more to come, more to be had, more to be dreamed.

And Americans are a violent people. H. Rap Brown was not wrong when he said, "Violence is as American as cherry pie." George Washington did not lead a nonviolent revolution; and slavery, which preceded the creation of the United States on this continent by more than a century and a half, was not a nonviolent institution. Surely the relationships of the early immigrants with the people whom they found here—the people whom the Declaration of Independence characterized as "the inhabitants of our frontiers, the merciless Indian Savages"— were not always nonviolent. Indeed, it could be argued that those who urged the Reverend Dr. Martin Luther King, Jr., to remain faithful to his nonviolent instincts were urging upon him a profoundly un-American course of conduct.

Domination of both nature and people has been a hallmark of American development and has left indelible marks on our national character. The manner in which the issue of slavery was handled at the Constitutional Convention is instructive. There were few men at that convention who could conceive of Africans in America as full human beings. Discussions about slavery were not permitted to balloon out to their full moral dimensions. When moral qualms were expressed, as when the issue of banning the slave trade arose, John Rutledge, a former governor of South Carolina, responded with what James Madison called "cold precision":

> Religion and humanity have nothing to do with this question. Interest alone is the governing principle with nations. The true question at present is whether the Southern states shall or shall not be parties to the Union. If the Northern states consult their interest, they will not oppose the increase of slaves which will increase the commodities of which they will become the carriers.

The issue of slavery was addressed three times in the Constitution, but the word was never used. The practice, however, was legitimated in our great organic document. A great conflict between human rights and property rights was thus sewn into the fabric of the union by means of compromises that glued the states to one another. With this conflict came an enduring ambivalence about the value of human beings and the amount of nurturing and care they were due within our national framework. Moreover, a habit was entrenched, particularly—but not exclusively—in racial matters, of denying the stark and sometimes ugly realities offered by daily life by finding intellectual abstractions and euphemistic words that permitted lies to be told about ugly deeds that were being done.

Not all human beings brought here to be slaves submitted to the condition of slavery docilely. Repressive violence had to be continued in our laws and in the dailiness of life in the slave states, therefore, in order to continue the practice, which, as John Rutledge correctly pointed out, was helping to build the economic foundations of the whole nation. Then, in the early nineteenth century, when Eli Whitney's invention truly made cotton king, there was a powerful southern push westward. With it came the need for brute force to level forests, lay roads, dredge canals, and build towns, so the internal slave trade flourished. Mothers, daughters, sons, and fathers were sold down many rivers for profit and development.

The miracle of America was being created out of a wilderness by force. Those who lived in the path of expansion were either subdued, killed, or driven away. As Harvard historian Nathan Irvin Huggins described them in *Black Odyssey*, white men of the time were "men who, more and more, would presume to be not only masters of other men but of their own world and their destiny."

The habits of mastery and control are as deep as our entire history on this continent and as wide as the land. After slavery was over, there was a West to be won, civilization to be expanded, a destiny to be achieved, heroic lives to be led, the most wretched cruelties and hypocrisies to be inflicted, and myths to be made. John Wayne, Shane, the Lone Ranger, and Joe DiMaggio light up male delusions of where we have come from and who we might be. The lone, taciturn, strong, and self-sufficient man can handle anything—a raging cattle herd, a gang of wild Indians, a curvacious miscreant, or Bob Feller's fastball.

American men were bright, brave, and, above all, masterful. They were also wonderfully individualistic, because power went to the quickest mind, the strongest will, and the most ruthless spirit. And besides, who needed to make a fetish about cooperation or conservation when there were millions of square miles of opportunity just over the horizon to the west? Freedom came to be internalized by many as the power of the individual to work out his fortune unimpeded by government or, for that matter, the weak and the slow.

We in the Kennedy administration were bright, brave, and masterful, or so it seemed to us. Our beau ideal was the dashing young president who was sometimes seen alone, reflecting at a White House window or steering his sailboat, face to the wind, always gallant, slim, and handsome. We knew that our ideals were universal, our ideas good, and our energy boundless. The torch was in our hands now, and our generation would set the world right. We would master our foes wherever we encountered them—on the nuclear gaming boards or in the back alleys of the world—and we would go on to remake the rest of the world in our image.

John F. Kennedy accepted his party's nomination at the far rim of the country in Los Angeles, which, although a village of five thousand people in 1880, was in 1960 growing rapidly toward becoming the country's second-largest city. Kennedy called us to a new frontier. The old frontier was gobbled up now, but its spirit was in us, so the man who would be president chose the frontier image as the spiritual vehicle for his trip to the White House.

Once there, he chose old American patterns for facing the threat that might obliterate us. While Kennedy called for a nuclear test ban, his administration produced nuclear weapons and fancy nuclear strategic theories faster than anybody previously could have dreamed possible. And why not? Kennedy had come to power charging General Eisenhower, of all people, of having neglected the nation's defenses by permitting us to endure a humiliating gap of missiles between ourselves and the thrusting Soviets.

But the nuclear peril was not all. Kennedy and his people spotted back-alley problems in Laos, in Vietnam, and in Cuba. For these problems, the whole panoply of national-security-state incantations was called forth. We had Green Berets and Operation Phoenix and military training advisors and CIA operations and Mafia hit men employed around the globe, projecting American power and protecting American security. Although some ultimately advocated "nuking" the Vietnamese, Kennedy's successors settled for Agent Orange, napalm, and carpet-bombing the Ho Chi Minh Trail. John Kennedy and his successors were not about to be measured and found shorter than the men who had tamed the old frontier. One of the most frequently asked questions about a prospective New Frontier appointee was, "Is he tough enough?"

The really tough guys in those days—the grown-ups—were the ones who worked with the secrets. With all that frenetic national security activity, there were secrets upon secrets. It was a subtle business. Those who were close to the president and presumably in on the main secrets formed almost a secular priesthood, standing above and apart from the rest of us. They moved their bodies through the town as if carrying precious cargoes, and when they moved off to corners of public rooms to whisper among themselves, the rest of us looked away in almost reverential deference. They all had coteries of young, trim, tough, well-tailored assistants—acolytes, full of their own secrets and their own arrogance. Although we hardly knew it in the beginning, these men were the ones who were crafting the Vietnam War for us.

Although nominally there was only one government in town, it was a two-tiered operation. There were those who operated the national security state and kept its secrets—the grown-ups—and there were the rest of us, who worked on such things as education, airline safety, civil rights, and the like. The divvying up of priorities, prestige, money, and status clearly demonstrated that.

The cultural roots of President Lyndon B. Johnson, who implored American servicemen to bring back a coonskin to tack to the wall, need not be elaborated here. There were many examples in the Johnson years of how unequal the competition was between the claims of the national security state and the claims of ordinary people trying to live their lives in America. In the late spring of 1968, two conflicting events occurred in Washington. The president sent up a bill seeking more taxes to finance the Vietnam War. Almost simultaneously, some people in the government wanted to respond to the Poor People's Campaign by asking Congress to authorize free food stamps for Americans who earned a dollar a day or less. When we had persuaded the president to take that action, he called Representative Wilbur Mills, chairman of the Ways and Means Committee, and told him of his plan. Mills told the president that if he wanted his war tax, he'd better forget his new idea. And that—despite the fact that Lyndon Johnson truly understood and cared about the plight of the poor—was that.

The belief of these two presidents, and many of their subordinates, in the efficacy of American violence was very strong. In December 1962, Admiral U.S. Grant Sharp, commander-in-chief of the United States forces in the Pacific theater, consulted all of the intelligence available to him (which undoubtedly was everything then available) and said flatly that the Vietnam problem would be solved by sometime in 1965. I found a contempt high in the American military for the Vietcong and its guerilla tactics. In this connection, it is useful to recall the full reference to Native Americans in the Declaration of Independence: "merciless Indian Savages, whose known mode of warfare is an undistinguished destruction of all ages, sexes and conditions."

In discussing in the *The Powers That Be* his time in Vietnam, David Halberstam (who won a Pulitzer prize for his reporting there) tells us that most Americans in those days subscribed to "the raggedy-ass theory of the Vietcong," which he described as a belief "that a light touch of American power and determination would bring them to heel very quickly."

A number of the original American flaws, embedded in the cultural configurations that were confirmed and propelled into the life of the new nation in the late eighteenth century, reappear here. Our generation of Americans believed in violence, just as the Founding Fathers did, and we used euphemisms for things too ugly to look at, just as they did. When we talked about a touch of American power, we meant wading into the jungle and splattering everything in sight—which is what, sometimes, our forces did. And some of our political and military leaders took a look at our foes—who were not white—and were unable to judge accurately their abilities as fighters or as men (and sometimes as women). The errors and sufferings these flaws caused were, of course, substantial.

One of the things the violence of those days did accomplish was to drown out the echoes of Eisenhower's last warning about the military-industrial complex. Ike was a war hero, after all. His successors had to demonstrate that they were strong, and strength could best be demonstrated by bloating the accounts of the Pentagon. As that was done, the monster that Ike had described grew to be the military, industrial, political, and job-preservation complex, with its tentacles (hardened like concrete) reaching into enough congressional districts to guarantee that promiscuous Pentagon spending would remain a permanent and obscene fixture in the mostmodern presidential equation.

The fact that the United States was neither smart enough nor strong enough to succeed in Vietnam was a shock to the culture and a shock to the mostmodern presidency. It led Richard Nixon to conjure up the specter of the United States as a "pitiful, helpless giant." Nonetheless, Nixon, who may have been the most complex of all our presidents, conducted foreign affairs in a brilliant, sophisticated way, creating the opening to China and constructing détente with the Soviet Union. Those initiatives, it seems to me, constituted a semibreakout from the mostmodern pattern. Yet, in other ways, Nixon was true to it, immersing and enmeshing himself in secret machinations and then trying to protect himself by throwing the mystical and magical words *national security* in front of his dirty deeds.

Jimmy Carter tried to break the mold by emphasizing human needs at home and making peace abroad. But he had neither the political skills nor the vision to succeed, and he had some bad luck as well. By the time he had gotten through telling us how complex the world was and had then run into the Iranians, the shadow of the pitiful, helpless giant fell large across the land. The sand-trapped helicopters at Desert One conjured up the vision of John Wayne's being outdrawn and having his six-shooter blasted out of his hand by some savage. Unthinkable and unforgivable. The stage was set for Ronald Reagan—his simplicities and his violent impulses.

In many ways, Reagan was the quintessential mostmodern president. He tried to restore the certainty that our oceans had once provided by creating a sky shield. He threw money at the Pentagon and then did it some more. He recommissioned obsolete battleships and then sent one of them to lob Chevy-sized shells into the hills above Beirut in an ineffectual display of strength. He invaded Grenada, launched a covert war against Nicaragua, and tried to kill Quadaffi in a bombing raid. His administration had a greater penchant for the secret side of the national security apparatus than any other we have known about, and Reagan had absolute contempt for governmental activities that were designed to improve the lives of ordinary Americans. His preference for the interests of property to investments in human beings would surely have found favor even with John Rutledge of South Carolina (quoted earlier).

Similarly, President Reagan wanted a six-hundred-ship navy, because he worried about all the "choke points" in all the seas and oceans in all the world. A remark in congressional testimony by Frank Carlucci, Reagan's secretary of defense, spoke volumes. When told that the defense budget could be cut, Carlucci responded that of course it could: The congressman should just specify what part of the world he was willing to give up.

The sense of American exceptionalism, coupled with the growth of the national security state and our material and emotional investment in it, has laid an awesome burden on the spirit of the mostmodern president. He has the Pentagon and all its forces; the CIA and its dark arts; and the National Security Agency with its electronic marvels, the power of all the secret national security directives, and the means to carry them out. It is now clear that Reagan, at least, had an entire off-the-books government. With all of that at hand, a president is tempted to feel that, if he is not omnipotent, he is a failure. And so, in the name of national security, it was permissible to attempt to murder people who were inconvenient to some U.S. policy goal or other. Castro, Trujillo, Lumumba, and Qaddafi are some of the people who were, at one time or another, in the way of our mostmodern presidents.

After Reagan came George Bush. It seems to me that he is the apotheosis of the mostmodern president. He has inherited all of the cultural baggage hidden in the nooks and crannies of the oval office over the last three decades and the ossified symbiosis of the government and the arms industry. Moreover, he is a true national security creature, having served as director of Central Intelligence in the 1970s and as vice-president during the Iran-Contra operations. Jim Hoagland, former foreign editor of the *Washington Post*, wrote in the early period of Bush's tenure that Bush, unlike Reagan, did not recoil from the Mutually Assured Destruction strategy, but rather had moved back toward it.

But there is more. I am indebted to Professor Todd Gitlin of the University of California at Berkeley for an analysis of mostmodernism in the Spring 1989 issue of *New Perspectives Quarterly*. Although Gitlin, along with most other commentators, calls the deconstructive approach he has in view "postmodernism," it is, from the standpoint of the constructive postmodernism reflected in this volume, more appropriately called "mostmodernism," because it results from taking some of the premises of modernity to their extreme conclusions. And although Gitlin writes of literary and artistic mostmodernism, it and the political vision we are pursuing here arise from the same sources, the knowledge that modern humankind has imperiled the future. Thus, this other form of postmodernism (which I am calling "mostmodernism"), running as it were on a parallel track, gives us some useful insights on the problems before us. Think, for example, of George Bush's 1988 campaign for the presidency and his program for the country as he has revealed it to us over the past years, as you read Gitlin's words.

> In the [m]ostmodern sensibility, the search for unity has apparently been abandoned altogether. Instead, we have textuality, a cultivation of surfaces endlessly referring to, ricocheting from, reverberating onto other surfaces. The work calls attention to its arbitrariness, constructedness; it interrupts itself. Instead of a single center, there is pastiche and cultural recombination. Anything can be juxtaposed to anything else.

Willie Horton, the pledge of allegiance, Boston Harbor sludge, a kinder and gentler America, an expressed desire to be "the education president," a budget with education cuts in it, Donald Gregg, clean air, pork rinds and troop cuts in Europe, John Tower, a true Klutz (African American) as chief civil rights enforcer, and No New Taxes! are some of George Bush's offerings. You figure it out. A cultivation of surfaces?

Part of the way to figure it out is to go back to another of John Kennedy's legacies: the new technologies of politics. Kennedy did not invent television, and he did not invent using the primary system to subvert the party system, either (Estes Kefauver did that), but he took those routes to political power to a point that changed presidential politics forever. After JFK used the primary trail so successfully in 1960, no candidate was ever going to be able to ignore places like New Hampshire and Iowa. And once Kennedy had leapt from the back benches of the Senate to the White House, a premium was put on telegenic politicians.

In the old days, the "old pols" had a large hand in picking candidates, but primaries and television eliminated the role of the old pols in delivering the candidates to the people. The old pols, however, had had another job: telling the candidates what the people were feeling. Kennedy took care of that too. He had learned to rely on Louis Harris's polls in his last Massachusetts race for the Senate. He made sophisticated use of them in the primaries, particularly in Protestant West Virginia, where he rolled right over Hubert Humphrey's last chance for that year. And that was the last chance for the old pols and the beginning of the new technology of politics. Nothing much stood between the candidate and the people but the television cameras and skill in raising money.

George Bush was elected president twenty-five years after John Kennedy was murdered. In that quarter of a century, the technology of politics took off. By 1968, the Republicans had learned how to package a candidate like a product. By 1988, there were not just political pollsters: There were professional political handlers, professional political television people, and professional managers of focus groups.

There did not have to be any guessing about what the people wanted and were feeling. The polls and the focus groups could pinpoint the answers to these questions. The handlers could tell the candidate how to say what the public wanted to hear, and the media people could put it on television in the most attractive way. The Willie Horton issue, for example, was discovered, according to the Republicans, in focus groups. And the rest, as they say, is history.

Values, themes, convictions, and visions do not matter much in this kind of politics. Images do. Or, in Professor Gitlin's words, it is "textuality, a cultivation of surfaces endlessly referring to, ricocheting from, reverberating onto other surfaces." It is the politics of the nine-second sound bite and the thirty-second commercial. It is the politics of images, not messages. It is the politics of politician as reflector, not as leader.

What is President Bush reflecting? In part it could be the young urban professional whom Gitlin describes this way:

> They were born in the late 1950s and early 1960s. Theirs is an experience of aftermath, privatization, weightlessness. They can remember political commitment, or images of it, but were not animated by it. The association of passion and politics rubs them the wrong way.

Even if Gary Trudeau's invisible version of President Bush has proven untrue, it is hard not to ascribe a sense of weightlessness to him. Finally, Gitlin suggests that the mostmodern attitude—an "all-consuming and all-corroding irony," he calls it—is a way of dealing with powerful feelings and fears unleashed in the '60s:

> [There is] the fear of destruction, the fear of powerlessness, the loss of identity. Men fear women; whites fear blacks; at some level everyone fears that nuclear war or the greenhouse effect will destroy the future.

President Bush seems to be waiting, holding his breath, at least with regard to environmental and domestic issues, hoping it will all come out all right. He is a man of his electorate; a man of this moment.

But this moment is a failure of nerve and this electorate has been blind to its own best interests. All-corroding irony will not do in the face of a growing hole in the ozone layer, or in the face of hospital nurseries filled with newborns dying of AIDS. Polished surfaces will not confront the epidemic of drugs sapping the strength of our society. The land is all filled up with people, with debt, and with garbage.

II. TOWARD A HOPEFUL POSTMODERN CULTURE

The strand of our culture that has been shaping our presidents recently is out of date. We need new themes and better models because we have different tasks. We should have learned by now not to yearn to dominate. We cannot do it. We once dreamed we could master nature when the task was to flatten forests or alter river channels, but we know now that that dream was folly. The planet has told us so. And the using and discarding of human beings is not only immoral; it is wasteful and stupid, as is the business of judging a human being's worth by gender or color. If the twentieth century has taught us nothing else, it should have taught us those things. So there are new tasks requiring new modes of thought, tasks of conserving, restoring, preserving, nurturing, cooperating, and finding one's place peacefully and constructively—not bombastically and domineeringly—in the societies of nature, humans, and nations.

President Reagan may, in fact, have done the nation a favor by reveling so hedonistically and so primitively in the mores of the old culture. The results for the nation may come to be so catastrophic that no other demonstration of the obsolescence of the old patterns will be required. President Bush seems in part to sense this as he pointedly repudiates some of the old Reagan patterns. But he keeps other patterns and does not seem to be able to define what ought to come next, aside from vague talk about a "new world order" and mostmodern, chauvenistic rhetoric about the twenty-first century as the "second American century."

But that is just fine; defining what the future should be is not his job. It is ours. We elected George Bush president, but we did not cede to him our senses of peril and possibility, nor did we cede to him our political heritage and our freedom. If we do not believe that the values and the assumptions that have informed the presidency over the last three decades will serve our nation and our planet well over the centuries to come, it is up to us to change the cultural context in which we do our politics as well as the policies that we live by.

The insight that informed the conference out of which this book arose is that we live on a fragile planet that humankind has imperiled. That insight does not translate automatically into a self-effectuating program. Nor, indeed, does it suggest easy individualistic answers, such as "Live simply so that others may simply live." Rather, it suggests the need for profound cultural transformations, the inevitability of hideously difficult policy conflicts, and the requirement for more arduous cultural, political, and intellectual work on national and international levels than Americans, so far, seem capable of undertaking or sustaining.

There was much talk at the conference about "the polity," by which, I suppose, one means those Americans eligible to vote. That polity is a lethargic, sleeping entity that barely rouses itself to vote for president—"the most personal vote Americans ever cast," the pundits tell us. It is a passive electorate, tailor-made for consumer politics and perfectly prepared between elections to cede the identification and shaping of critical issues to officeholders, experts, and self-seekers.

Democracy, like the genuinely postmodern sensibility to which we look forward, is not self-actuating. If we are to change our cultural habits, members of the electorate must be immersed in the long-term problems of humankind as antidotes to the short-term scripts that political handlers provide our candidates. They must also become convinced that what each of them thinks counts and that what each of them does can make a difference.

In a nutshell, I believe that the only effective antidotes to our bad and ancient cultural habits and the tattered state of our democratic practices is to take democracy seriously. That is not an original idea or even a new one. Thomas Jefferson expressed it almost two hundred years ago. In today's context, it means to stop taking our sovereignty for granted and to begin to educate our youngsters at the earliest age to think seriously about issues, to participate fully and effectively in politics and the business of governing their country.

If we are to replace the arcane and deadly abstractions of the national security mentality as the central focus of our politics, then ordinary people must come to believe that their concerns belong in politics. Our most decent attitudes about human beings and our common-sense views about the planet are rooted in peoples' actual lives and their desires for themselves and their children. Our national cultural memory, containing as it does so much violence and racism, has required Americans to invest enormous psychic energies in denying much of our historical baggage and the ways it affects us today.

Thus, when we look at the F-14 and its Top Gun pilot as bearers of the torch of freedom around the world, it bolsters our prettified historical myths and helps deny both the old burden of slavery and the contemporary burden of its legacies, the gross imperfections in our democracy: The world's foremost defenders of freedom could not possibly have had such a horrible history of unfreedom, and surely they are too busy to worry about ghettos! But if people actually got down to working together on the quality of their schools, the safety of their neighborhoods, or the quality of their water, they would undoubtedly be much more realistic about how problems developed and what the nation's priorities ought to be. The F-14 might then be seen as a poor alternative to expenditures on housing, and the training of the Top Gun as a waste of a good brain that might otherwise have taught high school physics or social studies.

In my own experience in grubbing around in local political issues, I have learned that good and tough politics knocks the edges off racism, the rosy glasses off our vision of the state of our democracy, and the national security detritus off people's priority lists. Politically involved people also often begin to identify common interests across racial lines. Finally, they come to understand that the words *provide for the general welfare* in the Constitution stand for at least as powerful a set of American values as the words referring to the "common defense."

If such values are to become the central focus of our politics, the polity has to wake up and place them there. Our schools teach people to drive, to operate computers, and to use condoms, but not to be citizens. That is absurd.

It is beyond my competence to outline a curriculum for democracy. Suffice it to say that I believe that democratic practice and theory, in age-appropriate dollops, should be inserted in school curricula from kindergarten on. American pupils must be convinced that they are both sovereign and free and that to remain that way will require a great deal of effort and time throughout their lifetimes. They should be taught that their heritage of freedom was not drafted in the eighteenth century and perfected and defended over the ensuing centuries merely for the gratification or pacification of their personal lusts, insecurities, and desires. American citizens should come to maturity with the understanding that their political system is precious and only briefly in their safekeeping.

The question then becomes: Politics for what and how do we do it? My own sense is that a broader, more active, and more potent electorate would come to understand that, important as realistic issues of defense are, issues such as regenerating the nation, nurturing our people, and protecting the planet are the only realistic pathways to the future. Moreover, such an electorate would understand that vitally important politics can be practiced at the local as well as the national and international levels.

Public education, for example, is an issue that currently cries out for sustained popular local political attention. For at least a decade, the nation has possessed the information that its public education system was in a shambles. Now big business executives have taken a look at the state of our public school systems and at our national demographics and have concluded that, unless this crisis is addressed, in a few years the nation will not have the quality of work force needed to sustain a healthy economy. Most advocates of better public education are ecstatic about business executives weighing in on this issue.

But wait! Shouldn't we ask: Education for what? Will not CEOs want education to produce a larger gross national product? Some of us might argue that it should be education for the planet, education for the future, education for citizenship. The fact is that those who are deeply involved in the political fight for better education, not only at the national level but also at the local level all over this country, are the ones who are going to answer the question: Education for what?

I mention education as a possible entry point for new political activism on local and national levels. Ecology, human development, zoning, health care, and the shape of economic development initiatives are among the plethora of other possibilities.

Finally, as I urge you to consider politics as the bridge to get us from where we are to where we want to be, I have to say something about the audience at the conference, composed, as it was, almost entirely of affluent, well-intentioned, white North Americans. I can assure you that politics emanating only from this segment of our population will not get us anywhere. The people in our inner-cities do not see these things the same way. Neither do the recent immigrants to this country from the countries just south of our borders. Finally, the majority of the people in the world are poor citizens of poor countries whose perspectives are vastly different from those of white, affluent, North Americans.

I should imagine that our message about adopting a postmodern value system in the name of conserving the planet would sound to the poor people in our nation and around the world like the captain of a team that is ahead by ten runs declaring in the fifth inning: "Game's over." Somehow, you have to find ways to make coalitions with others.

And I have a suggestion about where you can start. If you are going to try to get people to face the future, you have to face the *whole* future. So, I would suggest that, before you do one thing on a postmodern sensibility inspired by this book, you go to the poorest school in the poorest neighborhood in your city and look carefully at the children. Look into their faces, their eyes. Take it all in, because that, too, is the future.

Then imagine what words you would use to sell your postmodern concepts to a working-class black woman who has struggled to get her daughter to the verge of graduating from college. How would you formulate your arguments as you looked into her face and saw her dreams for her child? Then think of mothers in Bogata, Lusaka, Bombay, and Manila. Trying to imagine the appropriate words gives us a sense of the dimensions of our political and cultural problems.

You have to find answers to these questions if you want to get from here to there. The '60s taught us that single-issue political obsessions get beaten. There were the civil-rights people and the new-culture people and the anti-war people and the women's-movement people and the gay-rights people and the Native American people and the Hispanic people and the environmental people. And we all felt too much self-righteous urgency about our own causes to make effective coalitions with each other; and so the right wing knocked us all off in 1980 and set us all way back in the ensuing decade. We have to build coalitions at home and abroad in order to do the politics that will ensure the future of the planet. That means learning about and coming to terms with the needs and the aspirations of a lot of people who are very different from us.

In doing so, we may learn some things that might be useful in altering the culture that has produced our mostmodern presidencies. For example, the culture that produced me contains lessons that may be helpful and, in fact, parallel to some of the thoughts we have examined here. We have been asked by Joanna Macy in her essay to place ourselves as specks along the longest spectrum of time we can conceive. I do not live in a spectrum that long, but I do live in one that is considerably longer than the today-and-tomorrow frame in which so many of our fellow citizens seem to wallow. That frame of immediacy, it seems to me, serves to perpetuate modern postures of arrogance and lack of regard for the future. Mostmodern presidencies designed to appease the immediate lusts of the polity are the sure result. A longer frame and a different cultural orientation are required if we are to have better policies and better presidencies.

My culture is American—African American—and my spectrum is framed by my acute awareness of the continuing climb of my people and my family out of slavery, past our hideous inequities toward something far better in generations to come. My values in that frame are shaped by the slaves Harriet Tubman, Sojourner Truth, and Frederick Douglass, who escaped to freedom only to spend their precious freedom giving back to those still in shackles.

My reach in time goes back to my great grandmother, who was born sometime in the middle of the nineteenth century and who carried to her grave a burn scar inflicted on her in childhood by a cruel mistress. GreatGrandma could have fallen apart or jumped in a river to escape her fate, and who could have blamed her? But she didn't. She held herself together and raised Grandpa to be the strong, brave man who got our strand of the family out of Mississippi.

And I have a young daughter who, in the course of a normal life, might have a child—my grandchild—who might live into the twenty-second century. I have debts to people like GreatGrandma who survived slavery and made me possible. I can only pay that debt by using my freedom in ways that infuse her struggle for dignity within slavery with meaning. And I have obligations to that grandchild to do my part to make life in her centuries tolerable and to leave a record that can help guide her as the lives of Tubman, Truth, and Douglass have guided me.

The culture and the values of my blackness have given me the strength to spend a lifetime slogging away at the kind of political work I have suggested here as a bridge to get us from where we are to where we want to be. But my culture is not the only alternative to the frontier culture of dominance and control. My point in discussing it is to illustrate that there are many lessons in American life other than the cultural patterns that threaten us all. *We need not be prisoners of the currently prevailing culture.* We must *identify the alternatives* that work for us and draw strength and guidance from them.

Only then will we be able to get ourselves presidents who are humble about themselves and about the present, and who understand their debts to the past and are determined to meet their obligations to the future.

8

POLITICS FOR A TROUBLED PLANET: TOWARD A POSTMODERN DEMOCRATIC CULTURE

Frances Moore Lappé

Laments about political apathy among Americans are about as common as surfers on a Santa Barbara beach in July. The near-record-low turnout of voters in the 1988 election fed these laments. But it is not apathy many Americans feel; it is anger. Americans feel insulted by our political process. During the 1988 presidential race, the daily news story was not the candidate's latest position on critical issues, but an analysis of how the candidates' managers were manipulating us that day. No wonder people feel angry.

And no wonder so many feel disconnected from a system when it has contempt for them. Young people polled recently by Peter D. Hart Research Associates said that they do not see a connection between their concerns about, for example, "homeless people walking the

street" or "kids selling drugs" and government policies—either as causes or as solutions. The young people polled "do not see political participation as a way to address the problems," Hart noted.

Reinforcing their feeling of distance from politics, most of the
young people have a negative, cartoonlike image of politicians, the poll
found. Words like *dishonest, corrupt,* and *liars* were commonly used
descriptions.

The concept of citizenship reflected in this poll is notably passive.
When asked if they are good citizens, the participants reported that
they are because they "don't do anything wrong" or "don't do anything
to hurt anybody else." Citizenship means avoiding trouble, not taking
active responsibility.

But if many Americans do not see a connection between their
concerns and government, it does not mean that we are not active in
our communities. Roughly half of all adult Americans are volunteers in
an incredible variety of causes, giving an average of almost five hours a
week. Three-fourths of us give an average of almost $800 a year to
charities.

What then is the problem? Why do our political institutions
appear unable to reverse the downward slide we feel ourselves on?
Why do Americans not perceive the political process as a vehicle for
expressing their anger, their concerns, and their values?

These questions are at the center of my own current work in
which I seek to address the challenge of this book: to rethink America's
political culture. My work is based upon this simple hypothesis: *Only
with a deep democratic renewal can we as a people begin to conceive of
meeting the unprecedented threats to our society and our planet.*

Precisely because of their scale and complexity, today's problems
cannot be solved outside of a social process of growing citizen knowledge and responsibility—what I call "citizen democracy" and what
political philosopher Benjamin Barber calls "strong democracy."[1]

However, the transformation of today's passive, thin democracy
into a vital civic culture faces enormous ideological obstacles deeply
embedded in the modern worldview. This worldview carries ideas
about human nature, the nature of our ties to one another, and the
nature of our place in nature that justify and reinforce the thin, lifeless
shell that passes for democracy today. These ideas are difficult to confront, in part because they are so taken for granted as to be practically
invisible; they are the unspoken assumptions that shape and limit the
very questions we are allowed to ask.

In this essay, I first focus on what I see as the most challenging of
these obstacles: the hidden assumptions that block our creativity. Sec-

ond, I ask how we can retrieve the best *within* our own alternative political philosophic tradition to transcend these conceptual straitjackets. I suggest that we can draw from recent, constructive developments of democratic theory and practice emerging from community-based organizing today. Finally, I hold that, despite the temptation to meet unprecedented global threats by imposing seemingly expedient solutions provided by "experts," such an approach is doomed to fail. It is what got us into our present mess. We must instead rebuild democratic culture, not by creating new institutions or new language as much as by learning and teaching the political arts through all existing organizations with a stake in civic life.

I. OBSTACLES TO A DEMOCRATIC RENEWAL IN THE MODERN WORLDVIEW

Social Atoms Ruled by Absolute Laws

The modern worldview, emerging from the seventeenth century and defining both liberal and conservative views today, holds within it at least two core assumptions that make genuine democratic civic culture unthinkable.

First, the modern worldview conceives of human nature as atomistic. Encapsulated in our isolated egos, we are unable to know each other's needs. Our self-centeredness is not a moral failing; we are simply capable of nothing more.

Second, laws governing the interaction of these isolated social atoms parallel laws governing the Newtonian physical world. They are absolute. At least they must be held as such, lest the tampering of self-seeking individual atoms distort them for private gain. In our culture, perhaps the two most important of such laws, placed above human interference, are *market exchange* and *the right to unlimited accumulation of, and rights over, productive property.* We absorb as by osmosis the view that, as long as these rules are intact, individuals remain free to pursue their private interests and out of this pursuit spontaneously emerges a workable whole.

Such a notion of absolute economic rules carries several critical consequences. I will mention two.

We're off the hook! If laws of property and the market govern our interaction with one another and, say, the housing market prices some people out (and onto the street)—well, that's the marketplace law at work. It is not *my* doing. Or if Exxon chooses to put its profits above the cost of keeping oil-spill equipment at hand or the cost of doubled bottomed tankers to avoid spills—well, there is little I can say. After all, Exxon has determining authority over its property.

The modern paradigm relieves human beings of responsibility for moral reasoning and action as it relates to the well-being of the whole.

Politics is suspect. Equally important to any vision of citizen democracy is the fact that the modern worldview's stance toward the process of conscious, group decisionmaking toward common goals—usually called "politics"—is profound suspicion. Given our atomistic separateness, politics can only be a ruse, used by some people to manipulate others. By all means it must be kept outside our economic lives, that sanctuary of individual, private decisionmaking.

Now, if human responsibility for social outcomes is denied, on the one hand, and politics, by its very nature, is suspect, we are really in trouble! The problems facing us require *both* much greater conscious responsibility (beyond our immediate families' welfare) than perhaps human beings have ever before carried *and* highly developed group processes to conceive and carry out solutions.

Moreover, the core assumptions mentioned above—which define human beings as isolated atoms and social processes as ruled by absolute laws—block the development of a conceptual framework in which we might begin to conceive of solutions to today's multiple crises.

Paralyzing Social Trade-offs

The core assumptions of the modern worldview lock us into simplistic either/ors, constricting our imaginations. As long as the individual is conceived of as poised defensively against other social atoms, and thus against society, the most critical questions facing society get posed in terms of trade-offs. For example, we ask:

> Do we choose individual responsibility *or* social responsibility? Do we opt for government solutions that coddle people *or* for market solutions that spark individual initiative?

> Similarly, do we choose private, dispersed economic decisionmaking through the free market or do we choose centralized, governmental decisionmaking that undercuts the market?

In each, the answer is predetermined in the question itself. Encouraged to believe that we can only make the best of bad trade-offs, what we have now, no matter how bad it is, appears to be about the best we can hope for. Paralysis results.

The Public/Private Confusion

Yet another critical obstacle to a conceptual framework in which to seek solutions is the confusion over what is public and what is private. In our society, we absorb the notion that the more decisions we can keep private, the freer we are. The more decisions we allow to become public (that is, political), the less freedom we enjoy as individuals. Economic life is part of the private realm; government, part of the public. And so it follows that protecting freedom means keeping government out of economic life.

As the pieces of the modern worldview were taking shape in the seventeenth and eighteenth centuries, such a stance did indeed reflect the experience of many. Property holders sought backing for their right to control their own property, free of interference from the Crown. Small farmers, shopkeepers, and cottage industries were the heart of economic life, in which the economic unit was the family. Even as late as the 1870s, two-thirds of American workers were found in agriculture, forestry, and fishing.

But economic life has evolved. Today's primary economic decisionmakers are large economic bureaucracies, many with resources and power exceeding that of major nation-states. The annual revenue of Cargill, the world's largest grain trader, for example, exceeds that of the gross domestic product of Egypt, Greece, or Pakistan. The world's four largest corporations have a combined annual revenue greater than the combined gross domestic product of eighty countries comprising half the world's population. Yale political philosopher Robert Dahl argues that these large corporate bureaucracies have in many ways more influence over our well-being than does government.[2]

Today large corporations love to cloak themselves in private garb to maintain their privileged unaccountability to the well-being of the community. A few years ago, for example, Dow Chemical went so far as to protest that the Environmental Protection Agency had no right to inspect its operations because it was a legal "person" protected by the Fourteenth Amendment to the Constitution. In fact, it may be in assaults on the environment that we are paying the highest price for the myth that "private" economic decisionmaking by large corporate bureaucracies is outside the bounds of public deliberation. Barry Commoner estimates that chemical companies in the United States every year dump approximately eighty-five million metric tons of waste into the environment, furthering environmental decline. Treating that waste, he says, would consume the entire profits of the chemical industry.[3] In other words, no acceptable solutions are possible once such an enormous problem has been created by entities unaccountable to the common welfare.

Clearly, the past two centuries' transformation of economic life makes the old paradigm's distinction between public and private highly misleading and a major obstacle to our capacity to conceptualize solutions.

II. A DEMOCRATIC RENEWAL DRAWING ON ALTERNATIVE STRAINS WITHIN OUR CULTURE'S TRADITIONS

Given these long-standing, deeply embedded conceptual obstacles to democratic culture, how do we proceed? How do we even begin to think about addressing these inherited, now-dysfunctional, assumptions?

It has become a cliché of "development" experts who invade foreign cultures to "do good" that one first must appreciate the local culture in order to build on the best of inherited wisdom. It is understood that attempting wholesale introduction of new, foreign strategies is doomed. If this is pretty obvious advice for working in an alien culture, it surely applies to those who would seek to change their own. To be effective in moving our own culture toward greater democracy, we must build on the best of what has gone before. Arrogant dismissal of American culture as innately bad—mired in narrow individualism, materialism, and racism—will not take us far.

I am suggesting that, to move beyond the limitations of the modern worldview, *we must uncover constructive, alternative understandings within our own cultural traditions and build upon these.* We must see the alternative worldview, a postmodern worldview, that is implicit in our positive values.

Rethinking America's Public Values

All well and good, but how does one get at a worldview? Is it really possible consciously to address something so ubiquitous, amorphous, and vague as a worldview?

My suggestion is that we take it apart. The pieces of our worldview are reflected in what I call our *public values*. If a worldview is made up of unquestioned assumptions, they are manifest in our common definition of those values that knit the social fabric, those common definitions and rules that make our common life possible. Here in America such values include freedom, democracy, and fairness, to name only three. If we are to address the crisis of public life in America, we must therefore bring into open debate the meaning of such core public values.

My current work is precisely this: to cast our public values in sharp relief through dialogue. So my recent book, *Rediscovering America's Values*, is written in two voices. It is a dialogue about freedom, democracy, and fairness. One voice is my representation of the modern worldview (or what I there call the "Liberal paradigm"). The other voice is my own, hoping to express an emerging alternative perspective, one grounded in a view of human nature as socially constituted, not atomistic. The goal of my dialogue is to surface the largely unspoken assumptions embedded in our culture.

Let me touch upon two key public values—freedom and democracy—to give a flavor of what I mean.

Freedom: unlimited accumulation or unfettered human flowering? In late twentieth-century America, one definition of freedom has come to dominate. If in the modern worldview we are isolated egos and our stance toward one another is defensive, private property is a good weapon of defense. The more we have, the freer we are, the less we have to listen to others. Freedom easily becomes defined as *unrestricted accumulation*—a view captured particularly well by Ronald Reagan when, in 1983, he proclaimed: "What I want to see above all else is that this country remain a country where someone can always get rich."

So by 1989, the gap between rich and poor had become a widening chasm: A Michael Milken made $1,000 a minute. In 1960 a chief executive officer made forty-one times as much as the factory worker. That was no small gap, but by 1988 it had more than doubled, to ninety-three times as much![4]

This view of freedom as individual freedom for unlimited accumulation is an aberration. We have a much longer tradition to turn to. In it freedom means freedom for human growth. What would it mean to reclaim a more ancient and yet newly emerging concept of freedom?

For many people—and in most religious traditions—freedom is not an end in itself. Rather, its purpose is the development of the uniquely human potentialities and of the individually unique potentialities of each person, be they intellectual, physical, artistic, or spiritual. Prerequisites to such development include freedom of expression, religion, and participation, and more basically freedom from physical assault (both direct assault and indirect assault through deprivation of life's necessities).

Freedom so understood is not finite, so there are no trade-offs. My artistic development need not detract from yours. Your intellectual advances need not reduce my ability to develop my own intellectual powers. Assurances of my protection from physical assault, including my right to subsistence, need not prevent you from enjoying equal protection. This is true because sufficient resources already exist in virtually all countries to guarantee basic economic rights for everyone, as our institute documents in *Food First* and *World Hunger: Twelve Myths*, among other works.

Not only is freedom so defined not a zero-sum equation, but its sum is greater than its parts. Not only does your freedom to develop your unique gifts not have to limit my expression: My development in part *depends upon* your freedom. How, for example, can I deepen my appreciation and enjoyment of music unless you, with much greater musical talent, are free to develop your gift? Or how can you develop your full potential physical health unless someone else, with talents in science and medicine, is free to cultivate those talents?

Expanding our understanding of freedom, we can see that, as the freedom of the poor is being thwarted by poverty and hunger, *so is the freedom of those who are well fed.* The failure of our society to protect economic rights means that all of its members are deprived of the intellectual breakthroughs, spiritual insights, musical gifts, and athletic achievements of those whose development has been blocked by poverty and hunger.

Freedom understood as the right to unlimited accumulation of productive property is finite and divisible. Freedom so understood produces a trade-off, competitive mentality. But freedom to develop our unique capacities is infinite and indivisible. Freedom so understood produces a cooperative spirituality in which mutual aid is predominant.

Democracy: particular institutions or principles defining a way of life? A second of our public values is democracy. What is it? Is it an institution? Elections, political parties? In many societies there are both of these institutions, while the vast majority of citizens live in misery, unable to ensure that these institutions answer to even their most minimal needs. I think of the Philippines and many of the countries in Central America.

Have we mistakenly conflated our institutions and our values themselves? Perhaps democracy is *not* particular institutions after all. It might better be conceived as a set of working principles that determines a way of life.

The central principle of democracy is accountability, the linking of rights with responsibility. Those empowered to make decisions are responsible to all who must live with those decisions. Accountability requires, of course, the sharing of power. Although an *equal* sharing of power is beyond human reach, democracy means that no one is denied *all* power. Because eating and feeding one's offspring come first for all living creatures, people have been robbed of power wherever they go chronically hungry amidst adequate food. Democracy, so understood, is belied by the very existence of hunger.

Once we have grasped democracy as a set of interlocking principles, much changes: We discover that these principles apply equally to economic as to political life. Indeed, a most fatal mistake in the history of our democracy has been its narrowing, its constriction, so that we have come to see its application only in political life.

With freedom understood as freedom for human growth and democracy understood as a set of principles, we gain confidence to meet today's crises. We need no longer cling to economic dogma, be it the market, unlimited control of property, or any other simple formulation. We are free to ask *how* such economic devices can be made to serve our deeper values, such as freedom and democracy, and adapt them to do just that.

With this relook at our core public values we are equipped to return to those obstacles that the modern worldview places in our paths: the paralyzing trade-offs and the confusion about public and private economic entities.

Beyond the Paralyzing Trade-offs

Government's role to foster individual responsibility. Once we have probed our public values, we can reframe the most basic questions facing every society. Above I suggested that the modern worldview sets individual responsibility off *against* government responsibility. From a social understanding of human meaning, we can now ask, rather: How can public responsibility *enhance* individual responsibility?

Responsibilities shouldered by government need not make people dependent. Rather, it is too often the *neglect* by government of its responsibilities that creates dependency. Some examples are reflected in today's horrifying statistics: Almost one-quarter of American children are now born into poverty; twelve million are not protected by health insurance; half a million are malnourished; and poor children are twice as likely to be below normal in their physical development.

Inadequate social provision hampers the ability of individuals to develop the self-esteem and practical skills essential for human beings to become responsible adults. There is less a trade-off than a *complement* between social responsibility and individual responsibility.

From the viewpoint of the modern paradigm, premised on suspicion of government, such social protection places too great a burden on society—it just costs too much! We can respond with some common sense: Let's tally up the burden on society in dollars of, say, providing a child with prenatal care, Headstart, a subsidized summer job, and four years of public college education. Now that total, roughly $40,000, comes to about what the government spends to keep one inmate in prison for just *seventeen months*. Society *will* pay, regardless, and it will pay more, much more, for its failure to aid the healthy development of its citizens.

So, postmodern politics requires, very practically, an entirely new approach to public fiscal planning. As long as the task is balancing the public ledger this year, we will continue to cut our own throats, neglecting the social investments in health, education, basic public infrastructure. This neglect drains us of future wealth. We must design a long-term approach to government budgeting that allows us to calculate the long-term gain and to invest in ourselves accordingly. But we will be unable to do so as long as we are unable to perceive the "social commons" in the first place, as long as we are trapped by an ideology that reduces society simply to its individual parts. We need a postmodern vision of our interrelatedness and mutual interests.

The market and government: complementary roles. In the same vein, we can go beyond the market-versus-government trade-off. If both are seen as mere tools in the service of community, rather than as absolutes, we can ask: How can these two useful features of our common life—market exchange and government—reinforce each other? What is the appropriate role of each?

We can see that a healthy market economy *depends upon* a democratic government, one actively ensuring that income and wealth are spread widely. Otherwise, we face what we have today: an economy in which 10 percent of the population controls 86 percent of our financial wealth. Many are made too poor to participate in the market. So the market is stymied and highly skewed. And demand for caviar at Bloomingdale's booms while soup-kitchen lines lengthen. We have luxury condos spreading but little housing that hourly-wage working people can afford.

The market and the government have distinct and complementary, not contradictory, roles in a healthy society: a democratically accountable government ensures the widest *distribution of resources*, so that all citizens have access to the means of self-reliance and self-development; whereas the market ensures the efficient *distribution of goods.* These functions complement each other.

The market and the polity govern different arenas of our lives. The market is most useful in expressing our private interests. We need the polity to express our values. As citizens we set the value parameters within which the market works, deciding what carries value in and of itself and therefore must be governed by decisions made through dialogue about principles—about what we believe *in*, not just about what we will pay *for*.

In 1987, for example, nearly three-fourths of Americans polled agreed that the Constitution should be amended to include the right to health care. Was this idle wishing? No, Americans were expressing the view that life—protection of life through health care—is of intrinsic value and therefore inappropriately left to market distribution. As philosopher Mark Sagoff has written: "A market . . . in anything we consider 'sacred' is totally inappropriate. These things have a *dignity* rather than a *price*."[5]

Beyond the Public/Private Confusion

But such thinking is only possible as we are, at the same time, clearing up our deep confusions about the very definition of public and private. We need publicly to explore *how to apply in economic life the principles of democratic accountability* now taken for granted in political life.

To face this challenge takes courage: We must reconsider the very governing structure of the corporate backbone of our economy, certainly the one hundred corporations that control 60 percent of all industrial assets.[6] Professor George Lodge of the Harvard Business School suggests, for example, that such firms be chartered nationally as well as by the local polities in which they operate. Their charters would spell out their responsibilities to the community. And governing boards of major firms would be elected in such a way that all long-term employees would have a voice in selecting management.[7]

In so doing, we move not toward an economy in which the distribution of goods is planned by a central agency, an idea that has been discredited throughout most of the world. As I have stated, the distribution of goods is well suited to the market governance. However, distribution of wealth and income, capital investment, job creation, and environmental protection belong to the domain of public concern.

III. RETHINKING POWER AND SELF-INTEREST: AN EXAMPLE OF POSTMODERN POLITICS

A reasonable challenge to all that I have said might well be that, no matter how "correct" the conceptual framework, it is far removed from daily life and suggests no means of actualization. In fact, however, I am suggesting a framework rich in possibilities for immediate application.

In the last several decades, we have seen in communities throughout America the emergence of a highly developed theory *and practice* of democracy reflecting many of the challenges to the modern worldview I have just outlined. In this theory and practice, human beings are understood as intensely social beings with innate needs not only for meaning but also for self-discovery and transformation in community.

One example is the network of community organizations—from Los Angeles to San Antonio to Brooklyn—associated with the Industrial Areas Foundation (IAF). The IAF was founded by the late Saul Alinsky, who is remembered for helping poor people get justice by confrontational techniques, overcoming wealth and official power by sheer numbers, doggedness, and ingenuity. Since Alinsky's death in 1972, his organization has moved far beyond its founding premises in a postmodern direction. It understands effective citizenship as a learned art, built upon specific concepts, skills, and values. This concept of citizenship offers a powerful challenge to the modern worldview.

Let me briefly note a few of the fundamentals of this emerging theory of democratic life. The IAF names as its core concepts public life, diversity, power, and self-interest.

Public life is no longer automatically suspect. It is understood to be as essential to our humanity as is private life. If, however, in private life we seek familiarity and homogeneity, the world of public life is *diversity*. Moreover, different values apply. In private life, loyalty and forgiveness are key virtues. In public life, these virtues are replaced by accountability.

Perhaps even more telling is the IAF concept of *power*. In the modern worldview, power is one-directional. It is the ability to make things happen: The cue-ball sinks the eight-ball in the corner pocket. That's power! Once we perceive the human essence as social, however, this unidirectional notion of power becomes unthinkable. Categories of actor and acted-upon are no longer mutually exclusive. Every interaction changes all parties involved. And from these insights it follows that no one is ever completely powerless, completely unable to influence others.

Equally important, the understanding of *self-interest* is transformed. In the modern worldview, self-interest and selfishness are indistinguishable, as simply that which serves the private gain of the individual "atom." But in the emerging alternative, represented in the organizing theories of the IAF, self-interest is much richer. Self-interest is one's arena of meaning, all the things that matter—one's family, friends, religious faith, work commitments, security, health, and so on. It is one's identity. So understood, self-interest is impossible to further except in relationships, both public and private. Selfishness becomes the enemy of self-interest. Rather than squelched or venally indulged, self-interest must be nurtured and developed in relationships with others—the very basis of constructive political engagement.

Actualizing such concepts, which underpin democratic culture, requires specific skills, taught and developed through practice and reflection. Such skills include listening, critical thinking, bargaining, and reflecting.

Such an approach to public life leads to a political practice in striking contrast to most of what passes for politics today. The modern worldview has led, not surprisingly, to a politics increasingly reduced to a marketplace model—that is, the selling of political ideas (or should I say images?) and candidates to passive consumers. Left and right alike have accepted this model, as soundbites and direct-mail pitches take the place of political discourse, debate, and reflection on public values.

What might a postmodern politics look like? Let me answer with an IAF illustration. In the fall of 1988, BUILD, an IAF affiliate in Maryland, defeated a slick, $6 million National Rifle Association campaign against gun control. Organizer Gerald Taylor explained BUILD's upset victory:

> BUILD's relational canvass differed significantly from a conventional canvass rap, where tightly time-bound, highly structured and mainly one way interaction takes place. In the BUILD-organized precincts, public discourse took place. Thousands of people were talked with and listened to. Questions about the nature of community and the relative merits of a law that was not perfect were discussed. In short, people were taken seriously as citizens. Time spent was more important than how many people were talked at.[8]

Not only are ordinary citizens involved as full human beings, instead of as market segments; public officials are also approached differently. When BUILD members held their first meeting with Senator

Paul Sarbanes, he began by asking them what demands they brought with them. "None," they responded, to the senator's amazement. "We came here to find out what *your* interests are: Why you ran for this office, and what you hope to achieve."

I suggest that a postmodern worldview opens the door to a new, yet very old, conception of citizenship and public life. In it, the political process is legitimate. Because our nature is social, politics is no artifice or threat to our autonomous nature. It is an expression of our social nature. The democratic process is no longer simply a means of protecting our individual selves. It is prized in its own right: Through it, we make and remake our social reality, and, in the process, remake ourselves through interaction with each other. Herein lies our hope.

IV. Concluding Remarks: No Shortcuts to Democratic Renewal

In the awareness of planetary crisis lies an unprecedented opportunity. The shock of realizing that humanity now faces ultimate stakes can force us to admit that the old approaches have failed. It can produce openness to new thoughts. This is good. But urgency has its pitfalls as well. In an era of awakening to catastrophic threats, the temptation to seek shortcuts is strong. If the sky is falling, have we time even to be talking about democratic renewal? Such suspicion only reinforces passivity, as the not-so-hidden message is that the "experts" must decide. Moreover, such a sense of crisis can lead to scorn for our own culture, seeing its presently dominant values, rightly, as part of the problem. In so thinking, we make ourselves blind to those strains in our cultural history that can be part of the *solution*.

Yet there can be no answer to any of the threats facing us outside a reinvigorated public life. Nothing less can challenge the myth that large corporate bureaucracies are private and thus outside public accountability. Nothing less can challenge the deepening chasm, worldwide, between wealth and life-stunting deprivation. Nothing less can reshape the choices we make each day that determine our impact on the biosphere.

In short, there is no way to short-circuit the re-creation of a democratic culture, reshaping our concepts of ourselves in relation to one another, if we are serious about addressing the threats to the biosphere itself. But where and how do we participate? In asking this question, I think of *Washington Post* columnist Colman McCarthy's recent reminder to me: "The trouble with all good ideas is that they soon degenerate into hard work." Indeed. So in closing I offer some thoughts on that hard work.

Work with Existing Organizations

First, more important than creating new institutions or organizations perfectly reflecting an emerging constructive postmodern vision, we need to infuse alternative understandings into all *existing* organizations and institutions that bring people together and form our sense of the possible.

To be specific, I am now co-convenor (with Harry Boyte of the Humphrey Institute in Minneapolis) of a national project, Project Public Life, reaching out to include organizations as disparate as the YMCA, the American Library Association, the 4-H Clubs, the youth service movement, community colleges, and the Industrial Areas Foundation network I highlighted above, among many others. Our goal is to create a national facilitating structure for what we call "schooling in the political arts," including the concepts of power, diversity, and self-interest and the skills of listening and reflection that make good judgment possible. Our project seeks to help existing organizations founded with a public mission to return to their original purpose of enhancing active citizenship, armed with new concepts and new capacities for teaching skills.

In such work a most obvious place to begin is where people are already engaged in discussion of civic life. The classroom is one. I wrote *Rediscovering America's Values* as a dialogue on public values in part to stir up such classroom discourse. An immediate goal is to transform dull, detached courses in government, political science, and philosophy—courses now reinforcing a sense of politics as a spectator sport—into charged interactive sessions. Young people can be challenged to grapple with their own values and life's purpose and begin to learn the skills for effective public life.

Also, through this process, issue-driven organizations—from toxic-waste to campaign-reform groups—can deepen their understanding of their own purposes. Issue campaigns can become tools not just for winning specific battles but for dignifying and deepening public life itself. This requires that the one-directional approach to communication—canvass and direct mail—be supplemented or replaced with emphases on (1) stimulating dialogue on values toward a deeper sense of purpose, (2) creating ongoing public spaces where such dialogue can occur, and (3) learning the concepts and skills necessary to sustain citizen engagement over time.

In such work, a caveat: While it may be appropriate to supplement conventional language in order to convey a postmodern vision—to popularize words such as *communitarian, bioregional, decentralism,* and *win-win*—let's restrain our temptation to create a new language. By all means let's not abandon the terms that evoke the best of our people's traditions. If we are to reach beyond the narrow circles represented by the already converted, we must learn to define and use in liberating ways the language of our own culture. *Freedom, democracy, fairness*: these beautiful words we must reclaim for a postmodern vision.

We Need Not Change Human Nature!

Now, my final point. The democratic culture that is the subject of my talk presumes that our very survival depends upon our capacity to transcend the modern paradigm of social atomism. Let us be careful to make clear, however, that this path does *not* require remaking human nature. Throughout modern history those seeking social change have been attacked for seeking to reconstruct human nature, leading inevitably to totalitarian impositions—creating the "new socialist man," for example.

Let us make clear that we are building on traits already embedded in the human psyche. I will mention three.

First is an innate sense of connectedness to each other's well-being, intuitive feelings evolving from our tribal origins. Indeed, it is the modern paradigm's notion of the autonomous individual that now appears as philosophical and biological flight of fancy. Even Charles Darwin—misused for so long to defend dog-eat-dog individualism—believed that evolving human beings could have sustained and expanded our societies only because of "moral sense . . . aboriginally derived from the social instincts." Among primeval people, Darwin observed, actions were no doubt judged good or bad "solely as they obviously affect the welfare of the tribe."[9] Similarly, Adam Smith, so long identified as the celebrator of individual self-seeking, argued that human beings deeply appreciated their interdependency. He wrote in *The Theory of Moral Sentiments* (1790):

> [Man] is sensible . . . that his own interest is connected with the prosperity of society, and that the happiness, perhaps the preservation of his existence, depends upon its preservation.[10]

And this view of our nature is increasingly confirmed by comparative sociology, anthropology, and psychology. Recent studies find the roots of empathy in infancy, noting that infants react to the pain of others as though it were happening to themselves.[11]

My point here is that the challenge is not to *create* the "social instincts," as Darwin called them; it is to ask how we have denied them and how we call them forth again, now that they are so crucial to our survival.

Second, the approach to the future I am suggesting assumes a human need for *purpose*. Again, I rest not on wishful thinking. Psychologists now confirm that most people have a greater sense of well-being when they contribute to something they care about beyond themselves. In fact, many psychologists argue, our mental health depends on it.[12]

Third, and finally, an approach based upon the possibility of profound historic, personal, and social change assumes—does it not?—that we human beings are not only capable of feeling our interdependency, are not only creatures in need of purpose, but are also *creative* beings. And here, above all, we can turn to our own society's roots. I love to remind Americans that our nation was founded on the belief that indeed something new is possible under the sun. At the time, many considered the principles of our Declaration of Independence to be utter madness! James Madison near his death said that Americans proved what before was believed impossible. And Thomas Jefferson believed people to be capable of infinite creativity, writing that "laws and institutions must go hand in hand with the progress of the human mind."[13] Our very birthright as Americans is the capacity to envision and consciously create historic change.

As we face today's enormous challenges to ourselves and to our planet, as we realize the profoundly constraining assumptions within the modern worldview, I leave you with the provocative words of philosopher Lewis Mumford:

> [In such a time] our main handicap will be lack of imagination. . . .
> This is one of those times when only the dreamers will turn out to
> be practical men.

NOTES

1. Benjamin Barber, *Strong Democracy: Participatory Politics for a New Age* (Berkeley and Los Angeles: University of California Press, 1984), especially chap. 8.

2. Robert A. Dahl, *Dilemmas of Pluralist Democracy* (New Haven and London: Yale University Press, 1982), 184.

3. Barry Commoner, "A Reporter at Large: The Environment," *New Yorker*, 15 June 1987: 52.

4. Roy A. Schotland, "Rich Get Even Richer," letter to the editor, *New York Times*, 14 May 1989: E22.

5. Mark Sagoff, *The Economy of the Earth* (New York: Cambridge University Press, 1988), 69.

6. Nancy Folbre (Center for Popular Economics), *A Field Guide to the U.S. Economy* (New York: Pantheon, 1987), figure 1.8. Data are from *Federal Reserve Bulletins* and refer to all nonbanking corporations. For a comprehensive study of concentration, see Edward S. Herman, *Corporate Control: Corporate Power* (New York: Cambridge University Press, 1981), especially chap. 6.

7. George C. Lodge, *The New American Ideology* (1975; New York: New York University Press, 1986).

8. Gerald Taylor, "Preliminary Notes: Democracy and Organizing in the '80s," *Democracy Notes* 1/1 (February, 1989): 8.

9. Charles R. Darwin, *The Descent of Man and Selection in Relation to Sex* (New York: D. Appleton, 1909), 121.

10. Adam Smith, *Theory of Moral Sentiments*, part 2, section 2, chap. 3.

11. Daniel Goleman, "The Roots of Empathy are Traced to Infancy," *New York Times*, 28 March 1989: B1.

12. For an introduction and excellent bibliography to the debate on human motivation, see Michael A. Wallach and Lise Wallach, *Psychology's Sanction for Selfishness* (San Francisco: Freeman, 1983).

13. *Thomas Jefferson: Writings*, ed. Merrill D. Peterson (New York: Library of America/Liberty Classics), 1401.

9

A POSTMODERN PRESIDENCY FOR A POSTMODERN WORLD

Richard Falk

I. PROLOGUE

While I was first beginning to work on this paper some time back, a friend during dinner asked the dreaded question, "What are you working on?"

After a few seconds of nervous hesitation I responded confidently, "A paper on the postmodern presidency."

As might be expected, my friend, high spirited yet focused on immediate concerns, responded, "What on earth is that?"

"Well," I said, rather lamely, "that's what I'm trying to write about; it's really an attempt to discuss the sort of leadership we need for political life in the next century."

"Oh, now I know what you're talking about," said this now quite animated lady, herself a prominent writer, "you mean a president who could talk to the American people the way FDR did at his weekly fire-side chats. That would be wonderful. We need a president who spoke to citizens as if they were *really* people."

"Yes, that would indeed be helpful," I responded, "but that's not what my paper is about. You are imagining a more admirable or suit-able person filling the post, but that, in my way of thinking, is a longing for a good, as distinct from a bad, *modern* president, decidedly not a postmodern president."

Growing restive, if not impatient, my friend muttered, "There you go again, Richard, living in a California dreamscape instead of leading a march on Gaza or Johannesburg, something real and useful."

I protested one last time, "No, I think this is useful. I am trying to describe the kind of president we will need if my grandchildren are to have the sort of leadership that will be necessary and desirable early in the next century, and I am convinced that the requirements for such a presidency cannot be derived from the models of greatness we have in the past, that Washington, Jefferson, Lincoln, and Franklin Roosevelt were all great *modern* presidents, and we now require something quite different, even for the survival of our species, and for the well-being of this particular country."

Whether wearying or convinced, my companion revived, replying, "Yes, I see, but tell me one last thing. What can you possibly add to the discussion by using that fashionable, yuppy, New Age, literary-chic word *postmodern*?"

By now fervently wishing I had fended off the initial question, I remembered Marianne Moore's famous line about poetry—"I, too, dis-like it"—and I responded almost as if I enjoyed this third-degree set piece: "I, too, dislike *postmodern* for all the reasons you say, and I even have a few more of my own, but still in the end it remains efficient, seemingly indispensable, if specified carefully.[1] I am trying in this paper of mine to argue that there was a cultural posture and ascendent mind-set connected with being 'modern' that gave us the world we inhabit, with some of its glories and many of its dangers. And further, that this modern world as now constituted and functioning is not sustainable, that it has been moving rapidly into a self-destructive mode that seems quite irreversible, and that something quite new must soon emerge to enable human intervention on the basis of sustainable and constructive behavior, including a mind-set that transcends modernism by recon-ceiving the character of reality itself. A postmodern president, then, would be infused with this reoriented consciousness, and since we can't specify its properties except in relation to modernism, and because it comes after modernism, historically, it makes sense to convey what is meant by this admitted millstone of a word, *postmodern.*[2] Now, let's order dinner. Even if you beg me, I won't say another word about postmodernism, except that I'll send you the paper if it ever gets finished."

Despite this dismal prelude, we actually had a pleasant meal discussing such standard modernist concerns as the plight of the democracy movement in China and whether we as a people will end up being "bored" by the Vietnam War, with all the movies and postmortems. Pondering the overall rhythm of our conversation, I realize that it is not at all necessary to give up modernist concerns just because I feel strongly the magnetic pull of postmodernism.

II. FURTHER CLARIFICATIONS

Any inquiry of this sort is bedeviled by the claim that the term *postmodern* means something decisively different from *modern* when it comes to presidential leadership. Of course, a postmodern sensibility may influence or even dominate the outlook of someone who looks, speaks, and dresses in a typically modern fashion.

Consider the example of Mikhail Gorbachev. He briefly captured the political imagination of the world in the late 1980s by innovative leadership of the then Soviet state, as well as by bold vision of an altered order of relationships in world politics. Was he a great modern leader, or postmodern, or some confused combination? How are we to classify such a phenomenon of recent history? And if we can't, what can it possibly mean to contrast modernist with postmodernist?

The safe answer is that Gorbachev seems a bewitching mixture. He embodied the constructive potential of modernist leadership, yet perceived some of the needs of a postmodern world. Gorbachev was modernist insofar as his energies were devoted to the hopelessly difficult task of reforming the Soviet state. He failed dismally to make the Soviet economy work better and was utterly unable to improve the life of the Soviet people. Yet, there was always more to Gorbachev than this struggle to make the Soviet system work better. It is all but forgotten that in the early years of his presidency Gorbachev was prepared to repudiate nuclearism altogether and even to commit the Soviet state to the startling notion that war had become obsolete as a viable and rational instrument of statecraft; and further, Gorbachev better than his Western counterparts seemed to understand clearly that global-scale environmental problems can be overcome only if a more centralized system of world order is brought into being.[3] Of course, these perceptions were obscured and tempered somewhat by efforts to make his leadership credible for "modernist" constituencies, especially in his own country. Gorbachev's credibility, such as it was, depended on such diverse matters as adhering to a conventional dress code and continuing to act as if territorial sovereignty remained a viable basis for national security and as if potential enemies were more dangerous than the world political system itself. It is too early for a political leader of an important state to embrace fully the posture of a postmodernist.[4] Anyone who went beyond what Gorbachev attempted would be quickly discredited as "unstable" or "utopian"; the claims of modernism to dominate our sense of "the real" remain powerfully entrenched, especially in reigning governmental bureaucracies and their generally supportive and pliant media infrastructures.

It is still far too early to assess Gorbachev's legacy. We are now understandably entranced by the Soviet collapse and by Gorbachev's disappearance from the political scene. Gorbachev is remembered now largely for his failed attempt to bring about economic and political reform in the Soviet Union and for his refusal to reverse course in response to pressures mounted by hard-line reactionary forces in the Kremlin. Forgotten, at this stage, were the postmodern initiatives in foreign policy that Gorbachev launched with such imaginative flair—the acceptance of the restraints of international law, the engagement with nuclear disarmament, the sense that the United Nations needed to evolve into a mechanism that sustained global security, and, above all, the bold appreciation of the high seriousness of global-scale environmental challenges that could be met only by a combination of ambitious cooperative mechanisms and a shift away from consumerist values. We need to recover this attempt to initiate postmodern leadership and wonder why its emergence has been so slow in the capitalist West.

We have confirmations of this concern under the far more muted circumstances of U.S. presidential leadership. Leaders await their retirement to warn us of the dangers of the nuclear age, or they leave their postmodern concerns behind as soon as they enter the White House door. Even Ronald Reagan, a conservative president, could not escape the stern discipline of modernist guardians of realist orthodoxy. Returning from Reykjavik in 1986 after having endorsed a Soviet proposal to eliminate *all* nuclear weapons by stages before the year 2000, he was attacked from all sides of the political spectrum, and most fiercely by Democrats, as "unprepared" or incompetent. Suddenly, this leader, who until then had effortlessly deflected any criticism and withstood snafu after snafu, had now challenged, surely unwittingly, a major tenet of the modernist consensus, and had to be made to back down by the keepers of geopolitical orthodoxy. And, indeed, Reagan got the message and turned his back on what the world had found so hopeful and exhilarating about the Iceland summit. Bush's rejection of the Earth Summit consensus on the need to cut back on carbon dioxide emissions is one more confirmation that the cult of the modern continues to dominate the corridors of power in the United States.

The most we can expect by way of postmodernist leadership these days are "intimations" (veiled indications of a radical shift in style and substance), "closet adherents" (disguised and suppressed reorientations), "apocalyptic warnings" embedded in farewell speeches, and "voices from the wilderness" (the prophetic cries of those situated beyond the corridors of power).[5] Possibly, one can imagine a Shakespearean fool infiltrating the White House as a consultant and gaining access to the inner recesses of presidential power, then using her wit to deflower the vain pretensions of modernism, especially in some of its more lethal forms.

To be postmodern is not necessarily to be ethically superior. Let's express the position differently: It will be inevitable that the next century will be postmodern *in some sense* as modernism is being superseded by various levels of globalism. A positive variant of postmodernism is far from inevitable and seems unlikely from our present vantage point.

As matters now stand, "the lords of the global village," to use Ben Bagdikian's expressive phrase,[6] may well emerge as the nonterritorial media moguls who are moving rapidly to monopolize control of images and information on a "for profit" basis, wiring the planet into a single grid. Such reconfigurings of "power" seem likely to supersede modernist hierarchies and to reduce the presidency of even a powerful state to "an office" responsive to the wishes of a newly ascendant economic elite with a transnational base of operations and loyalties.[7] It is unlikely to be responsive to human suffering or ecological decay, but it is likely to be dedicated to achieving degrees of technocratic stability sufficient for the maintenance of this new, globally constituted, economic hierarchy.

Such a postmodern presidency could be little more than a ceremonial nexus, essentially diversionary, serving to pacify mass attitudes. Modernism—with its stress on territorial efficiency and materialist satisfactions—earlier overwhelmed the feudal order and in Europe reduced the absolute royal leader to such a ritual figure.[8] The king or queen of England has continued to be the subject of veneration within the British domain, but the power of governance shifted elsewhere in the glorious Revolution of 1688 and its aftermath. Leaders such as Mitterand, Kohl, and Reagan have succeeded by becoming ceremonial presences rather than true centers of authority and legitimacy. Power has passed elsewhere, especially to the media lords, but generally to the cutting edge of financial and business operations, quite literally to the peddlers of "junk bonds" and the master manipulators of "insider information"; the criminalization of such scapegoated antiheroes as Ivan Boesky or Michael Milken is but a small diversionary maneuver in the forced march to the new capitalist wonderland of electronic information providing a charismatic possibility of generating fantastic paper wealth. Without satisfying a single basic need or even producing one more product, the players in this new game (called "casino capitalism" by Susan Strange) have, for the moment, found an alchemical formula by which money begets money. In the meantime, misery persists, homelessness grows, the environment decays. Statistical data are to the decline of modernism what steel, coal, and oil were to its ascent.

Perhaps, in this very negative interpretation of the future (as present), we have already achieved a postmodern presidency of sorts, and the use of words like *teflon* to describe the role captures something of this development. It was not Reagan, as much as the office itself, whose role had changed. The original notion of government anchored upon an energetic executive was a modernist fable no longer applicable.[9] George Bush's rudderless leadership seems also expressive of a disturbing and disorienting form of postmodern emergence. Is Bush a nice guy because he smiles well and looks fit for his age even if his first veto was cast to prevent raising the minimum wage to a level enabling tolerable subsistence?

Of course, the citizenry is as much to blame as the presidency. A symbiotic relationship is present, sustained and construed by the media. We, as citizens, get from the White House what we seek, and this has been systemized in the form of pricey media consultants and celebrated interpreters of public opinion polls. If we want a more responsive presidency, we must begin by awakening the citizenry from its long sleep. At this stage, this sedative image of the modern presidency is no more than a partial tendency—at worst, a robust conjecture. It is surely possible, even likely, that a modernist restoration will occur, especially in face of external challenge and fully justified renewed fears of an "imperial presidency."[10]

My intention in this essay is to proceed along a normative line of vision. I believe that the superseding of modernism is occurring before our eyes and that it is not generally a pretty picture, but I see also the possibility of preferred forms of postmodernism emerging and informing the political life of the future, including that of the governing process in this country.[11]

It is also accurate to regard the perspective taken here as postmodern rather than antimodern.[12] The modern mind-set brilliantly enabled a surge of materialist progress that mitigated the hardship of premodern life for the great majority, undermined the economic basis of slavery, and extended and enriched life through the formidable agency of technological innovation. In political settings, modernism functioned most successfully at the scale of the territorial state, rendered secure by its military prowess and by achieving through diplomacy "a balance of power."

Until this century, the United States could remain on the sidelines and observe the often costly workings of balancing mechanisms as operative in Europe. The United States was blessed in these modernist senses with a naturally insulated geography, abundant resources, and an inspired and inspiring initial political leadership (the revolutionary generation of "the framers"). It is no wonder that the United States is perceived by others and itself as the miracle of modernism and remains, accordingly, reluctant to prepare itself for the approaching sunset. The American version of the Edenic myth is so strong that no amount of contrary experience seems capable of dispelling it.

Such reluctance is especially strong in relation to political institutions. The U.S. government has proved remarkably durable over time and has exhibited considerable flexibility during periods of stress and crisis. There exists an almost mystical belief that great presidents emerge in U.S. history as needed—Lincoln at the time of civil war, Roosevelt at a moment of severe economic depression and overseas challenge. Such an optimistic outlook anticipates a continuing capacity to find the leaders we need and to associate that inherent strength with the nature of the political system. Waiting for a postmodern presidency then consists in just that, waiting. If needed, she or he will appear. There is no occasion or opportunity to intervene by way of institutional reform.

There are two related aspects of this modernist argument:

(1) Modernism need not be repudiated in its historic mission in building strong, prosperous territorial states nor in its encouraging the creativity and individuality of the human person; the process of surveying the prospects of postmodern politics is based on the existence of a *different* historic mission for the peoples of the next century.

(2) The United States' political adaptation of modernism in its constitutional process has been particularly successful in creating an engine of prosperity and happiness for the great majority of its people,

and the presidency has been properly understood as integral to this success. Those who suffer are generally regarded not as "victims," but as "losers," having been given in some degree "an opportunity." The continuing moral, as well as political and economic, validity of the American claim to have achieved a superior polity is confirmed by the flood of immigration (legal and illegal), the relatively greater willingness of the United States to invite refugees and immigrants to share in its blessings, and the validation of market-oriented constitutionalism associated with the ending of the cold war.

Despite this resilience, the modernist path to the future is blocked at every step. The new circumstance of modernism is evident in the opening sentence of an editorial appearing in a prominent newspaper: "It is ironic—tragic, in fact—that new generations of US nuclear weapons coming off the assembly line seem to be more of a threat to Americans than to any perceived enemy."[13] Such an assertion, made before the disappearance of the Soviet threat, is not an anomaly, as the editorial implies, but a metaphor for dying modernism. How can an American president lead unless he supports policy adjustments implied by this metaphor? Yet if he were to do so, he would no longer be "fit" to be president. Catch-22 is not just a wry commentary on military life. It is at the core of our intellectual and political confusion about a situation in which old values and beliefs remain entrenched in existing institutions while new values and beliefs are still in their infancy or even struggling to be born.

A final image might clarify my understanding of the radical separation of modern and postmodern when it comes to presidential role and identity. During the closing stages of World War II, the U.S. government made two momentous decisions that seemed to carry into history the extreme, absurdist logic of wartime modernism: a refusal to "waste" bombs, planes, and pilots by destroying the tracks carrying trainloads of Jewish refugees to Auschwitz, and the decision to use atomic bombs against Hiroshima and Nagasaki, despite the incipient military defeat of Japan, based on the principal rationale of "saving lives," mainly American lives. (This rationale was based, in turn, on the highly conjectural assumption that otherwise the main islands of Japan would be invaded, allegedly generating far greater overall casualties.)[14]

It is, of course, hopelessly speculative to insist as a matter of empirical prediction that a postmodern president could not endorse comparable policies in circumstances of perceived emergency to the political future of the United States. The argument developed here is normative and conceptual. A postmodern president would not deploy violence through reference to a *calculative logic* about war goals, but would at the very least regard *innocent civilians* as impermissible targets under *any* circumstances, nor would civilian victims of Hitler's genocidal policies be regarded as less valuable than combat troops, including those who are American citizens.

A postmodern president would act on the basis of a *normative* orientation toward the value of human life without sharply distinguishing "friend" and "foe," "us" and "them."

A postmodern president in our understanding is *conceptually incapable* of neglecting the claims for relief of those faced with threats of genocide and *could not* decree the use of weapons of mass destruction against cities, people, and animals.

III. THE MODERNIST PRESIDENCY

To comprehend the American presidency as a political institution, it is helpful to reconsider the leading idea that animated the approach taken to the whole project of establishing a new political order in the United States as a sequel to the American Revolution. Those much-celebrated Founding Fathers were deeply influenced by the intellectual climate associated with the Enlightenment, especially by an implicit confidence in the motive force of human reason as an assured vehicle of progress.

What held sway in this constitution-building moment was reason, not as an abstraction but as an expression of political identity and historical experience. America of the 1780s and 1790s was constituted by thirteen separate sovereignties that had cooperated to prevail in a war of independence, and much of its then current leadership had come to realize that the survival and well-being of these immigrant nations could be best safeguarded if they formed some more durable form of union. This union needed to occur in a form that vindicated the repudiation of British rule and expressed something distinctively American about the nature of political community. Such an outlook helps explain the emergence of *American exceptionalism*, the claim that the United States has a special reformist mission in the international order, early formulated as a city on a hill, a light unto the nations, even a new Jerusalem.[15]

The U.S. Constitution represented a brilliant, inspired response to these requirements, embodying reason, reconciling the constituent sovereignties of the former colonies with a newly conceived shared sovereignty, learning from Britain while basing government on a republican conception of legitimacy, and yet not challenging dubious features of existing societal practices, including slavery, exclusion of women, and denial of rights to, and displacement of, Indian nations.

Such difficult societal tensions were buried in the constitutional process, lurking within broad abstractions. There were two understandings of "reason" that exerted influence then and have remained active in the life of American society. There is the Jeffersonian view of reason as eventually ensuring human mastery over nature, with science enabling reality itself to be comprehended as a series of "laws," and of human history as unfolding as if guided by a kind of machine. Such a view was highly secular, pushing religion into the background, and tending to suppose that education of the citizenry would ensure a steady improvement in the human situation, especially as a consequence of the inventiveness of the technological imagination. This image of the role of reason was basically optimistic about the future and has provided the ideological underpinning of industrial civilization and its materialist ethos.

The second image of reason was far more troubled about the human situation. Its basic perception was that of powerful destructive tendencies arising from the fallen condition of humanity and from within the human psyche itself. The contrast is well expressed by Adam Gopnik: "The ideal of reason celebrated in David and in Diderot— clear purpose, expressed in purified form—is far from the tragic ideal of reason that moved Burke and Voltaire, whose sense of the overwhelming power of the irrational in life made them see reason not as a firm ground of human action but as a bridge across the abyss of human fear."[16] A contemporary political figure such as Henry Kissinger personifies this darker view of reality and regards the future as fraught with danger. Reason is an indispensable tool in the ongoing struggle to impose some temporary order on the chaotic forces of nature and human impulse, mainly by instilling fear in the minds of militarily weaker rivals. The ultrarationality of deterrence theory as a management technique for nuclear weaponry during the period of the cold war is illustrative of this second conception of reason. As Gopnik suggests, this outlook is "tragic" and generates pessimistic assessments of the future.

The political arrangements that have produced our constitutional order embody this tension without ever attempting to resolve it, and the political history of our country exhibits both of these central tendencies of reason. On the one side, as Garry Wills puts it, "The Constitution was an ingeniously constructed Enlightenment machine of 'counterpoises.' "[17] On the other side, it was dominated by a concern about excess and abuse, exhibiting little confidence in enlightened leadership or in the capacity of an educated citizenry to provide "reasonable" leadership or guidance. The relevance of such concerns was addressed by James Madison in his famous essay in *The Federalist*, No. 10, which specified the menace of "faction" (that is, "a number of citizens, whether amounting to a majority or minority of the whole, who are united and actuated by some common impulse of passion, or of interest, adverse to the rights of other citizens, or to the permanent and aggregate interests of the community").[18] Reason is balanced by the dark unknowns connected with public passions, and, more remotely, with original sin; government is presented simultaneously as a vehicle for assured progress and as a desperate defense against the irrational.

The presidency emerged out of these unresolved tensions. Its outward form represented a compromise between those who wanted a king and those who believed in legislative supremacy. As originally constructed, the president was generally perceived, except during wartime, as definitely subordinate to Congress. Tocqueville ruefully observed: "This dependence of the executive power is one of the inherent vices of republican constitutions. The Americans could not eliminate that tendency which leads legislative assemblies to take over the government, but they make it less irresistible."[19] Yet from the outset of the republic, a series of strong presidential personalities defied these perceptions by focusing our understanding of political authority in this country directly on the person of the president.

Hamilton in *The Federalist*, No. 70, declares that "All men of sense agree in the necessity of an energetic executive" and suggests that the only concern is how to reconcile such an objective with "other ingredients which constitute safety in the republican sense." As elsewhere in the constitutional arrangement, the challenge is met by offsetting capabilities and by specifying limits on authority. The president functions within the system of checks and balances associated with the separation of powers as between legislative, executive, and judicial branches, and within a framework that includes the acknowledgment of inalienable rights of the citizenry.

The evolution of the presidency has not challenged these basic parameters. The constitutional arrangement has seemed validated by its unsurpassed durability and by its capacity to generate effective responses to serious internal and external crises. The American Civil War, cyclical economic downturns, but especially the Great Depression, the two world wars, and the management of both the cold war and nuclear weapons, are seen as the essential tests.

An impressive aspect of the presidency has been the emergence of gifted leaders at times of crisis who have enhanced the office, accepting the popular mandate of leadership, while turning back from any fundamental encroachment upon the basic system of checks and balances, including the fundamental commitment of government to electoral challenge and oppositional activity. Certainly Lincoln and Franklin Roosevelt rose brilliantly to the occasion of crisis. When Richard Nixon was deeply challenged by the Watergate disclosures, he was persuaded to resign from the presidency.

The presidency has definitely expanded over time, both relative to the other branches and absolutely. Its control over resources and instruments of destruction has grown well beyond earlier expectations. The complexity of society, the weakening of statehouse government, the extension of national security concerns to peacetime, and the active overseas role of the United States in all regions of the world have given the presidency a particular salience in the contemporary world. To the extent to which foreign affairs dominates the public agenda, the president dominates government. These developments are strongly reinforced by the centrality of visual mass media, especially given the media's tendency to be preoccupied with the center of the center.

At the same time, there is some sense that the presidency has entered an entropic phase in recent decades. First of all, as a consequence of emergency powers, an enormous peacetime military budget, the routinization of covert operations, and the antidemocratic character of war making (especially relevant to possible uses of nuclear weaponry), a genuine concern has surfaced that the original scheme based on balance and coordinate branches of government could no longer protect the citizenry against abuses of governmental authority.[20] The government is becoming a presidential system—an elected king of temporary tenure proposed by political parties that offer the citizenry a choice of tweedledee and tweedledum on fundamental issues of governance. Presidential campaigns have become media contests, and public discourse has become trivialized, generating disaffection and widespread indifference among the public. This assessment does not imply that elections and the socioeconomic and geopolitical outlook of the president are of no consequence. Reagan's White House years were a disaster for the poor, brought much added bloodshed to Central America and South Africa, and accelerated the arms race. A more liberal president would not have duplicated these policies but might well have produced equivalent suffering by finding it more difficult than Reagan did to allow an ally like Marcos to collapse in 1986 and by being less able than a conservative to let go of some weapons systems or of the cold-war approach to U.S./Soviet relations. That is, the identity of the president has some definite policy significance, but the net assessment of these policy effects does not produce clear normative results.

Two related processes of deterioration have converged: Presidential encroachment under the banner of national security eroded the premises of republicanism, and contemporary political rivalry entered a phase in which issues of principle were subordinated to matters of time and image. Alongside an anxiety about an "imperial presidency" has appeared a complementary concern about a "trivial presidency."[21]

Interpreting this kind of institutional entropy from the perspective of modernist orientations suggests a line of explanation. The more assertive features of the departure from the earlier constitutional conceptions of equilibrium are a consequence of the breakdown of "normalcy" in international relations, especially with respect to war and peace. The technology of war, the interpenetration of political and economic forces, and the transnational visible and invisible flows of money, people, drugs, poisons, and images across state boundaries produces the multilevel penetration of territorial sovereignty that threatens the fundamental function of government to defend territorial boundaries and uphold security. An aggressive assertion of new executive powers is a desperate, yet futile, attempt to respond to this challenge by conventional means, that is, by unilateral regulatory and defensive capability of sufficient magnitude. The response is both "unconditional" and a failure if measured pragmatically.

The situation can be summarized: The modern presidency was conceived to facilitate "life, liberty, and property" for citizens (an elite, patriarchal category) in a republican form of democratic polity. This project rested upon the premise of defensible, impermeable boundaries and a widely shared sense of public satisfaction within domestic society. Ultimate security was associated with waging and winning wars overseas and sustaining a healthy economy at home. In this respect, World War II and its aftermath represented the apotheosis of the American achievement but also initiated processes that have subverted the stability of the original conception.

As matters now stand, the only way to protect the well-being of Americans is to uphold the global interests of humanity as a whole, an essentially nonterritorial imperative. There is no sustainable way of creating territorial enclaves of "security" by walls and military capabilities. The territorial state has become an illusion and has been silently replaced by the porous state.

At the same time, the continued territorial, military orientation of the United States encroaches both on popular sovereignty and civil liberties at home and on the autonomy and well-being of foreign sovereign states caught up in the maelstrom of destructive geopolitics. There is a mismatch between exposure to destruction and harm and the distribution of political authority associated with the territorial state and the states system. The constitutional problem is in its essence a world-order problem.

Similarly, preservation of the global commons (air, water, resources, space, polar regions) is marginal to the traditional concerns and operations of the states system. Some flexibility and resilience have been displayed by states in their unilateral and cooperative efforts to regulate some activities pertaining to the global commons, but there is such unevenness of perception and responsibility as to what should be done by whom that it seems unlikely that desirable forms of community intervention will be forthcoming.

The modern presidency cannot reasonably be expected to cope with such a situation, for at least three reasons:

(1) The modern presidency was conceived in an atmosphere in which foreign affairs were peripheral to the conduct of government and international concerns were exceptional and short-lived; now it is subject to a situation in which foreign affairs are central to domestic governance and in which the territorial integrity of the country, despite its unprecedented level of military prowess, is being constantly undermined and is vulnerable to external influences in a variety of serious, multiple respects.

(2) It was conceived in a setting in which the engagement of politics to advance the well-being of citizens could be meaningfully undertaken within the scope of territorial boundaries, especially because the United States enjoyed advantages of geographic isolation and abundant natural resources; now it is evident that an ambitious global regulatory capability is necessary to protect all peoples, as well as future generations, against the risks of ecological collapse.

(3) It was conceived under the sway of a politics of *space.* Now the prospect for a hopeful future involves a politics of *time.* The territorial state, as expressed by electoral cycles, conceived of time as almost irrelevant to the serious challenges confronting society, whereas danger to the global commons requires responses that envision decades of commitment, including present costly investments and adjustments for the sake of deferred gains in life prospects.

The modern presidency cannot be easily reoriented, except rhetorically. The original constitutional arrangement retains an important range of positive features (as deeply committed democratization and human-rights drives elsewhere in the world bear witness, and as patterns of economic emulation imply), but it is gravely insufficient in conception and tradition for the array of postmodern challenges. A modern presidency acting in a postmodern world is bound to produce popular disappointment over time, leading many citizens to disillusionment with politics and feeding a self-fulfilling expectation of terminal catastrophe. If we cannot learn to see beyond modernism, we will by default be subscribing to one or another form of apocalyptic scenario. Envisioning postmodern transformations is itself part of the process of avoiding the influence of those eschatologies that might otherwise confuse the end of a civilizational era with the end of the world.

IV. A POSTMODERN PRESIDENCY FOR A POSTMODERN WORLD

It has been frequently remarked, that it
seems to have been reserved to the people
of this country, by their conduct and example, to decide the important question,
whether societies of men are really capable
or not, of establishing good government
from reflection and choice, or whether they
are forever destined to depend, for their
political constitutions, on accident and force.
—Alexander Hamilton
The Federalist No. 1[22]

This country, with its institutions, belongs to
the people who inhabit it. . . . The chief mag-
istrate derives all his authority from the people. . . . His duty is to administer the present
government, as it came to his hands, and to
transmit it, unimpaired by him, to his successor.
—Abraham Lincoln,
First Inaugural Address, 1861[23]

The constitutional experiment that created the United States of America definitely succeeded in establishing "good government" by a deliberative process. Hamilton's expectations were more than met in relation to the challenges of his day, although such "success" overlooked those categories of inhabitants denied the full benefits of citizenship. Shortcomings of equity and efficiency existed from the outset, but neither tyranny, anarchy, nor vulnerability to either foreign or domestic adversaries threatened the security of the country or its republicanism. The new question posed toward the end of this millennium, not much more than two hundred years after the constitutional arrangement was put into operation, is whether this system of government can be transformed to meet the challenges of the postmodern world as effectively as it met the challenges of the modern world back at the end of the eighteenth century.

Lincoln reposed his confidence on the people of the country to renew and transform political arrangements as often as necessary. His stated conviction that the government belongs to the people is easily dismissed as mere oratory at this time of bureaucratic centralism and manipulative mass media; even if verbally acknowledged, it seems virtually impossible to implement by appropriate tactics. Lincoln in his First Inaugural Address, intent on avoiding civil war, restated the prevailing view of his day that the citizenry possessed final authority and responsibility for the shape and reshaping of the governing process: "Whenever they shall grow weary of the existing government, they can exercise their constitutional right of amending it, or their revolutionary right to dismember or overthrow it."[24] Lincoln's concern at the time, of course, was the threat of dismemberment and civil war; he was dedicated to sustaining the original concept of federated unity. His vain effort to discourage secession included invoking hallowed tradition in the form of "the mystic chords of memory," thereby hoping to entice "the better angels of our nature."[25]

Never have we, as a people, more needed to feel empowered to exercise this critical role of creative renewal, heeding these better angels of our nature. Noting a mood of passivity and despair when it comes to issues of governance, it is easy to feel discouraged, even irrelevant. Listening to the political discourse of recent presidential campaigns is to be almost completely cut off from the postmodern aspects of our world. *There is a dangerous split between the porousness of civil society in relation to the world and the rigid impermeability of the modern state, especially here in the United States.*

Comprehending this split may help us rethink the place of the presidency in the postmodern world. First of all, the presidency is embedded in the state structure, and both media and political parties, the main influences on electoral choices, are resistant to a postmodern reorientation. The presidential outlook continues to be territorial, short-term, and premised on a flag-waving patriotism that finds its greatest sources of satisfaction through military victory in war.

If the state is rigid, and the presidency is caught within its bureaucratic web, then it would be naive to expect political leaders to be receptive to postmodern priorities. The most that could reasonably occur is a modernist rendering of adverse trends giving rise to various efforts to alleviate the worst symptoms and a desperate search for technological fixes. Such an approach treats each catastrophe as an anomaly rather than as a warning or sign of systemic weakness. In this regard, presidential rhetoric may accommodate postmodern priorities to a certain degree, but policies, programs, and resource allocations are not adjusted, except perhaps at the margins.

Two preconditions for infusing the governance process with the implications of multdimensional porousness are to nurture a *genuine* democratic process and to acknowledge a cultural need for imaginative approaches. The vitality of civil society is indispensable for regenerating activity within the public sphere. Democratic process in this respect is more a matter of attunement to the changing historical context than it is the panoply of civil liberties guaranteed by the Constitution and protected by courts. It is the citizenry, or sectors of it, that are most likely to be vigilant and agitated, exploring a variety of ways to meet the postmodern challenge. These initiatives take advantage of the availability of experimental space, creating a political pedagogy that proceeds from the bottom up.[26]

This pedagogy devoted to entering the postmodern world is developing rapidly in the United States, Europe, and to some extent elsewhere. Of great benefit has been an astonishing array of voluntary associations addressing informational issues involving environment, development, democracy, and human rights. The activities and impact of Worldwatch Institute, Amnesty International, and the Overseas Development Council are illustrative of different types of undertakings here in the United States. These reinterpretations of "reality" have been reinforced by U.N. conferences and by international commissions that build a wider understanding of serious global trends. The report of the Brundtland Commission on the world environmental situation (*Our Common Future*) has gone a long way toward creating an informed consensus that environmental decay requires massive commitments of resources and energies by leaders of states or else irreversible catastrophe will ensue, that environmental restoration must proceed, at least in part, on the basis of global coordination; and that environmental reform, to succeed, must be connected positively with equity and developmental concerns.

A complex process of revisioning civilizational values is also necessary. The dominant message of popular culture is that the modern world is on a ghastly, terminal death trip; the rhythms and lyrics of hard rock, however distasteful and often artless, exhibit this pervasive sense of impending doom. More reflective elements in civil society have been reconsidering the nature and meaning of life, moving from the material to the spiritual, from the growth imagery of industrialism to ideas of sustainability implicit in ecological ethos. A receptivity to non-Western worldviews facilitates the process. The experience and outlook of pre-modern indigenous peoples and non-Western civilizations are being studied and affirmed, not only for their own sake, but as affirmative models embodying cultural and ecological wisdom. At times, the exotic quality of otherness is being romanticized. Nevertheless, an apprecia-tion of the primacy of nature in human experience is being rediscov-ered in many settings, and human relations to animals are being consid-ered seriously from a variety of ethical standpoints.[27]

These developments have been reinforced by the emergence of transnational and domestic social movements, especially those con-cerned about women, environment, peace, democracy, and human rights. These movements are serving as vehicles for new values and pri-orities, often ones arising from postmodern appreciations of reality.[28] This ferment in civil society is altering the character of political life and expectations in the United States, mainly by fostering an image that postmodern adjustments can occur more easily at the periphery and grassroots than at the center. The presidency becomes a passive force historically, at least temporarily, despite its continuing command over frightening destructive capabilities as well as its extraordinary media potency. There is a range of attunements possible for any given presi-dency, and in the light of altered circumstances: For instance, the calm-ing of East-West tensions gives salience to other societal concerns, and the occurrence of ecological disasters provides leaders with occasions to insinuate into the work of the presidency the concerns of postmod-ernism: globalist perspectives, ecological preoccupation, a lengthening time horizon, and a recentering of national security away from mili-tary/territorial concerns.

The institutional and media gatekeepers will continue to insist on a hard-core modernist president and presidential style for the foresee-able future, but it is difficult to ensure that no closet postmodernist will slip by under these evolving conditions. And if such a leader were to find herself in the White House, and were skilled in the exercise of state power and used it to confront crises of modernism, then a post-modern presidency might be born more quickly than could have been reasonably forecast.[29] Gorbachev is an instance of attempted drastic modernist reform from within under far more unlikely circumstances than exist here.[30]

In their own quite distinct styles, Franklin Roosevelt and Ronald Reagan both exhibited the potential for presidential leadership by their ability to grasp and stimulate the symbolic unconscious of the American people. A postmodern president would need such an aptitude, but would put it at the disposal of a new ideological emphasis that might be described as *ecological populism*. The initial task of presidential leadership in a postmodern world is to foster wide public understanding of the altered political agenda and of the shifting character of effective instruments of governance.

V. PREEMPTING THE PRESIDENCY: A NOTE ON POSTMODERN POLITICAL IMPERATIVES

Nation-bound citizens will have to rise to a
yet higher perspective, to a yet wider civic
awareness, to a yet tighter self-discipline.
          —Theodore H. Von Laue,
    The World Revolution of Westernization.[31]

As Von Laue expresses the growing concern, "Surely, if there is no massive change of mind among the peoples in the leading industrial countries, there will be unprecedented gloom."[32] The creative potential for change involves a dramatic reactivation of popular sovereignty infused with the spirit of a positive postmodern future.

Any indication that postmodernist attitudes in civil society are penetrating the governance structure will be fought at every stage by the citadels of modernism. *The Wall Street Journal*, perhaps America's most influential newspaper these days, complained bitterly in 1989 that George Bush's modest program to combat water and air pollution has the appearance of "a sellout to the environmental apocalyptics."[33] To invest in a safer and cleaner environment on a territorial basis is thus repudiated because of its adverse effect on short-term profitability of industrial enterprise. Not surprisingly, *The Wall Street Journal* has also been a consistently keen advocate of high levels of defense spending and technological innovation, of military intervention overseas, and of skeptical attitudes toward arms control and most forms of internationalism, and has displayed enthusiasm for crime control and traditional social and family values as understood by the middle classes. Late modernism and ardent militarism go hand in hand.

There are, then, two Americas: The first endorses the future as a continuation of the past, but seeks a less intrusive state in relation to business and financial activities and a more assertive state overseas to protect American imperial interests and spread the ideological gospel of market-oriented politics. This America firmly controls both the seats of power and most avenues of access, although not with the dogmatic rigor of *The Wall Street Journal* editorial pages. Locked into an outmoded geopolitics, this America exaggerates the stability and adequacy of current governmental arrangements and underestimates postmodern actualities and opportunities.

The second America is currently struggling to find a more unified voice. It consists of many disparate strands of conviction and practice. Its political coloring is partly green, partly rainbow, and partly blue, corresponding respectively with an emphasis on ecological, equity, and world-order priorities. At present, the second America tends to revision the future from some fixed point, whether it be that of social ecology, cultural feminism, or creation theology. There are many overlapping elements: a rejection of patriarchal forms of order, the rediscovery of mythic accounts of the sacred center of human existence that draw inspiration from scientific frontiers in physics and biology, a relocation of human meaning within the workings of nature, and the search for community based on the extremes of local commitment and an overarching species destiny, as enriched by particular racial, ethnic, and national experiences.

Mediating between these two Americas are those who believe it is possible and necessary to reform the first America in the light of certain insights derived from the radical perspectives of the second America. These mediating forces seek to use information and reason to make a case for adjustment—how security is conceived, how resources are allocated, how sovereignty is protected, and how supplies of energy and food can be sustained. Even these mediating forces grow strident if their efforts are deflected and the dire consequences of inaction become more evident.[34]

In any event, exploration, relevant political discourse, experimental undertakings, and exemplary action are mainly confined to the domain of civil society at this time in the United States. Such a generalization is strengthened by comparing Western Europe, where the Greens are having a direct impact on the public sphere by participating in the formal electoral process and by inducing center parties to adopt an ecological outlook. In several recent European elections, environmental policy has often topped the agenda of public concerns. The American circumstance is also different from that of the former Soviet Union (and some other socialist countries), where aspects of a postmodern reorientation of politics were endorsed at the highest levels of government, by the supreme leader. If the U.S. president were to speak of global issues in a mode similar to that used by Mikhail Gorbachev in the late 1980s, *The Wall Street Journal* would likely be calling for a bill of impeachment.

Thus the American situation is distinctive, if not unique, in the world. There is present a vital societal impulse toward a postmodern reorientation, but it remains confined to the margins of civil society or harmlessly deflected in popular culture. To be sure, environmental anxieties mount, but their relevance is treated by leading social forces as mounting a claim on modernist resource allocations (that is, recast the budget to protect the environment) and ingenuity (that is, devise technological innovations that are profitable and effective).[35]

Such a circumstance could change rapidly. Additional ecological trauma might lead to a populist eruption of a green variety. The very dynamic that has quarantined these concerns and values could under greater stress generate a dialectical shift in political consciousness that repudiates modernism abruptly. To prepare for such a possibility encourages those of us who are "premature postmodernists" to think ahead, even constitutionally. If a postmodern mandate is given to the leadership, what might it imply for constitutional arrangements?

VI. A FEW NOTES ON CONSTITUTIONAL REFORM: FORMING AN IMAGE OF THE POSTMODERN PRESIDENCY

When Khomeini recently told Gorbachev he should look to Allah rather than the market reforms to solve his problems, Gorbachev knew instinctively that Khomeini was right.
   Of course, Gorbachev is not about to embrace Islam. My point is that Gorbachev knows Khomeini is right to pose questions in the overall frame of human existence.
—Rudolf Bahro,
"Theology not Ecology."[36]

Garry Wills observes that Patrick Henry's nationalism was pragmatically disguised by his idealistic rhetoric of statebuilding. Henry seemed to be looking beyond the separate sovereignties of the colonial and revolutionary eras:

The distinctions between Virginians, Pennsylvanians, New Yorkers, and New Englanders are no more. I am not a Virginian, but an American.[36]

Virginia, as the most populous state, would exert its greatest influence if relative legislative influence was based on direct representation rather than on the basis of constituent electorates representing each state. As Wills says of Henry, "He had discovered a way to help Virginia by *not* being a Virginian."[38]

In some ways, we need similar political understandings to inform the outlook and behavior of political leaders. In the deepest, most pervasive ways, a leader can most help America and Americans by *not* being an American! Not in Henry's sense of preserving Virginia's influence, but in a postmodern sense of constructing a future world in which Americans can be secure and even serene (thereby shifting the axis of politics from space to time). Such security can only be achieved within a political community that is truly global in scope.

There are some more tangible moves that would be inherently valuable and would facilitate transition. We are not yet at a stage to write "The Federalist Papers II" or "Planetary Papers for a Postmodern World," but we may be at a planning, conjectural stage. Perhaps, even the consideration of the presidency as postmodern is an early step in the process.

From a constitutional perspective, the following building blocks can be briefly mentioned in relation to fundamental topics.

Representation. The idea of governmental representation remains purely territorial in relation to sovereign states and statist in relation to world political institutions. Both forms of representation are modernist in the extreme, appropriate to a world in which territorial allocations of political authority were both efficient and generally accurate. But now critical behavioral patterns are nonterritorial in their locus of effects, the state is porous, and many negative effects of current practices will fall heavily on the future. As a result, patterns of representation are neither efficient nor equitable.

To suggest alternative forms of representation, we need a variety of concrete proposals adapted to various discrete settings. Two sets of ideas seem helpful. First, add a new legislative chamber to the U.S. Congress, a House of Overseas Delegates. Its members would be drawn from foreign countries, partly by election, partly by appointment. Second, add to the United Nations a third chamber constituted by representatives of the peoples of the world and of the nongovernmental sector of human affairs, selected by voting and by appointment.

The initial rationale is to widen policy debate, as well as to give expression not only to the twin postmodern realities of porousness of territorial units and the interactive destiny of peoples situated in various regions of the world, but also to the failure of modernist governments to represent the human interest and to the long-term effects of present undertakings.

International Law. Encourage the idea that foreign policy should be carried out within the framework of law and that citizens have the right to expect such adherence as a matter of constitutional guarantee. To give assured substance to such an expectation requires a judicial procedure of an appropriate sort that not only acknowledges the legitimacy of citizen challenges but also is empowered to assess and repudiate presidential initiatives that are found to violate international treaties and customary rules. Building such a tradition of *inner* accountability, an enforceable duty to respect international law, would impose a world-order discipline on governments and revitalize democracy by giving citizens a genuine role in establishing limits on official action. If constitutional democracy were extended to foreign policy, it would be a virtual Magna Carta for the Postmodern World!

This orientation could also be extended in two directions. First, it could give non-Americans a remedy in the United States legal system in the event that a foreign policy initiative seemed "illegal" under international law. For example, a Nicaraguan citizen during the period of Sandinista governance could have appealed to the American legal system to challenge aid to the Contras, or could have insisted through U.S. judicial procedures on implementing the World Court decision rendered in favor of Nicaragua. Second, the United States government, in the company of other sovereign states, could be expected to accept the compulsory jurisdiction of the International Court of Justice and make an unconditional obligation to comply with its judgments. Failure to uphold such a judgment would be treated by the United Nations as an automatic breach of the peace and would constitute a Crime against Peace, for which the relevant political leadership would be personally and criminally responsible—not only conceptually, but by remedies provided in American law.

Responsibility. Political leaders would uphold their commitment to carry out international law as well as to execute domestic law in a faithful manner. In this regard, the Nuremberg Principles, as enunciated after the trials of surviving German (and Japanese) leaders in World War II, would be adopted as binding internal law in the United States and elsewhere. Further, an international criminal court would be constituted to deal with complaints of crimes of state. U.S. leaders would not be eligible for public office unless they explicitly accepted in advance the validity of procedures of accountability evolved to implement the Nuremberg Principles. Such claims would take precedence over assertions of sovereign prerogative.

Sovereignty. The idea of political authority would need to be adapted to this new global setting. The basic objective of upholding the well-being of the citizens within a particular community could be satisfied only by a dedication to the well-being of all the peoples in the world and of their descendants unto several generations.

To achieve such results requires greatly increasing reliance on international cooperation and strengthening the mechanisms to achieve these goals. A stronger United Nations with its own revenue base and peacekeeping forces is one obvious policy direction. In effect, the territorial community can be best protected by promoting nonterritorial approaches. Traditional military capabilities, while not irrelevant, would be of declining significance over time, being neither needed nor effective.

Citizenship. The idea of loyalty and citizenship would reflect these basic shifts in perspective. There would continue to be a primary connection with an American experience, but this would be qualified by an unconditional acceptance of the primacy of international law and by the long nonterritorial shadow of the future. The character of political identity would also shift from space to time, making for a new constellation of attitudes toward government. I have discussed elsewhere the emergence of a new political identity, that of "citizen pilgrims" whose commitment is to a future community built around ideas of sustainable peace, justice, and ecological relations.[39] It is such a mode of citizenship that establishes a postmodern presence in the midst of civil society long before formal and official changes occur.

The ideal postmodern president would embody these changed ideas about structure and identity. Her leadership would be intended, above all, to strengthen this pattern of postmodern techniques and images of governance. A postmodern president would, almost inevitably, be female and feminine to express the cultural resolve to move decisively beyond the modern world.

NOTES

1. For example, see Ralf Dahrendorf's complaint that adding the modifier *post* is to be afflicted with what he regards as "a veritable author's disease," meaning intellectual weakness. Indeed, he says that attaching the word *post* is a shabby way "to impress on us that unheard-of-things have happened in recent

times." Being unable to "put their fingers" on exactly what's going on, the writers "settle for the claim that we are therefore living post-some-other-time" (*The Modern Social Conflict* [London: Weidenfeld and Nicolson, 1988], xiv). Actually, Dahrendorf is correct in relation to some recent writing on "the postmodern presidency," which turns out to be little more than a claim that what's going on in the present period is new and different from what preceded.

2. See the quite different presentations of the juncture of modern and postmodern in Jean-François Lyotard, *The Postmodern Condition: A Report on Knowledge* (Minneapolis: University of Minnesota, 1984) and Todd Gitlin, "Post-Modernism: The Stenography of Surfaces," *New Perspectives Quarterly* 6 (1989): 56–59. Both authors view postmodernism as already embodied in our cultural circumstance in which the only political task is one of negation, whether it be claims of meaning and aspiration or hierarchies of power. In my understanding, this stance is an aspect of late modernism or a manifestation of the disintegration of modernism (or realism, see Gitlin, "Post-Modernism," 56), but not yet a genuine alternative ethic and metaphysic, a true postmodernism. If one adopts Lyotard's or Gitlin's orientation, then Reagan and Bush are postmodern presidents acting in a postmodern world. My usage insists that a postmodern president would have the skills and normative vision to provide the sort of leadership required to act successfully in the postmodern world. Such a president would not be image-fixated, but would have intergenerational sensibility. See, section IV for specification.

3. See Gorbachev's 7 Dec. 1988 speech at the United Nations.

4. See Morris West's novel *The Clowns of God* (London: Hodder & Stoughton, 1981), which suggestively explores the extent to which a leader—in that instance, a pope—could go beyond the limits of conventional wisdom.

5. See Robert Jay Lifton on "the retirement syndrome," in Lifton and Falk, *Indefensible Weapons: The Political and Psychological Case against Nuclearism* (New York: Basic Books, 1982), 96–98.

6. Ben Bagdikian, "The Lords of the Global Village," *The Nation*, 12 June 1989: 805–20.

7. See Robert Gilpin on the resilience of statism in relation to multinational corporations, in Gilpin, *U.S. Power and the Multinational Corporation* (New York: Basic Books, 1975).

8. "Flexible" means that it could absorb Marxism. See also Samuel Clemens (Mark Twain), *A Connecticut Yankee in King Arthur's Court*, in which an allegorical account of the triumph of modernism over feudalism reached its climax when the pre-Rambo hero wielding a Yankee machine gun mowed down masses of knights in a final battle scene.

9. See *The Federalist* (New York: E. P. Dutton, 1929), No. 70.

10. See Arthur Schlesinger, *Imperial Presidency* (Boston: Houghton Mifflin, 1973).

11. See my essay, "In Pursuit of the Postmodern," in *Spirituality and Society: Postmodern Visions*, ed. David Ray Griffin, (Albany: State University of New York Press, 1988), 81–98; reprinted in Falk, *Explorations at the Edge of Time: The Prospects for World Order* (Philadelphia: Temple University Press, 1992), 5–23.

12. Compare the analogous point in Allan Megill, *Prophets of Extremity* (Berkeley: University of California Press, 1985), 34.

13. *Christian Science Monitor*, 14 June 1989: 20.

14. For persisting controversy among historians as to motives, see G. Alperowitz, *Atomic Diplomacy* (New York: Simon & Schuster, 1965).

15. See Loren Baritz, *City on a Hill* (New York: John Wiley, 1964).

16. Adam Gopnik, "Goya Today," *New Yorker*, 19 June 1989: 88–92, at 92.

17. Garry Wills, *Inventing America: Jefferson's Declaration of Independence* (New York: Doubleday, 1978), 356.

18. In Jacob E. Cooke, ed., *The Federalist* (Cleveland: World Publishing, Meridian edition, 1961), 56–65, at 57.

19. Alexis de Tocqueville, *Democracy in America*, 122; see also 130: "In America the President exercises very substantial influence on affairs of state, but he does not conduct them; the preponderant power resides in the representatives of the people as a whole."

20. See Richard Falk, *The Promise of World Order* (Philadelphia: Temple University Press, 1987), 77–92.

21. See Jeffrey K. Tullis, *The Rhetorical Presidency* (Princeton: University Press, 1987).

22. In Cooke, ed., *The Federalist*, 3.

23. In Philip Van Doren Stern, ed., *The Life and Writings of Abraham Lincoln* (New York: Modern Library, 1940), 655–56.

24. Ibid., 655. This affirmation is repeated at Gettysburg in 1863 in the famous concluding phrase: *and that government of the people, by the people, for the people, shall not perish from the earth.*

25. Ibid., 657.

26. The Soviet experience seems to suggest the possibility of an effective top-down pedagogy under certain conditions—here the crisis of the Soviet state that opened up political room for maneuver available to an imaginative leader with the requisite skills; ironically, Gorbachev has so far acknowledged the postmodern imperative to a far greater extent than any leader operating within countries with strong civil societies.

27. Christopher Stone, *Earth and Other Ethics: The Case for Moral Pluralism* (New York: Harper & Row, 1987).

28. Part of the ferment is antimodern, not postmodern, relying on violent tactics and fundamentalist understandings to impose a reign of terror on modern society in the name of a higher truth, a hallowed tradition.

29. Actually, a woman is less likely to escape detection by the gatekeepers, because she would be scrutinized with especial care to ensure mainstream credibility, whereas a man would seem to have a slightly better opportunity of hiding postmodern tendencies until in office. In fact, the women who have become leaders of their countries thus far have all lived up to modernist expectations.

30. Soviet society had submerged civil society under the dead weight of the state for decades and the Soviet gatekeepers—party bureaucrats—had displayed an aptitude for identifying and eliminating any aspiring leader with pretensions of an imaginative approach.

31. Theodore H. Von Laue, *The World Revolution of Westernization* (New York: Oxford University Press, 1987).

32. Ibid., 362.

33. "All Apocalyptics Now?" *Wall Street Journal*, 16 June 1989: A6.

34. These issues are interestingly discussed in *New Perspectives Quarterly* 6 (Spring 1989). This issue of *NPQ* is devoted mainly to contrasting views of "the new ethological ethos"; see especially Wolfgang Sachs's critique of ecodevelopment orientation ("The Virtue of Enoughness," 16–19). Sachs criticizes mediational approaches (e.g., Worldwatch Institute) as managerial rather than as transformative, contributing to essentially futile modernist tactics of adjustment rather than a transition to postmodernism. In Sachs's language, "though the curtain of silence has finally been pulled away from the global environmental crisis, current policy proposals ignore the option of intelligent self-limitation and merely reduce concepts of ecology to blueprints for greater efficiency. Such policies implicitly reaffirm a particular economic *worldview* and risk the further Westernization of minds and habits—cultural fall-out that fundamentally threatens the goal of sustainability" (16). This is an important critique

although the contrast and opposition between ecodevelopers and true ecologists seems overstated.

35. See the cover story in *Time*, 2 Jan. 1989.

36. In *New Perspectives Quarterly* 6 (1989), 39.

37. Quoted by Wills, *Inventing America*, 12.

38. Ibid., 12.

39. See Falk, *Promise of World Order*, 25–31.

10

SEARCHING FOR A
PRESIDENT WITH A
GLOBAL VISION

Frank K. Kelly

I. THE NEED FOR NEW TYPES OF
PRESIDENTIAL CANDIDATES

The signers of the American Declaration of Independence—the founders of the United States—were sure that they were launching a revolution that would have repercussions around the world. In the centuries since that bold statement was signed in Philadelphia, the words and actions of American leaders have stirred people on all the continents.

People in China, in East Germany, in Hungary, in Poland and in other countries have engaged in massive demonstrations, proclaiming their determination to obtain the freedoms guaranteed to Americans under the Constitution with its Bill of Rights. Applauding the Chinese rebels, one American observer said: *"They want what we've got."* Judging by the decline in American participation in presidential elections, it might be more realistic to say: *"The Chinese want what they think we've got."*

Only a small percentage of voters took part in the nominating process in 1988, which was dominated by the power of money and the tricks of expert manipulators. The crucial problems facing the United States and the world were rarely discussed by the candidates of the two major parties, who evaded the fundamental issues and appealed to the emotions of prospective voters. Half of the eligible voters—disillusioned or disgusted by the campaign—did not even bother to vote.

According to opinion polls, many Americans did not think the candidates offered to them were really qualified to serve as chief executive of the United States at a time when many critical decisions had to be made on national and global problems. They did not find in George Bush or Michael Dukakis the capacities for long-range thinking and vigorous presidential leadership urgently needed in the 1990s.

At least $100 million were spent in the 1988 campaign by the two leading candidates. Other millions were raised and spent by others who sought the nominations of the major political parties. Images and image making dominated the efforts of all the candidates. Candidates were "packaged" and sold on commercial television stations in competitions with advertisements for soap, automobiles, microwave ovens, and other products.

Increasingly skeptical about all products sold on television and radio, American voters became deeply doubtful about all the candidates sold in the same way. Yet the candidates were persuaded by their advisors that the "selling strategy" was the only way to win. Plunged into this process, candidates spent two to three years in exhaustive tours of the country, appealing to special interests, making deals, raising millions of dollars, sanctioning television "spot messages" with distorted images of other candidates, and engaging in maneuvers to manipulate pressure groups.

While the nominating process has become heavily professionalized, the ability of candidates to focus upon the crucial issues in the nuclear age has been steadily reduced. Candidates who are willing to spend years in an atmosphere of fakery may be fundamentally dedicated public servants who simply engage in flummery to win necessary votes—or they may have enormous egos. In any case, they tend to gather around them staff members with limited objectives—or cynical technicians who become rich by selling people as merchandise.

Is this nominating system the best one that can be devised in a time of rising conflicts and rapid changes? It seems to me that much evidence now exists to demonstrate that this system is sapping the strength of American democracy and endangering the future of this nation and its leadership role in the world. I believe that we now need to offer suggestions for an alternative process that might offer new avenues of participation for millions of Americans.

All human beings are more than citizens of nations. We are inhabitants of a small planet now endangered by nuclear weapons and the threat of environmental destruction. In such an age, we need a national and even international discussion of the kind of president the United States should have, and an organized, systematic search for the men and women who may be potential candidates.

It is essential to find candidates with far-ranging visions of global cooperation—candidates with the qualities evidenced by Franklin D. Roosevelt and Harry S. Truman, who took the lead in founding and fostering the international organizations established during and after World War II.

Roosevelt's statement of the "Four Freedoms" prepared the way for the eventual adoption of the Universal Declaration of Human Rights under the leadership of Eleanor Roosevelt. In an address to Congress in January, 1941, Roosevelt dedicated himself to these freedoms: "The First Freedom is freedom of speech and expression—everywhere in the world. The Second Freedom is freedom of every person to worship God in his own way—everywhere in the world. The Third is freedom from want—everywhere in the world. The Fourth is freedom from fear—which, translated into world terms, means a world-wide reduction of armaments to such a point that no nation will be in a position to commit an act of physical aggression against any neighbor—anywhere in the world."

"That is no vision of a distant millennium," Roosevelt declared. "It is a definite basis for a kind of world attainable in our own time and generation."

Harry Truman, Roosevelt's successor, also had a deep sense of responsibility to humanity. When I worked as a speech writer for Truman in 1948, I admired his vision and his determination to work for peace. His first act as president was to give immediate support to the formation of the United Nations. He told me in the Oval Office that he knew he had done a hellish thing by dropping atomic bombs, but he quickly reminded me: "War itself is hell." He believed that nuclear weapons would finally compel nations to accept the necessity for a global federation.

Truman was well aware of the flaws in the American nominating system. He did not regard himself as the best qualified man in the United States to serve as president. "I've got the job and I'm doing my damnedest," he remarked to me. "But there are people in the country who might do better." He regretted the fact that many well-qualified persons would never be considered. He said: "We should find the best candidates and get them to run."

When Truman decided that he would not run again in 1952, he offered his support to Governor Adlai Stevenson of Illinois, a strong advocate of international cooperation. When Stevenson seemed unwilling to run, Truman urged Averell Harriman to get into the race. Harriman asked me to be the Washington director of his campaign, and I accepted because I shared Truman's respect for Harriman. He had the experience to be a global leader.

Harriman had never been elected to any public office, so his entry into a presidential campaign surprised some of the leaders of the Democratic party. But he had a remarkable background. He had been chairman of the Union Pacific Railroad; he had been the administrative officer of the National Recovery Administration under President Roosevelt. In World War II, he had been the U.S. ambassador to the Soviet Union and to Britain. After the war, he had been one of the administrators of the Marshall Plan, which stimulated the revival of the devastated countries in Western Europe. He was known and admired by people in many fields and in many countries.

At the Democratic convention in 1952, Stevenson first backed Harriman and then decided that he would accept the nomination himself. He was defeated that year by another man with international experience—General Dwight D. Eisenhower, the Republican nominee. Eisenhower was another candidate who had never held an elective office. He was persuaded to run by other leaders.

I cite these examples not to suggest that these men were without serious faults—they were not—but only to indicate that the American nominating system can be opened up for unusual candidates—for leaders not regarded as professional politicians, for candidates chosen on the basis of wide experience in significant positions, not for their abilities to "perform" on television or to wrap themselves in the American flag.

II. Bringing Forward New Candidates
in the Nuclear Age

In an age of planetary crisis, at a time when an American president must be a global leader, I think we must launch a systematic search for extraordinary candidates, as quickly as possible.

To begin the discussion of what needs to be done, I suggest the formation of a Council of Citizens—composed of leaders of many organizations, representing Americans with a broad variety of views and backgrounds—to conduct an ongoing hunt for notable men and women who have the qualities of leadership and wisdom to help the people of the United States and the world move toward the future envisioned by Franklin Roosevelt in the Four Freedoms.

The first board of directors of the Council of Citizens should be drawn from all regions of the United States and should assemble a board of advisors drawn from outstanding people from all regions of the earth. At its first meeting, the council should announce that all Americans would be invited to participate in the search for potential presidents. It should also acknowledge that American presidents affect the lives of people around the planet, so the people of the rest of the world should also be given a chance to be heard.

The council should focus national and international attention on two urgent questions: What persons should be considered as potential presidents, expected to be leaders of humanity in a time of global transformations? How should presidential campaigns be conducted, in order to give the American people (and people everywhere) opportunities to bring out the fundamental questions to be faced, and to illuminate the ideas, actions, and leadership capacities of the candidates?

In the course of the search for new candidates, public hearings would be held by the council in all the regions of the United States. Prospective candidates, chosen by the council on the basis of suggestions from the people, would be presented at these hearings. The candidates would be asked to discuss questions submitted to them in advance by the council, and then respond to other questions offered by the audiences at the hearings. These hearings would be broadcast.

At each regional hearing, the candidates would be presented on television and radio broadcasts apart from the hearing itself. The candidates would be asked to comment on questions telephoned to the broadcasting stations by viewers and listeners.

After a year of such public hearings and broadcasts, the council would ask the people who attended the hearings and those who heard or watched the broadcasts to name the candidates who were most impressive. The council would then present these candidates on a series of national radio and television programs, with viewers and listeners again invited to question them. After these programs, the council would conduct a series of public opinion polls, surveying not only the popularity of the candidates but their handling of the basic issues.

The council would then convene a Citizens' Assembly to be held in March or April of the presidential election year. The five thousand delegates for this assembly would be elected at meetings sponsored by the Council of Citizens in all regions of the United States. All members of the council, which would consist of five hundred persons drawn from many fields and many achievements, would also be eligible to participate in the assembly.

The twelve candidates regarded as the best qualified persons— who would be chosen by majority votes in the council, after the procedures previously outlined—would be presented to the assembly.

After six days of intensive serious discussions of the merits of these candidates and of their views on the crucial issues facing the United States and the world, the delegates at the assembly would vote on the candidates, considering each one as a possible president and each as a possible vice president with the qualifications to become president. The balloting would be done openly and individually (not by states) on television. The delegates would vote first for a presidential candidate and then for a vice presidential nominee. The results would be immediately tabulated and announced. Delegates would be free to vote for more than one candidate for each office.

During the balloting in the assembly, members of the radio and television audiences would be asked to give their preferences by calling telephone lines operated by the staff of the council. These would be toll-free lines to encourage maximum participation. These votes would also be tabulated and announced publicly at the assembly after the delegates had completed their voting.

The results of the Citizens' Assembly and the preferences expressed through other channels would be called to the attention of the national committees of all political parties and other leaders in the parties. In the months between the assembly and the party conventions, polls would be taken regularly by the council to show the relative standings of the candidates endorsed by the assembly (and those selected by the broadcasting audiences) in comparison with the standings of the Democratic, Republican, and Independent candidates contending for presidential nominations through the state primaries and other channels.

The candidates emerging from the search conducted by the council would be encouraged to have their names placed in nomination at the party conventions. If they indicated their willingness, efforts would be made to find party delegates who would put their names forward, thus making it possible for one or both of the major parties (and any independent party) to consider such candidates.

After the party conventions had chosen their candidates, the Citizen's Assembly could be reconvened to review the records of the nominees. The assembly would be asked to vote on a possible endorsement of one set of candidates, or to take no position, or to form a Campaign Committee to support highly qualified candidates ignored or rejected by the parties. *The purpose of the Citizens' Campaign Committee would be to make voters aware of the potential presidents available to them, and thus to encourage more active participation in the whole process of choosing a president with a global vision.*

The formation of such a Council of Citizens could bring new life and new hope into the nominating system and into the subsequent elections. The council should be funded initially by grants totaling $50 million from a group of foundations and individuals. If the search for potential presidents drew the support of millions of citizens, the council could operate on a year-to-year basis with funding from individual gifts.

In a nuclear age, in a time when the very survival of the earth depends in large part upon the leadership and policies of the United States, the search for an inspiring president demands a continuing program of information and discussion to engage the thoughts and stimulate the activities of millions of concerned people.

A systematic hunt for candidates with the highest qualities for national and global service could have far-reaching effects on the selection of nominees and on the level of the debates conducted by the candidates in the campaigns. In time, the national political parties might form search committees that could bring forward candidates who might be overlooked otherwise.

Members of the party organizations might be reluctant to examine such ways of opening up the nominating process, but candidates with outstanding abilities could not be easily dismissed or resisted. Wendell Willkie in 1940 and George McGovern in 1972 showed that the traditional party leaders could not always control the major parties.

Throughout the history of the United States, new movements have arisen to meet the needs of the times. It is obvious that tremendous changes are ahead for this country and the world. It is urgent to develop new ways of moving to meet the challenges of this age.

III. IMPORTANT QUESTIONS FOR THE
POSSIBLE CANDIDATES

In the search for nominees, the Council of Citizens should develop a comprehensive list of questions to be used in evaluating all of the persons under consideration, including the avowed candidates (senators, governors, and others) striving for the nominations of the major parties.

Here are some of the questions that should be considered:

1. Does the person have a record showing a global awareness: an understanding of the interdependence of nations, the connections between the United States and the ecological problems of the earth, and the necessity for American commitment to international cooperation in every field?
2. Does the public and private life of the person show a consistent adherence to high moral standards?
3. Does the person have a comprehensive vision of the American constitutional form of government and of what might be done to improve it?
4. Does the person have access to an international range of advice and to the many sources of knowledge that are necessary for tackling planetary problems?
5. Are the views of people from many areas and many backgrounds— young and old, male and female, black and white, brown and yellow, poor as well as rich—actively invited and thoroughly examined by the possible candidate?
6. What kinds of materials (pamphlets, fund-raising, letters, telemarketing efforts, advertisements, public relations plans, TV programs) have been used by this person in public activities?
7. What uses has this person made of nonpartisan research projects and reports on national and global issues prepared by "think tanks" and by U.N. agencies and other international organizations?
8. How does the person deal with critics and opponents? Does the person clearly appreciate criticism and learn from opponents, or are such critics and opponents downgraded, disregarded, or attacked?
9. Does the person cling to slogans and platforms of the past, or show an awareness of the need for new thinking and new measures to meet new challenges?

10. Has the person shown calm strength in correcting mistakes and meeting emergencies, admitting errors and changing courses of action with reasonable flexibility?
11. Has the person been generous in giving credit to colleagues, advisors, and assistants at various stages of his or her life?

There are many other questions that could be explored. The eleven questions I have listed are simply examples of the kinds of inquiries that would be valuable. David Griffin (this volume) has pointed out that the president's symbolic-moral leadership of the nation and thereby the world is important in making every human being realize that environmental destruction is a process that is suicidal. Potential presidents should be considered in the light of the need for that kind of leadership.

Candidates Who See the Possibilities of a New Society

In his speech at the American University, in Washington, a few months before he was assassinated, President John F. Kennedy said: "Our problems are man-made. Therefore, they can be solved by man. And man can be as big as he wants. No problem of human destiny is beyond human beings. Man's reason and spirit have often solved the unsolvable—and we believe they can do it again."

In the violent decades after Kennedy's murder, many people lost confidence in American leadership. President Lyndon Johnson, who called for "a great society," lost sight of his global goals in his obsession with military power in the Vietnam War.

The presidents who came after Johnson's departure based their policies on two of President Truman's more questionable doctrines: security through American strength and the preeminent place of the United States in humanity's future. Truman asserted that national security and global security were closely linked. He established the National Security Council and made the quest for "national security" the central element in American policies. He declared: "The heart and soul of American foreign policy is peace. We are supporting a world organization to keep the peace, and a world economic policy to create prosperity for all nations." He did not foresee the dangers to the world's environment.

The men who carried out "national security" policies under Truman and his successors regarded themselves as "realists" who knew how to operate successfully in the "modern" world. The concepts of that world were built on quantitative measurements, on materialistic science and hard technology, on the assumption that the problems of the world could be understood and handled by "objective" methods that produce measurable results.

The national security policymakers were astounded and baffled by the revolutionary events in Eastern Europe and in China in 1989. The end of the cold war and the emerging possibilities of a new society caught them by surprise. Demands for freedom and human rights—for recognition of the essential unity of humanity— indicated that nonmaterial factors could become more significant than most of the policy "experts" had anticipated.

Many scientists and thinkers in other fields now cite evidence that humanity is moving from the "modern" worldview of quantitative measurements to a "postmodern" holistic worldview that retains the benefits of science but opens up a new awareness of creative evolution.

Dr. Willis Harman, a regent of the University of California and president of the Institute of Noetic Sciences, has classified scientific knowledge on four levels: the physical sciences, such as molecular biology; the life sciences, dealing with natural selection, system functions, and organ functions; the human sciences, concerned with individual biological health and individual purposes; and spiritual sciences, concerned with wholeness and universal purposes, honoring "the deep subjective experience of untold prophets, mystics, artists, and poets."

The current system for nominating presidents in American politics disregards what Dr. Harman calls "the spiritual sciences." Candidates are not expected to appeal to the high ethical standards proclaimed by the wisest leaders. They are simply expected to please or placate people with an immense variety of interests, promising voters a great future without requiring any sacrifices or dedication to the public service. They are taught to avoid the hard questions, to stick to platitudes, and to "come across" convincingly on television and radio.

The fact that half of the American voters, in 1988, refused to vote in that election—and millions of those who did finally vote expressed disdain for the two major candidates—makes it clear that new methods of bringing forward strong candidates could evoke positive responses from large numbers of people. Such candidates, supported by a Council of Citizens and a Citizens' Assembly, could make future campaigns exhilarating examples of candid debates and vigorous participation by citizens.

If candidates suited for the future of a new society are to be found, the search will have to go beyond the ranks of professional politicians. Environmental leaders, doctors, heads of foundations and other nonprofit organizations, business executives with global awareness, university presidents, scientists, and others in various fields should be considered.

The finding of these new leaders will come from the activities of millions of citizens, just as the tremendous events of 1989 came from the stirrings of people in many countries. All those who participate in the search will gain a deeper understanding of their own responsibilities for the future of the nation and the whole earth.

Participation by people in many countries against the nuclear arms race finally compelled governments to begin to halt that ghastly competition. John Tirman, director of the Winston Foundation, observed in an article in the *Los Angeles Times*:

> It was the massive demonstrations in Europe in 1981 that first riveted attention on the new and perilous nuclear stand-off on the Continent. At the same time, a similar if less strident movement was spreading through the United States, coalescing in 6,000 local groups that forcefully articulated their concerns: speaking to neighbors, writing pamphlets, lobbying Congress. Nuclear-freeze resolutions were placed on city and state ballots, and were victorious in nearly every test. A citizens' diplomacy grew quickly as well, establishing sister cities with the Soviet Union, beaming televised space bridges around the world, sending delegations to Moscow.

This writer took part in the nuclear freeze movement in Santa Barbara, became a founding director of the Nuclear Age Peace Foundation, and went to Moscow to speak on "The Role of the Public in Preventing Nuclear War." In that speech—given to seventy-nine officials, including members of the Supreme Soviet—on 26 April 1983 I urged the Soviet government to take the initiative by making reductions in nuclear arms, dismantling conventional weapons, and opening up new avenues. Other "citizen diplomats" offered similar advice. One of the Soviet officials who listened to these talks was Gennady Gerasimov, who later emerged as a spokesman for Mikhail Gorbachev. Gorbachev came forward with a global vision that gained the admiration of people around the world and set off an astounding series of events in China and Europe.

Through the initiative of citizens, expressed through the council and the assembly I have proposed, the atmosphere of the nominating process in the United States could be drastically changed. That could lead to the discovery of presidential candidates with the qualities of global leadership necessary for the survival of our planet.

Great awakenings have occurred in Europe and China, in Latin America and Africa. Great awakenings could be stirred here by an imaginative and hopeful search for women and men who could move with us into a new stage of explorations and high achievements.

"The time has come to adopt a more scientific method for selecting presidents," Daniel E. Koshland, Jr., editor of *Science*, declared in an editorial. He proposed that each candidate should be required to devise a total federal budget, revealing his or her priorities.

That suggestion is certainly worth discussion. The United States budget, with its enormous arms expenditures, has a major impact on people everywhere and on the global environment. President Truman used to spend many hours going over his annual budgets with the press. He took questions and explained how he had arrived at his decisions. He felt that the people were entitled to a full and fair examination of a president's programs and proposals. No other presidents have imitated him, but candidates in an age of planetary crises should be asked to present proposed budgets and defend them in public sessions.

It seems evident to many citizens that "the time has come" to adopt a better method of selecting presidents. I offer my suggestions with the hope of stimulating a national and international discussion of the type of systematic search we should have.

By engaging in this effort, or by developing an alternative way, the American people and all other members of humanity could be drawn into preparing themselves to meet the tremendous ecological, social, and economic challenges that are converging upon all residents of this planet.

The challenges cannot be evaded. The time for action has rushed upon us.

NOTES ON CONTRIBUTORS AND CENTERS

JOHN B. COBB, JR., is author of *Process Theology as Political Theology* and co-author of *The Liberation of Life: From the Cell to the Community* (with Charles Birch) and *For the Common Good: Redirecting the Economy Toward Community, the Environment, and a Sustainable Future* (with Herman Daly). He is professor emeritus of theology at the School of Theology at Claremont and founding director of the Center for Process Studies. In retirement he lives in Pilgrim Place at 777 N. Cambridge Way, Claremont, California 91711.

RICHARD FALK is author of *This Endangered Planet, A Study of Future Worlds, Explorations at the Edge of Time: Prospects for World Order* and *Revolutionaries and Functionaries: The Dual Face of Terrorism.* He is rapporteur of the Global Civilization Project, an undertaking of the World Order Models Project, and Albert G. Milbank professor of International Law and Practice at Princeton University, Princeton, New Jersey 08544.

DAVID RAY GRIFFIN is author of *God and Religion in the Postmodern World* and *Evil Revisited* and editor of *Spirituality and Society: Postmodern Visions* and *Sacred Interconnections: Postmodern Spirituality, Political Economy, and Art.* He is professor of philosophy of religion and theology at the School of Theology at Claremont and Claremont Graduate School and executive director of the Center for Process Studies, 1325 North College, Claremont, California 91711.

WES JACKSON is author of *New Roots for Agriculture* and *Altars of Unhewn Stone* and editor (with Wendell Berry and Bruce Colman) of *Meeting the Expectations of the Land.* Having established and directed the Environmental Studies program at California State University in Sacramento in the early 1970s, he is now the founding president of the Land Institute, Salina, Kansas 67401.

FRANK K. KELLY is author of *Court of Reason: Robert Hutchins and the Fund for the Republic, The Fight for the White House,* and *The Martyred Presidents.* He is the senior vice president of the Nuclear Age Peace Foundation and co-founder of the Council of Citizens, a nonpartisan organization working to increase citizen participation in American politics. He was vice president of the Center for the Study of Democratic Institutions for sixteen years, and previously served as a speech writer for President Truman and as staff director of the U. S. Senate Majority Policy Committee. He resides at 34 East Padre, Santa Barbara, California 93105.

FRANCES MOORE LAPPÉ is co-director and co-founder of the Institute for the Arts of Democracy (I.A.D.), 36 Eucalyptus Lane, San Rafael, California 94901. Best known for her 1971 book *Diet for a Small Planet,* Lappé co-founded the Institute for Food and Development Policy in 1975. The latest of her twelve books are *Rediscovering America's Values* and (with I.A.D. co-founder Paul Martin Du Bois) *Doing Democracy.*

JOANNA MACY is author of *Dharma and Development, Despair and Personal Power in the Nuclear Age, Mutual Causality in Buddhism and General Systems Theory, World as Lover, World as Self,* and (with others) *Thinking Like a Mountain.* Besides leading workshops on empowerment and deep ecology, she is an adjunct professor at the Graduate Theological Union and the California Institute of Integral Studies. She receives mail at 1306 Bay View Place, Berkeley, California 94708.

DOUGLAS SLOAN is author of *Insight-Imagination: The Emancipation of Thought and the Modern World* and editor of *Toward the Recovery of Wholeness: Knowledge, Education, and Human Values.* He is also author of works on American educational history. He is professor of history and education, and director of the Center for the Study of the Spiritual Foundations of Education, at Teachers College, Columbia University, New York, New York 10027.

JIM WALLIS is author of *The Call to Conversion* and *Agenda for Biblical People* and editor of *Waging Peace: A Handbook for the Struggle to Abolish Nuclear Weapons.* He is the founder and pastor of Sojourners, an ecumenical community committed to relationships with the poor and building community in the inner city, and editor of its magazine, *Sojourners*, Box 29272, Washington, D.C. 20017.

ROGER WILKINS is author of *A Man's Life* and co-editor (with Senator Fred R. Harris) of *Quiet Riots: Race and Poverty in the United States.* He is a commentator for National Public Radio's Morning Edition, host of WHMM TV's "Washington Leaders," a Fellow at the Institute for Policy Studies, and Clarence J. Robinson professor of history and American culture at George Mason University, Fairfax, Virginia 22030-4444.

This series is published under the auspices of the Center for a Postmodern World and the Center for Process Studies.

The Center for a Postmodern World is an independent nonprofit organization in Santa Barbara, California, founded by David Ray Griffin. It promotes the awareness and exploration of the postmodern worldview and encourages reflection about a postmodern world, from postmodern art, spirituality, and education to a postmodern world order, with all this implies for economics, ecology, and security. One of its major projects is to produce a collaborative study that marshals the numerous facts supportive of a postmodern worldview and provides a portrayal of a postmodern world order toward which we can realistically move. It is located at 6891 Del Playa, Isla Vista, California 93117.

The Center for Process Studies is a research organization affiliated with the School of Theology at Claremont and Claremont University Center and Graduate School. It was founded by John B. Cobb, Jr., Director, and David Ray Griffin, Executive Director; Mary Elizabeth Moore and Marjorie Suchocki are also Co-Directors. It encourages research and reflection upon the process philosophy of Alfred North Whitehead, Charles Hartshorne, and related thinkers, and upon the application and testing of this viewpoint in all areas of thought and practice. This center sponsors conferences, welcomes visiting scholars to use its library, and publishes a scholarly journal, *Process Studies*, and a quarterly *Newsletter.* It is located at 1325 North College, Claremont, California 91711.

Both centers gratefully accept (tax-deductible) contributions to support their work.

INDEX

225